Human Resource Management for the Event Industry

Human Resource Management for the Event Industry still remains the only text to introduce students to the unique application of HR principles in the context of a highly complex event environment. Linking theory, research and application it looks at the purpose and processes of managing such a sizable and varied workforce in a highly pressured environment through the differing and various types of events from sporting to arts to business events.

Since the first edition, there have been many important developments in the field, and this second edition has been completely revised and updated in the following ways:

- Extensively updated content to reflect recent issues and trends including: labour markets and industry structure, impacts of IT and social media, risk management, volunteer motivation, talent management, equal opportunities, and managing diversity; all explored specifically within the event industry.
- An extended volunteer chapter, including new material on ethics, volunteer motivation and satisfaction.
- A new chapter on internal communications looks at how an effective internal communication plan can be achieved, which is a critical part of HR strategy in the unique event environment.
- Updated and new international case studies throughout to explore key issues and show real life applications of HRM in the event industry.
- New Industry Voice case studies by HR professional Kerrie Nash, sharing her expertise and experience in the field.
- Supported with new lecturer and student online resources including: PowerPoint slides, suggested answers to review questions, and web and video links to additional resources.

Written in a user friendly style, each chapter includes international examples, bulleted lists and exercises to test knowledge.

Lynn Van Der Wagen is Head of Tourism and Events Management at the Northern Beaches College, Northern Sydney Institute of TAFE. She is the author of many highly acclaimed books on tourism and hospitality, among them *Hospitality Management and Event Management: For tourism, cultural, business and sporting events*.

Lauren White is a public relations and communications professional employed by a leading global law firm. She wrote the new chapter on the role communications strategies play in integrating the workforce (stakeholders, staff, contractors and volunteers) and provided input across all other chapters.

Books in the Events Management Series

Edited by

Glenn Bowdin, Leeds Metropolitan University, UK
Don Getz, University of Calgary, Canada
Conrad Lashley, Nottingham Trent University, UK

COMPANION @ WEBSITE   A range of further resources for this book are available on the Companion
Website: www.routledge.com/cw/wagen

Human Resource Management for the Event Industry

Second edition

Lynn Van Der Wagen and Lauren White

Routledge
Taylor & Francis Group

LONDON AND NEW YORK

Second edition published 2015
by Routledge
2 Park Square, Milton Park, Abingdon, Oxon OX14 4RN

and by Routledge
711 Third Avenue, New York, NY 10017

Routledge is an imprint of the Taylor & Francis Group, an informa business

British Library Cataloguing in Publication Data
A catalogue record for this book is available from the British Library

Library of Congress Cataloging-in-Publication Data
Van der Wagen, Lynn.
 Human resource management for the event industry / Lynn Van der Wagen
 and Lauren White. – Second edition.
   pages cm – (Events management series; 12)
   Includes bibliographical references and index.
   ISBN 978–0–415–72783–9 (hardback) – ISBN 978-0-415-72782-2 (pbk.) –
   ISBN 978–1–315–85196–9 (ebk.)   1. Special events industry–Personnel
   management.   I. White, Lauren (Public relations manager)   II. Title.
   GT3405.V36 2014
   394.20068'3–dc23
                                                                    2014012409

ISBN: 978-0-415-72783-9 (hbk)
ISBN: 978-0-415-72782-2 (pbk)
ISBN: 978-1-315-85196-9 (ebk)

Typeset in Helvetica Neue
by Cenveo Publisher Services

Contents

Plates

Figures

Tables

Preface

The second edition of *Human Resource Management for Events* has been enhanced by the contributions of Kerrie Nash who is arguably the most experienced HR professional in the world of mega events. She has over 20 years experience in establishing and managing HR/training operations in the following roles:

- Director of Games Services, Glasgow
- Head of Workforce, London Organizing Committee for the Olympic and Paralympic Games
- Head of Spectator Services, Doha Asian Games Organizing Committee
- General Manager, Event Services, Special Olympics World Summer Games
- Programme Manager, Spectator Services, Manchester Commonwealth Games
- Head of Workforce Strategy and Integration, Manchester Commonwealth Games
- Programme Manager, Human Resources and Workforce Training, Sydney Committee for the Olympic and Paralympic Games.

Kerrie Nash has shared her expertise across all areas covered by the text and her quotes from the field enhance every chapter. It is not often that an author is able to access the depths of knowledge of such a highly qualified industry practitioner; and the book is enhanced by her valuable contributions.

This edition has been updated with a new chapter on internal communications which is a crucial part of the HR strategy. Effective internal communications plays an important part in workforce engagement, and this should encompass the whole workforce, contractors as well as paid staff and volunteers.

From an academic viewpoint, recent research has been incorporated and discussed in the text, including the various studies on volunteer motivation and retention. It is hoped however, that this edition raises awareness of the wider scope of human resource management for events, with particular attention paid to the contractors and partners and their role in delivering the final event product. The crisis over G4S's Olympic security preparations in London which led to police and the military stepping in to fill the void left by the private security contractor is a case in point. Failure to meet last minute recruitment and accreditation targets meant that the G4S was unable to meet contractual obligations in this high-risk area. Legal and industrial relations issues, labour market conditions, logistics and risk management are all the remit of the HR professional.

Environmental targets are important aspects of most event bid processes and even the smallest community committee pays attention to environmental sustainability. However, social impacts of events are seldom afforded the same attention and it is here that there is scope for change in the event industry. The bid for the 2004 Olympics by Cape Town, South Africa, represented the first bid from Africa, and the focus of this bid was on urban and human development. Affirmative action principles were to be applied to employment and skills development in this unsuccessful bid. Today smaller events in South Africa are used for the sole purpose of building entrepreneurial skills. For example, Skills Village 2030 is a practical framework for workplace experience that utilizes festivals and events for social inclusion, cohesion and integration.

Brazil has been in the spotlight for mega events, and their government's endorsement of affirmative action in 2001, combined with more recent attention being paid to social issues may lead to an increased focus on the social impacts of these mega events, not only outside the organization, in areas such as sports participation, but also inside the organization, in the areas of recruitment and training. This requires a genuine commitment to diversity principles and selection of employment programmes with clearly defined social objectives.

It is hoped that this text will enable event managers to shift their attention from infrastructure and operational procedures to the important area of human resource management. People deliver an event and a highly professional standard of event service should become the norm. This is particularly important in the business events sector where there is considerable international competition.

People make events successful, and there are so many of them behind the scenes. There are ticket sellers, purchasing officers, technical assistants, media monitors, cleaners, cooks, accreditation experts, security officers, risk managers, creative designers, announcers, singers and sweepers. Mostly their skills are brought together for a very short time. There is no more challenging environment for human resource management than the event business.

Events celebrate our best moments: winning the World Cup, coming first in an Olympic 100 metre swim, watching children performing, receiving an award, holding a twenty-first birthday party, or a ninetieth for that matter. Small or large, events commemorate our most important moments, and they are significant in our lives and in our cultures. Because there is so much planning and organizing to be done – because the risks are high – event professionals are needed.

There are many books on event planning, on crowd management and on economic impact analysis. But to date, there has not been a book on human resource management for the event industry. The challenge for me was irresistible. I had a background in human resource management as a training manager and director of human resources for a five star hotel. This was early in my career, and I thought the hospitality industry was the most exciting one there was. This was until I worked for the Sydney Olympic Games and discovered the world of events. It was not a soft entry into the business; it was conflict ridden and stressful. But, hey, it was exciting. And as every event manager will agree, all the angst is worth it when the event is a success. So with the rosy afterglow of a flawless mega event, I continued to teach in this area and became increasingly enchanted with the event business, later becoming involved in the Beijing Olympic Games and the Shanghai World Expo, an event that surpassed all targets with an attendance of 73 million visitors. And of course who could miss the enchantment of the London Olympic Games?

This book is for anyone managing people at a festival, carnival, exhibition, show, competition, race, display, match, concert or convention. The work needs to be analysed and allocated, contracts prepared and signed, people hired, procedures developed, staff trained, uniformed and fed. Things change constantly; the structure (physical and organizational) is often not in place until days or hours before the event starts. In this controlled chaos, decisions are quick, clear communication is essential and people need to be upbeat all the time. I have to confess that when working as a volunteer for the Sydney Olympic Games I became so tired of smiling, nodding and answering questions on my journey to and from work (two hours each way) that in the final days I went in mufti, carrying my volunteer uniform in my bag and saving my emotional energy for my shift. My hope is that the bonhomie of your events is such, too, that it wears you out! That's the measure of success: everyone around you is uplifted and energized, and you know that this event will be fixed in everyone's memory for a lifetime. People said, 'this is a once in a lifetime opportunity'. If you are entering this profession, I hope that you have many such positive opportunities.

Finally, may I welcome my co-author, Lauren White, whose important task it was to highlight the role of internal communications in integrating the efforts of the diverse and often widely dispersed workforce. Internal communications (incorporating social media) works towards developing a work culture that contributes to the event's impacts, whether these are economic, social or environmental. Some events raise money for important causes, others exhibit and sell products on the world stage, and many events reinforce the branding of the organizing body. For mega events it is the country's reputation that is on the line. Who can forget the service of Olympic Games staff and volunteers? In each case the individual's patriotism and enthusiasm contributed to their country's image domestically and internationally. Commitment of team members, volunteers and stakeholders is the key to success; the audience will remember the service experience, not the width of the pathways or the number of flags flying, long after the event is over.

Acknowledgements

The help of many people and organizations has been essential in the preparation of this book, particularly Kerrie Nash, who provided the industry insights at the end of each chapter.

The author thanks the following organizations for their contributions: Alcatel Ottawa Children's Festival; American Express; Arts Council England; Better Festival Group; California Traditional Music Society (CTMS) Annual Summer Solstice Folk Music, Dance and Storytelling Festival; Beijing 2008 Olympic Games; Boat Magazine; Canmore Folk Music Festival; Chelsea Flower Show; Edinburgh International Book Festival; Edinburgh International Festival; European Youth and Sport Forum; FIFA World Cup Soccer 2006; Food Safety, Victoria; Good Vibrations Festival; HOTBOX; International Festival and Events Association (IFEA); International Special Events Association (ISES); Korean Film Festival; Lsionline; Manchester 2002 Commonwealth Games; Melbourne 2006 Commonwealth Games; Nonprofit Risk Management Center; North Devon Journal; Ottawa Folk Festival; Oxford City Council; People 1st; Rio Times, Showforce; Special Olympics; Studio Festi; TAFE NSW; Trade Union Congress (1UC); UK Sport; Vancouver International Writers and Readers Festival; Volunteering England; Wave Aid; and Westchester County Business Journal.

The organizations listed above gave permission for me to use their material. Every effort has been made to trace the owners of copyright material, in some cases with limited success, and I offer apologies to any copyright holders whose rights I may have unwittingly infringed.

I would also like to thank Ruth Blackwell, Glenn Bowdin, Matthew Lazarus-Hall, Rob Harris, Roy Masters, Nola Sher, Tony Webb, and the editorial and production teams who produced the book.

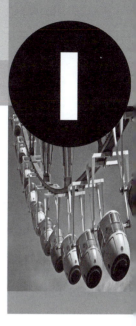

PART **I**

Human resource strategic planning
Establishing the context

Part I of this book establishes a context for human resource management in the event business. The different types of event include business events (conferences and exhibitions), sports, arts, entertainment and community events, street parades and festivals. These events may be commercial or not for profit. They may be fundraising events or simply big parties.

The functions of human resource management of recruitment, selection, induction, training and performance management are important parts of every event organizer's job. In the case of large events, including mega events such as the Winter Olympic Games or FIFA World Cup, the size of the event would clearly warrant a specialist human resources team. For smaller events, these functions would be undertaken by the organizer, organizing committee or area managers.

In this environment, there is typically a diverse range of employment arrangements and very frequently there are volunteers involved. Most events are project based, occurring once only or annually. Chapter 1 will discuss the unique features of the event environment that differentiate it from other traditional business environments in which human resource management is practised. Chapter 2 will look at planning from a macro perspective, looking at the whole workforce that could include paid staff, volunteers and contractors (vendors/suppliers) who provide event services such as catering. The growth of the event team over time and the phases of organizational development will be covered in Chapter 3, shortly followed by a discussion in Chapter 4 of the issues associated with volunteer management. Chapter 5 deals with the employment of event service providers such as security, cleaning, waste management and technical support (lighting and sound). Having developed an awareness of the overall responsibility that the event organizer has for the health and safety of everyone working on site, the following chapter, Chapter 6, will discuss employment legislation in more detail. Finally, Chapter 7 will discuss the process of job analysis, leading to the development of job descriptions that form the basis for many other human resource functions (such as training) which are covered in Part II when the text moves on to operational planning. Overall, Part I is largely focused on the development of a strategic plan for human resource management of one or more events.

The event environment

Learning objectives

After reading through this chapter you will be able to:

- Differentiate between events in terms of size, scope and type of event.
- Identify a range of factors that differentiate events from more traditional ongoing business enterprises.
- Discuss the management of events in terms of creative and organizational attributes of organizers.
- Describe contemporary, strategic approaches to human resource management.
- Differentiate between the different groups of people comprising the event workforce.
- Discuss the emergence of event management as a profession.

Introduction

International events such as the Olympic Games, FIFA World Cup, World Championship in Athletics, Americas Cup, Commonwealth Games and many other mega sporting events continue to grow in size and investment. Most importantly, this growth is matched by the almost exponential growth of the television audience that watches these world-class competitions. So much so, that the organizers of opening and closing ceremonies will freely admit that these ceremonies are no longer designed for the audience seated in the stadium, even if these spectators have paid thousands of pounds for their tickets. The ceremonies are designed with every camera shot in mind, and CAD designs are used to visualize the on-screen effects from the various camera positions well in advance, most particularly those from high vantage points above the stadium. Major sponsors want to know beforehand how their logos will appear in the footage of the ceremony – how they will be positioned and how long they will appear on screen. There are also all sorts of political pressures brought to bear on the design of the ceremonies programme, with the host country branding itself according to the images portrayed. There are athletes, performers, players, entertainers, ushers, security staff, police and a multitude of other staff, including volunteers, working behind the scenes and many others performing on the stage or field of play. Managing the interests of everyone involved, meeting deadlines on a multitude of projects that are codependent and immutable in their timelines are just a few of the challenges of this environment. The 2005 Live 8 Concerts were held in 10 cities, including London, Philadelphia, Paris, Berlin, Johannesburg, Rome and Moscow, and played to hundreds of thousands of people. A TV audience of several hundred million was watching the gigs. In this case, the event was not a sporting event but a social justice initiative to eliminate poverty in Africa. This example further illustrates the challenges of producing an event on such a large scale, with specific political and economic aims in mind. The workforce for mega events is similar in scale and composition, Beijing Olympic Games for example recruiting 70,000 volunteers for the Summer Games and 30,000 for the Paralympic Games (primarily students). However, it was reported that an additional 400,000 municipal volunteers provided other services outside of the venues and a record 1,125,799 people applied to be volunteers! The London Olympic Games recruited a similar number (70,000) but with a more diverse profile having received 240,000 volunteer applications. Rio's diversity manifesto is as follows: 'we demonstrate appreciation of human diversity. It strengthens friendship among all, welcomes and respects the participation of each individual in this collective movement, emphasizing the principle that we all belong to one single world'. The volunteers are however the friendly face of an event which is staged by a multidisciplinary team. There is the paid workforce of the organizing committee and the project management team to consider and they are the core staff carrying overall responsibility for a successful event.

The additional size and scope of the contractor workforce is generally underestimated, often as much as 50 per cent of the operational crew, including providers of goods and services, also known as vendors. Many services, such as catering and cleaning, are contracted out and there is sometimes debate about whose responsibility it is to develop the event-related knowledge and customer service skills required by contractor employees on the site. As Goldblatt points out,

> You are being paid for creating memorable positive experiences, and you and your staff are the critical resource that makes the guest's experience memorable. Issues such as your human resource organization, training, and employee retention are vital if you are to remain competitive.
>
> (Goldblatt, 2005b: 108)

Events: a new context for human resource management

Events are not only challenging in their size, scope and timeline. Many events are smaller, locally based and involve only a limited number of people compared with larger events.

However, human resource management remains a key success factor when the wide range of stakeholders and participants need to be brought to one purpose. Frequently, even the organizing committee cannot agree on the primary purpose of the event! Anyone who has sat on an event committee would know this.

Essentially, the biggest difference between the management of an event and the management of an ongoing business enterprise is that the event is generally intangible, untested and there is only one chance to get it right. In contrast, a retail store that doesn't sell the stock this month can put it all on sale next month and hope to at least meet its costs. Events are often high stakes ventures; at the mid-scale level, a festival can represent the labours and dreams of the whole community. At the lower-end, in terms of scale, the most obvious example is a wedding. Well, at least one hopes that this is a once in a lifetime celebration! Indeed this event, although small, may represent a family's life savings thus making it a high stakes venture that needs to run flawlessly. Only the scale differs.

Classification and characteristics of events

There have been many efforts to characterize events by type. The main classifications encompass business, sporting and cultural events. While technically, sports would come under the umbrella of culture, it is useful for us to differentiate this category. One further way in which events can be further classified by type is as not-for-profit and commercial/profitable events. An overview of event types is shown in Table 1.1.

Many event characteristics have already been discussed and these will be elaborated further. First however, it is important to attempt to define 'event' and 'event product'. As Brown and James (2004) point out, there are as many definitions as there are textbooks. For Goldblatt (1997) a special event is a 'unique moment in time celebrated with ceremony and ritual to satisfy specific needs'. While this definition clearly satisfies most events falling in the category of cultural events, it is not entirely satisfactory for many large-scale, commercial or corporate events such as product launches and other business events which are not necessarily celebratory. Perhaps a definition on which most writers would agree is that an event is generally a complex social endeavour characterized by sophisticated planning with a fixed deadline, often involving numerous stakeholders.

The event product is the whole package of goods and services. This is primarily the event programme but it also includes merchandise, food, service, the environment, transport, queues etc. Salem, Jones and Morgan describe the event product as 'a unique blend of activities, which are the tools for achieving the overall event aims and satisfying customer needs' (Salem et al., 2004: 19). In order to achieve its purpose, an event must meet human needs at all levels, and the management of human resources in order to provide an optimal experience for the audience is a critical part of product planning.

By way of example (and estimate) an annual festival might have the following income and staffing ratios:

- audience of 100,000 over five days (20,000 per day)
- 15 permanent staff

TABLE 1.1 Classification of events		
Business	Meetings, conventions and conferences	Many associations have annual conferences around the world and the bid process for these is conducted many years in advance. For example, the International Conference on Alzheimer's Disease and Related Disorders, presented by the Alzheimer's Association (USA), is the largest gathering of Alzheimer researchers. More than 3,000 scientists from around the world from 67 countries attend. However, in terms of conventions this is only mid-scale.
	Exhibitions	The world's biggest information and communication technology exhibition CeBIT is held annually. Firms from upwards of 64 countries present their products and systems at the Hanover show where about 850,000 visitors attend. Many agricultural fairs have animal exhibitions and competitions, this adding somewhat to the challenges for organizers. Bulls, horses and dogs all require careful handling!
	Incentives	Incentives are corporate events organized for high achieving staff, often held at a resort or holiday destination but including work related meetings and presentations. In 2011 CITS sent 10,000 participants to South Korea setting the record of the largest Chinese tourist group visiting South Korea.
Sports	Competitive sports events	All stages of sporting competition including amateur and professional fall into this category with a multitude of sports such as baseball, cricket, football.
	Non-competitive sports events	Fun days and non-competitive activities characterize this type of sporting event, runs and walks supporting charities, and dragon boat races of the non-competitive variety providing another colourful example.
Cultural	Arts	Arts festivals come in a multitude of formats including, for example, the Adelaide Festival of Ideas. Film festivals are popular around the world. The Edinburgh Festival, which includes classical music, opera, theatre and dance, would fit into this category.
	Entertainment	There are many music concerts held around the world, on a large and small scale with multiple different music genres represented.
	Virtual/hybrid events	Many live events are now broadcast on the internet leading to the use of the term 'hybrid event' to include the virtual audience. Many conferences now follow this format. The shows 'American Idol' and 'Super Voice Girl' merge live events with television broadcasts, also involving a wide range of social media.
	Community – historical and anniversary celebrations	Founding days and other anniversary days are popular for celebration, including centenary and bicentenary celebrations of community. Multicultural festivals are also popular.

Social action – cause related events	Generally fundraising in nature, this type of event can include those such as the Live 8 Concert. There have been relief concerts to raise money for the victims of the tsunami in SE Asia and hurricanes in the USA. This type of event is often directed at a specific and immediate humanitarian crisis.
Protests/political events	Many street protests, against globalization for example, fall into this category. There is an annual calendar of protest events and international days of action around the world.
Life cycle/ milestones	Baptisms, Bar Mitzvahs, weddings and funerals are all life cycle events. While most are small scale, the funeral of Nelson Mandela rivaled that of Pope John Paul II in 2005, which drew 5 kings, 6 queens and 70 presidents and prime ministers as well as 2 million faithful. Mandela's funeral was the world's largest gathering of Heads of State thus presenting high-level security risks.
Religious	Ranging from small to large scale including, for example, the Indian Kumbha Mela, which attracted 100 million people over 44 days in 2013.

- 700 temporary, seconded or contractor staff
- total revenue 8.7m GBP (of which ticket sales 70 per cent, concessions 20 per cent, merchandise 3 per cent, sponsorship 7 per cent).

However, there are few industry benchmarks as there are for example in the hotel industry.

The things that make marketing of event products complex are their features of intangibility, inseparability, heterogeneity and perishability, core service marketing concepts. In particular, the product leaves little that lasts, other than a few photos or memorabilia. One aspect of the event product that is seldom acknowledged in discussing event marketing is the anticipatory element of the product. Most events are something that the audience, and indeed the participants, will look forward to since they are significant and generally positive social occasions. By enhancing this part of the product one can enhance service and satisfaction. Staff training usually has the event programme and related service delivery as its focus. This needs to be expanded to cover the lead up period during which time staff are selling tickets, registering participants or providing information. Often the client works with the event management company over a long period. The service provided during this sometimes stressful time needs to be managed just as well as the actual event production.

Key characteristics of the event industry at the present time include the following.

Worldwide interest

Increasing globalization, a growing television audience and exposure to the web has led to increased interest in events as a reflection of contemporary culture. In some extreme instances, sporting events can stop the nation and the world. This is certainly the case

CASE STUDY 1.1
Bid to recruit 2014 World Cup volunteers

The Brazilian government last week launched an audacious bid to find 50,000 volunteers to help ensure the 2014 World Cup logistics run smoothly. In addition, 7,000 will be expected to lend a hand at the Confederations Cup this June.

Last August FIFA, the world football (soccer) governing body, set up their own initiative, but the Brazilian government have jumped on board. Headed by the country's Ministry for Sport, Aldo Rebelo, the two are now working in partnership.

Volunteers recruited by the government will be enrolled to aid both tourists and the general public during the events. Specific locations include airports, tourist points, public parties, of which there are likely to be hundreds during the tournaments, and well-known night spots. There will be three volunteer groups; management support, event task force and tourist support.

Ricardo Trade, chief executive of the Local Organizing Committee (COL), said: 'This programme is fantastic. Volunteers will be pivotal to the success of the events [the Confederation and World Cups]'.

As volunteers, those recruited will not be entitled to any form of financial remuneration for their time and effort. They will however receive meals, transport to and from their place of duty, an official uniform and insurance against accidents while working.

According to the Ministry for Sport, the Brazilian government will be spending in the region of R$30 million (7.7m GBP) during the recruitment process. These costs cover selecting and training volunteers, purchase of uniforms, meals, transport expenses and insurance cover.

Aldo Rebelo, the Minister for Sport, said, 'We want the volunteer scheme to reflect Brazilian society as a whole. It will be a celebration of football's greatest virtues: hope, optimism and a coming together of people'.

Source: Rio Times Online: http://riotimesonline.com/brazil-news/rio-sports/2014worldcup/bid-to-recruit-2014-world-cup-volunteers/

Reflective practice 1.1

Explain the difference between the volunteer programme proposed by the government and that run by the organizing body (FIFA) in general terms.

Many volunteers apply from outside the country to work at this type of event. Discuss the approach you would take to signing up volunteers from other countries for a major or mega event.

with some athletic events in the Summer Olympics. Two billion viewers watched Pope John Paul II's funeral. The execution of this event was doubtlessly planned in most infinite detail, an extraordinary ceremony attended by the world's leaders and watched worldwide. South African leaders said that the funeral of Nelson Mandela was larger than that of Princess Diana, Michael Jackson and Pope John Paul II combined. This event and the broadcast was marred by the 'fake sign language interpreter' but security fears for the event's assembly of world leaders were unfounded.

Competitive environment

Countries and cities involved in bid processes demonstrate the competitive nature of event procurement. Many conferences and exhibitions attract thousands of visitors and their expenditure is generally much higher than the average international visitor. All over the world, in Asia, and China in particular, there are initiatives to build bigger and better convention facilities in order to attract this lucrative segment.

Economic and tourism impact

Business events, cultural and sporting events also contribute in significant ways to economic and tourism impacts. Many cities and suburbs are branded by their hallmark events, including Edinburgh, Monaco, Rio, Calgary and Chelsea. Counted here is the direct expenditure of visitors and event organizers as well as the indirect (or flow on) economic effect on the wider community.

Consumers are looking for authentic or imaginative event products

Consumers look for a point of difference, and in particular look for authenticity when visiting an event as a tourist. When there are leisure options, an event needs to provide the motivation to attend. In the case of annual events, the visitor needs a reason to return. WOMAD provides an example of a popular and enduring event, held in several cities. WOMAD stands for World of Music, Arts and Dance, expressing the central aim of the WOMAD festival – to bring together and to celebrate many forms of music, arts and dance drawn from countries and cultures all over the world. The organizers say that they aim to excite, to inform and to create awareness of the worth and potential of a multicultural society.

Benefits to the host community

The community expects to be consulted when there is an anticipated impact on their local area. The community needs to know that the positive impacts will outweigh the short-term negative impacts. There are many residents of Melbourne who remain opposed to the motor race held annually in their city, the Melbourne Grand Prix. On the other hand, Chinese citizens displaced by the massive construction projects of the 2008 Olympic Games demonstrated resigned acceptance to the planning priorities established by their government. In Rio de Janeiro, protests were held against expulsions and demolitions and a public groundswell of protest emerged in response to concerns over government funding deployed from services to meet the costs of staging the World Cup and the Olympic Games. Even the smallest community event must be approved by local authority, whose role it is to ensure that the event is a good fit with the community, has minimal risk and, indeed, will contribute in a positive way to the social fabric of the region.

Minimizing risk

Public liability and other insurances are significant considerations for event organizers. Safety is a primary concern, particularly when there are additional risks associated with mass gatherings. Crowd behaviour and potential fatalities at sporting and music events are a worldwide issue.

Political influence

When many large events require government support at one level or another (including at local level) there are always political considerations. In Australia, for example, a regional event is much more likely to attract funding than a city event since regional development is a political priority. Naturally bidding for mega events such as the Olympic Games or FIFA World Cup requires government support at the highest level with countries being fiercely competitive. The hosting of 2020 World Expo in Dubai is expected to establish the city as an international business and sporting event destination as well as an economic hub for the region.

Complex design and execution

Most events do not carry a blueprint. They are often complex and risky artistic endeavours attracting media attention. They can involve hundreds of people as spectators, participants and workers. All of these people join together for a typically short period, ranging from a few hours to a few days. In that short time the purpose and aims of the event must be achieved. Plans are dynamic and the whole project is often quite organic, some might say chaotic.

Multiple stakeholders

Sponsors are the most demanding of stakeholders and rightly so if they have made a significant investment. In some cases, they compete against each other in terms of exposure if their expectations aren't carefully managed. Sponsors want signage, media coverage and a range of other benefits. Other stakeholders include government, tourism bodies, emergency services, roads authorities, contractors and the local community to name just a few. In the simplest example, at a music festival the teenagers want to go wild, their parents want them to behave like 50 year olds and the police would prefer that they stay at home. The bands encourage the fans to behave badly and the security staff have their hands full monitoring drug and alcohol abuse. For large events there are competing contractor organizations who have to submit tenders for event services such as security. This can become fraught with problems if the tendering is not above board and if the contracts are not awarded with sufficient time for effective implementation.

Volunteer management

Many events, large and small, are organized or staffed by volunteers. This brings further challenges as the event manager responsible for human resources needs to evaluate the specific needs of volunteers and ensure that they are met. Volunteers may be motivated by patriotism or a commitment to the cause behind the event, such as fundraising. In many cases, volunteers have high expectations of having a good time and will leave if this is not the case. Attrition rates will be discussed in a later chapter. The decisions relating to the size and scope of the volunteer workforce need to be carefully considered.

PLATE 1.1 Ambulance officer, surf lifesaver and volunteer, all part of the event workforce for a swimming event

Event management – art or science?

Attempts to describe the responsibilities of event managers often elaborate on the challenges of logistics and operations. Indeed, Brown and James suggest that many practitioners

> have put aside, ignored or failed to consider the conceptual development and design of their events – the very heart and soul, the raison d'être of any truly great event – in favour of artificially manufacturing events that try to meet the needs of clients and stakeholders.
>
> (Brown and James, 2004: 53)

Their position will be taken up here as a discussion about the art and science of event management. Other writers suggest that a project management approach such as EMBOK (event management body of knowledge) could be used to formalize and develop the professionalism of the contemporary event manager (Goldblatt, 2005a; Silvers et al., 2006). Clearly event management is both an art and a science. It is a science in the same way that meticulous project planning is applied to the building of a bridge. Indeed many events involve the building of infrastructure of one sort or another. However, this is only part of event management. The other part of event management is more akin to producing a movie. Here people and resources are brought together in a creative and costly pursuit in which the audience response defines success or failure. Thus event management is in some ways like engineering, while in others it is like movie making. The question is whether one and the same person can be the artist and the scientist or whether these roles are best separated. There has to be a tension between artistic vision and operational implementation. This is illustrated by successive Olympic Games opening ceremonies where in the short period of four years, the technology used surpasses that used in previous ceremonies. However at its essence the opening ceremony is a production not a project. In contrast, an exhibition such as CeBIT, the largest computer exhibition in the world, is more like a project of massive proportions. Events require vision, and a later chapter will revisit continuum of art and science as it applies to the design and management of events, and look in detail at the topic of event leadership. Figure 1.1 illustrates the continuum of creative and organizational input required for various different types of events, arts and entertainment events typically requiring extensive creative input while exhibitions require more attention to logistics.

Contemporary human resource management

The personnel function used to be associated quite narrowly with recruitment, selection and implementation of company policy. Indeed in some event organizations this is the role or function allocated to one or more individuals: to ensure that the event is adequately staffed and that policies and rules are put into place to manage the event workforce.

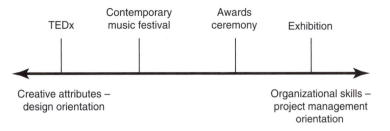

TEDx   Contemporary music festival   Awards ceremony   Exhibition

Creative attributes – design orientation   Organizational skills – project management orientation

FIGURE 1.1 Continuum of creative and organizational input required for different types of events

However, contemporary human resource managers see their role as being more strategic and business oriented. Where the event organization has this focus, whether in the form of a human resources department or in the form of allocating this function to relevant managers, there are considerable benefits.

Labour cost is frequently one of the most significant costs associated with running an event, complicated by the fact that such a large proportion of this labour cost is often hidden in agreements developed with contractors, such as catering contractors. This needs to be acknowledged when undertaking strategic planning for human resource management. Following a scoping exercise to determine the multitude of tasks that need to be undertaken, strategic decisions must be made about which of these tasks should be outsourced. A risk analysis is necessary to ensure that the job analysis is based on sound decision making. For example, it is commonplace to contract security organizations to manage this role. Their staff are adequately trained, carry the necessary licenses and are expert at this type of work. Well of course, this is what one hopes and plans for.

Thus at a strategic level, the event organization needs to decide which services should be outsourced to professional service providers and which kept in-house. These are critical decisions, driven by labour market forces, the most significant issue being the temporary nature of most event related employment. Maximizing performance and achieving optimal levels of service is only possible with strategic human resource planning. Risk management is a key aspect of this planning and at the end of Chapter 3 Kerrie Nash, whose expertise in mega-event HRM is unparalleled, lists her top six risks.

Human resource management of events

One of the most distinct features of events is the management of the people needed to design and stage the festival, exhibition, street parade or competition. This is no ordinary business environment. Most organizations hold onto their employees for months and years, giving them time to socialize and develop their skills and knowledge in the context of the business. In the event environment on the other hand, there is generally a handful of individuals on the planning team and a mass of paid, voluntary and contractor employees working on a temporary site for anything from a few hours to a few days. Developing a vision or purpose for the event, conducting a detailed job analysis, responding to constant

PLATE 1.2 Montage of workforce roles

changes in operational planning and meeting the communication needs of all involved are just some of the tasks of the human resource manager. Indeed, most events do not have a human resource manager, and this function is undertaken by the senior staff from the event manager down to the team leader. It is thus vitally important that each person in a management or supervisory role understands the human resource function and their contribution to managing the people in this extended and temporary workforce. This challenging and dynamic environment is one which tests people management skills to the limit. As one event manager describes it, 'something will always go wrong, it is how

TABLE 1.2 Event workforce
Event committee
The role of the committee is to formally identify the primary purpose and goals of the event and to monitor progress towards those goals. The committee members can take on responsibilities such as production, marketing, staffing, operations and finance.
Stakeholders
There are multiple stakeholders who impact on event planning from different directions, such as local government, emergency services, roads and transport, environment protection authority, police, sponsors. The owner/manager of the venue (facility) is one of the primary stakeholders and will be listed separately.
Event staff
The paid staff of the event organization (or collaboration of more than one event organization) share responsibility for designing and producing the event. Paid staff are usually experienced and qualified, if not in the events business, then in a related field. This group can remain quite small until close to the event. In some cases, the paid workforce includes staff on secondment, particularly from government agencies. This is the team that produces or stages the event, whether sporting, entertainment or business.
Venue (facility) team
The venue team generally co-ordinates venue operations. In the sporting world this could be a stadium in which services are provided to the audience. This could also be the staff of a convention centre or hotel providing a wide range of core services such as food and beverage.
Contractors
Few events run without the extensive use of contracting organizations (suppliers) to provide goods and services. These include for example, all temporary fencing and facilities. Lighting, sound, stage management, electrical, entertainment, catering and waste management are just a few examples of contractors and sub-contractors.
Volunteers
Many community events involve volunteers, sometimes from the committee down. The number of volunteers varies depending on the type and scale of the event. For many sporting events, the volunteers are specialists in their areas of scoring etc. Commercial events such as exhibitions seldom include volunteers.

you respond to it that matters'. As Table 1.2 illustrates, there are several different types of people involved in putting on the show. In some cases, their interests differ, particularly when safety issues are balanced with expenditure. Conflict is commonplace when there is a difference of opinion about for example, the choice of entertainment. In this case the committee might agree but the sponsor does not approve or endorse their choice.

As Drummond and Anderson point out, 'quality in the operational environment of events and festivals is directly related to the people delivering the service' (Drummond and Anderson, 2004: 88). The customer interacts with any number of service providers, such as ticket sellers, security staff and cleaners. These people could all work for contracting organizations and are therefore not under the direct control of the event organization. Managing the quality of such interactions is imperative, and the selection and training of contractor organizations and their staff will be discussed in detail in later chapters. In relation to the service staff whose role it is to manage customers at an event, these authors stress that 'the communication and professional skills of these people influence the whole understanding of the organization in the visitor's mind' (Drummond and Anderson, 2004: 89).

Event management as an emerging profession

There has been recent debate about the emergence of event management as a profession (Goldblatt, 2005a; Harris, 2004). If the level of interest by students in this area and the number of courses offered is anything to go by, one would have to accept that, indeed, this is a new profession. However, Harris (2004) analyses this issue in some detail to conclude that a lack of common purpose and unity precludes the development of the event profession in the current environment. This is largely due to the numerous industry associations representing different sectors such as conferences, exhibitions, special events, venue management and the like. While the industry is fragmented and lacks a common code, as you would find for example with the medical or engineering professions, there is little hope for the development of a single professional association and code of conduct. However, this author does provide a model for the professionalization of event management, illustrated in Figure 1.2. which takes into account the trait, functionalist and business approaches to emerge with a model for the UK event industry. Events carry with them a number of risks, most importantly risks associated with public safety and for this reason qualifications in both vocational and higher education sectors are becoming essential requirements for the aspiring event manager. Steyne (2012) identifies that a gap exists between the current event management curriculum outcomes at higher education institutions in South Africa and the expected competencies of sport event managers in practice.

Ethics and corporate responsibility

Ethics and corporate responsibility are key elements for an event organization, particularly human resources responsibilities such as occupational health and safety, volunteer management, contractor management and, indeed, people management in general. While Webb (2001) stresses the positive collaboration that occurred between stakeholders of the Sydney 2000 Olympic Games, particularly between unions and organizers, he does point out that goodwill played an important part in the few cases where staff were not paid for two weeks due to a range of glitches including time recording. While for this event, problems were overcome for bus drivers who were unhappy with their pay, accommodation, food and shifts, there are many smaller events where both employees and volunteers feel that they have been treated badly. This is seldom reported due to the short-term nature of the event, those involved simply deciding never to become involved again.

Of all HR responsibilities, concern for the safety of staff (and audience) is most important. Since the crowd crush at the E2 Night Club took twenty-one lives in Chicago

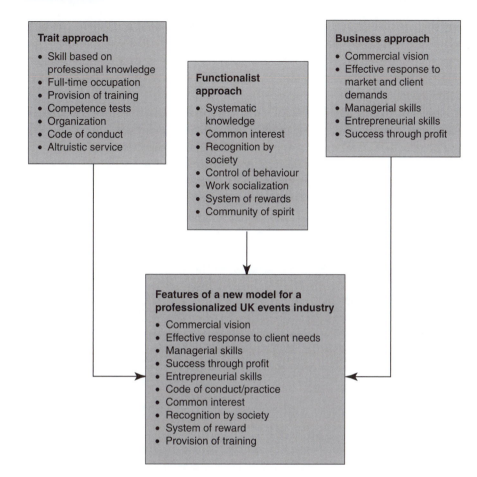

FIGURE 1.2 The new model: professionalization of events management

in 2003, and the inferno at The Station nightclub, also 2003, claimed 100 lives in the fourth-deadliest nightclub fire in US history, the National Fire Protection Association has enacted tough new code provisions for fire sprinklers and crowd management in nightclub-type venues. Crowd managers are required to control the crowd, keep egress paths clear and assist in rapid evacuation. The *Life Safety Code* calls for one crowd manager for every 250 attendees and that they undergo approved training in crowd management techniques. This has implications for recruitment and training, for HR risk management and for workplace supervision, including monitoring and control of contract labour. Across the industry there are moves to improve safety. The Crowdsafe website has guidelines for managing crowds and mosh pits and conducts ongoing research into crowd safety. Increased threats to mass gatherings are a major concern for authorities whenever large events are staged.

Finally, an emerging trend is the analysis of ROI (return on investment) or ROO (return on objectives) for the HR aspects of event planning. Clearly all initiatives, such as training the event project team or developing and implementing an internal communications strategy such as that discussed in Chapter 16, require a budget allocation. The question is whether the temporal nature of most events can justify this expenditure. This sits in contrast to the sectors of the industry such as business events (conferences and exhibitions) where a return on investment in people is likely to improve the organization's competitive position.

While the International Festivals and Events Association (shown in the case study) has a voluntary code, it is likely that higher levels of legislative compliance will become necessary in many countries as more event planning elements fall under the scope of legislation. It is really a case of 'watch this space' as governments and associations work towards developing legislation, recommendations, guidelines and codes of practice which will further develop the profession of event management and raise the status of organizations which demonstrate best practice. In the United Kingdom, several guides are available on

CASE STUDY 1.2
Code of conduct

The International Festivals and Events Association (IFEA) has a code of professional responsibility which includes the following standard specifically related to human resource management:

Principle/Standard #4: Members shall embrace and promote the highest standards of human resource training and management.

Consideration #1: In its development as an industry, festival and special event organizations and professionals must establish the highest standards of professional hiring, employment and development. As such, members should take such action as necessary to ensure that they, as individuals and organizations, establish and practice ethical hiring, termination and discipline practices for employees and associates. At a minimum, members and member organizations shall operate in compliance with all federal, local and state laws concerning the hiring, promotion, and discipline of employees. Because of the industry's commitment to social and community development, members and member organizations should take every reasonable opportunity to ensure and encourage the diversity of their membership, and employee and volunteer base.

Consideration #2: Members and member organizations should take such action as necessary to comply with federal, state, and local Equal Opportunity Employment laws and to avoid the practice and tolerance of discrimination based on race, creed, national origin, age, handicap, political affiliation, sex, sexual orientation, religion, parental or military status, veteran status, or disability. At a minimum, members and their organizations shall comply with all laws applicable to the jurisdiction(s) in which they conduct business.

Source: http://www.ifea.com/about/#27

Reflective practice 1.2

Explain why you think codes of practice should be necessary for event management.

This code looks at hiring, equal employment opportunity (EEO) and training. Suggest other human resource practices that could be covered by a code of practice.

the HSE (Health and Safety Executive) site to assist with safety and crowd management at events both large and small. However with the rapid growth of the industry in size and scale, including both mega events, such as the Olympic Games, and small community festivals, there will be moves to ensure compliance in a much more rigorous way all over the world. Recognized training will become a minimum requirement for many roles in the event industry. As outcomes of this training, Arcodia and Axelson show that organizations advertising for event managers rate the following five skills as most important, based on the number of times these skills were mentioned in their study of 1,002 job advertisements: organizational/planning skills; general communication skills; team skills; customer service skills; and computer skills (Arcodia and Axelson, 2005). In addition, a detailed knowledge of human resources/industrial relations legislation and codes of practice for staffing and supervision will be found on the job specification of every event manager and event human resources specialist.

Summary

Events celebrate, inspire and commemorate. To make them successful, the work must be planned and allocated according to the vision and goals of the event. Done strategically, this includes the management of contractor organizations and their staff as well as the relationships with key stakeholders. For all but the biggest events, there is no human resources manager. This function is undertaken by the event committee and the organizer. Each manager and supervisor is responsible for his or her people, making sure that they provide optimal service in a dynamic environment. With the emerging emphasis on professionalism in the event business, human resource management is a key element. Codes of practice and legislative requirements make it essential that event organizational planning is undertaken by people who are professionally qualified, in this case in Human Resource Management as it applies in the unique environment of event management.

Revision questions

1   Using the event classification (Table 1.1) listed in this chapter, identify a specific/real event to match each of the categories.

2 List and explain 10 characteristics of the event environment most relevant to human resource management.
3 Using a major or mega event, explain in detail how this event is structured in terms of staffing with for example, the names of sponsors or contractor organizations.

Industry voice by Kerrie Nash

One of the first things I would be doing in an event in any country would be commissioning a labour market analysis. This is in order to understand the skills in the local market that we are likely to need to access.

From there, you need to build a plan, working with local government and others, to ensure that opportunities for local employment and skills are maximized.

Another consideration is that when people come on board into functional areas, they can become very adept at putting up walls and defining what they do and don't do. That can leave gaps. I think it's an important part of HR's role to help break down some of those walls by setting expectations right from the attraction and recruitment stage. You need to explain that the expectation of the business is that employees look at what's going on around them, take on board the 'orphans', take on things which are closely aligned to their role, and do not build up the walls saying 'I only do this'. Collaboration and integration is a key aspect of event organizational development.

Discussion questions

Few events are large enough to make an impact on employment and skills in the region, although McDonald's (official sponsor and trainer of the London volunteer workforce) made a guarantee to offer every one of the volunteers that lived in an Olympic borough and who were not in employment, education or training to have the opportunity to receive a City and Guilds Level Two qualification in the principles of customer services.

See more at: http://www.hrmagazine.co.uk/hr/features/1020999/olympics-special-interview-jez-langhorn-vp-people-mcdonalds#sthash.F2LSRqg1.dpuf

1 Looking instead at smaller events of different types explain how these events can lead to positive social impacts for full time staff, volunteers, agency personnel and interns.
2 Kerrie suggests that HR plays a role in integration. Looking back at the key tasks of HRM described in this chapter explain how this can be facilitated.

References

Arcodia, C. and Axelson, M. (2005). 'A review of event management job advertisements in Australian newspapers', *The Impacts of Events*, University of Technology Sydney, Sydney.

Brown, S. and James, J. (2004). 'Event design and management: ritual sacrifice?' in I. Yeoman, M. Robertson, J. Ali-Knight, S. Drummond and U. McMahon-Beattie (eds), *Festival and Events Management: An International Arts and Culture Perspective*. Oxford: Elsevier Butterworth-Heinemann.

Drummond, S. and Anderson, H. (2004). 'Service quality and managing your people'. In I. Yeoman, M. Robertson, J. Ali-Knight, S. Drummond and U. McMahon-Beattie (eds), *Festival and Events Management*, 80–96.

Goldblatt, J. (1997). *Special Events*, 2nd edn. New York: John Wiley and Sons Inc.

Goldblatt, J. (2005a). 'An exploratory study of demand levels for EMBOK', *The Impacts of Events*, University of Technology Sydney, Sydney.

Goldblatt, J. (2005b). *Special Events: Event Leadership for a New World*, 4th edn. Hoboken, NJ: The Wiley Event Management Series.

Harris, V. (2004). 'Event management: a new profession', *Event Management*, 9, 103–109.

Salem, G., Jones, E. and Morgan, N. (2004). 'An overview of events management', in I. Yeoman, M. Robertson, J. Ali-Knight and U. McMahon-Beattie (eds), *Festival and Events Management*, Oxford: Elsevier Butterworth-Heinemann.

Silvers, J. R., Bowdin, G. A., O'Toole, W. J. and Nelson, K. B. (2006). 'Towards an international event management body of knowledge (EMBOK)', *Event Management*, 9(4), 185–198.

Steyn, E. (2012). *Training of Sport Event Managers for the South African Context* (thesis). Available at: https://ujdigispace.uj.ac.za/bitstream/handle/10210/8203/Steyn.pdf?sequence=1; viewed 14 January 2014.

Webb, T. (2001). *The Collaborative Games: The Story Behind the Spectacle*. Annandale, NSW: Pluto Press.

Human resource planning

After reading through this chapter you will be able to:

- Provide and discuss definitions of human resource management.
- Describe the strategic human resources planning role.
- Illustrate how human resource planning is linked to the event purpose and goals.
- Discuss issues relating to integrating human resources functions across projects.
- Describe key human resource functions.
- Conduct a human resources risk analysis.

Introduction

Human resource management is much more than recruitment and selection of staff and volunteers; it is a wide-ranging activity, involved with long term strategic development of the event organization. The expected outcome of this is a positive culture of commitment and cooperation developed in the process of managing the workforce. In the event business, there are diverse non-traditional employment contracts, and an extraordinarily complex workforce which needs to be integrated into one body working towards the same purpose and goals. For a mega event this collaboration and cohesion needs to occur over a long and stressful planning period which can take four years or more. It is entirely conceivable that the planning team becomes frustrated, particularly during the periods when the media is critical about issues such as budget overruns, and alternative options (jobs, lifestyle changes) are considered. In fact, a serious consideration for event human resource managers is the possibility that key staff will bail out shortly before a mega-event in order to avoid competing with peers in a flooded employment market soon after the event. One can easily conceive of an event where the infrastructure is not complete and the venues are still being constructed in the final days before opening. In the same way, human resources strategies can fail to meet their objectives and the human side of the event can spiral into disaster very quickly. The human version of the wet concrete syndrome must be avoided at all costs; people must be confident and ready to meet the opening deadline. One of the key lessons and recommendations from the Manchester Commonwealth Games Report (2003: 78) was that

> timely procurement of contractors and monitoring their recruitment are two crucial components of Games delivery for the accreditation team. This group, the biggest in terms of volume, need to be carefully monitored as their overall management can affect the effectiveness of the Games.

This recommendation points directly to the issue that arose with the security contractor at the Olympic Games ten years later. Scaling up the workforce at the last minute proved impossible and the military was brought in. In a broader sense, contractor workforce planning is just as important as that of the core team and any volunteer programme.

Definitions of human resource management

The range and variety of definitions for event management are matched by those for human resource management, which is problematic if a single definition is necessary, or indeed desirable. Armstrong (2012) suggests that the goals of HRM are to:

- support the organization in achieving its objectives by developing and implementing HR strategies that are integrated with the business strategy;
- contribute to a high performance culture;
- ensure that the organization has the talented, skilled and engaged people it needs.

Buller and McEvoy (2012) present a model to align organizational, group and individual factors with the organization's strategy. They redefine 'line of sight' as 'the alignment of organizational capabilities and culture, group competencies and norms, and individual KSAs, motivation and opportunity with one another and with the organization's strategy' (p. 43).

The external business environment will be stressed in this chapter where a detailed labour force analysis is often required to identify whether sufficient numbers of skilled individuals are available for short term employment with the event organization. Indeed for many of the larger events, senior event professionals travel the world to meet the temporary needs of event projects. While the need for specialist staff may be met overseas, the bulk of the labour force required for the very short period of event execution is typically large and unskilled. For this reason, consideration might be given to running the event during school and university holidays with a view to employing large numbers of students (90 per cent of the Beijing Olympic Games volunteers were students). This is only one of many considerations. For example, competitive forces can complicate planning when workers are in short supply and casual staff may be double counted if they work for more than one security or catering company.

In the event environment, an additional challenge is the logistics of staff planning, including uniforms, accreditation, transportation and meals. This is not unique to events such as the FIFA World Cup, events such as music festivals need to give similar consideration to the logistics issues that do not face human resource professionals in the conventional business environment. For example, students volunteering for work at a festival may be asked to arrive at the venue at 5am to assist with setting up the event. At this time of day, public transport systems are seldom working. Finishing very late at night presents the additional problem of safety when the event audience has already left the site leaving staff working for a further three hours or more. Food is an unusual topic to raise in a chapter on strategic planning, but it is an essential need which is costly to meet if 300 volunteers need two hot meals, outside normal catering hours at a temporary venue. The logistics of staff planning is thus an additional feature of human resource management that needs to be stressed for the event environment.

These issues can be summed up as leadership and logistics. A strategic approach to human resource management means taking a leadership role in the development of the event organization and the execution of the event plan. Furthermore, logistics of staff planning is far more complex in this environment of temporary structures and transient teams than it is for human resources professionals in traditional environments.

Strategic approach to HR planning

A strategic approach to human resources planning involves the following:

1   Formulating strategy, including an environmental assessment of the labour market, industrial relations framework, and the level of expertise required. This includes decisions regarding outsourcing components of the project to other organizations (see Case Study 2.1). It also involves working with stakeholders, such as government bodies and sponsors.
2   Developing a flexible and responsive approach to dealing with HR issues as they emerge in the planning period and providing advice at strategic level.
3   Ensuring that the event organization's vision, goals and objectives are the starting point for all human resources planning, incorporating the values of the organization.
4   Providing integration across a wide range of projects, all working at a different pace towards the target date for the event.
5   Focusing on customer service, internal and external in all elements of planning and delivery.

Analysis of the labour market is essential. In Atlanta in 1996, staff shortages were reported in many businesses such as hotels. As a result volunteers were poached (some being enticed by cash), leading to an unacceptable attrition rate (some rumours attribute this premature departure of volunteers to the baggy shorts they refused to wear, but that is probably a myth). If the event requires staff and volunteers to undertake police

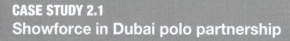

CASE STUDY 2.1
Showforce in Dubai polo partnership

Showforce was an official event partner to the Julius Baer Beach Polo Cup in Dubai. The two day event, which took place from 19–20 April on the sands of Mina A' Salam, was organized by mamemo productions, owned by Sam Katelia, who originally founded the sport in 2004. As an official partner, Showforce was contracted to supply stage and event crew for all aspects of the event including installation of 3,900m² structural decking, 4,000m² carpeting, 400 running metres of temporary walling and 2,000m² of high quality decoration. In addition, the Showforce crew also provided support to other event partners.

Sonu Bottom, mamemo productions said, 'It was an amazing experience to see the Showforce team lead and help all our suppliers achieve their goals. Showforce was the backbone of the event and I cannot thank them enough for accepting all the challenges, last minute changes, early starts and late shifts. The team was a pleasure to work with'.

Source: http://www.lsionline.co.uk/news/story/Showforce-in-Dubai-polo-partnership/-ABF3AI

Showforce: Red Bull's X-Fighters World Tour

Red Bull's X-Fighters World Tour began in Dubai (UAE), more than 20,000 spectators came to the stunning dirt track set up on the white sands of Dubai's Jumeirah Beach. We were appointed to provide a project manager, senior team members, international crew chiefs, riggers, stage managers and site crew and supplied 35 staff in total. Tasks included the loading and offloading of cargo, cable pulling and fixing, rigging, stand building, ramp maintenance, set up and dismantling and technical works. A big sand storm took place and our International Crew Chief used his leadership skills to make sure all safety procedures were being followed, his reaction towards the dangers that came with the storm were highly praised by the customers and fellow contractors.

In addition, complications with equipment being held in customs meant changes to the way the work was originally scheduled had to be made. We were able to rise to the challenge, supplying larger numbers of crew and were highly flexible with working hours.

Source: http://www.showforce.com/who-we-are/case-studies/#/red-bull-blink-events

Reflective practice 2.1

- List the professional expertise offered by Showforce for these two events.
- What were the logistics and other challenges presented by these two events?
- What are the advantages of using an organization with this track record?

checks for accreditation purposes, volunteers become a valuable and employable commodity. According to Webb (2001), Games contracting employers in Atlanta found that they needed to recruit up to 4,000 staff to be sure of having 1,000 employees at the event. Knowing this, the Sydney 2000 organizers developed two key strategies: first, they recruited many volunteers from out of town, leaving the local labour force intact; second, a formal industrial agreement was reached for paid and contractor employees which rewarded them for assigned shift completion with a bonus hourly rate, paid only after the event. For a large-scale event, an analysis of the skill requirements is an essential part of planning. Shortages of skilled staff such as chefs can be remedied through innovative approaches to menu planning and food storage (cook-chill). However, before specific solutions such as these are discussed, the impact of the event's staffing needs should be analysed in detail across the board, including the size of the labour pool; the knowledge and competence of those in the labour pool; the size and skill of a potential volunteer workforce; and the availability of contractor organizations to meet the short term demands of providing event services. This is particularly relevant when working offshore to run events in countries where expertise is limited.

The most significant role for human resource experts in event planning is that of integration. A major event comprises multiple projects with different timelines. Each of these has human resources components including staffing, development of policies and procedures, training, performance management and recognition. In some cases, these are similar for all projects while in others the project has specific and different human resources requirements. This effort needs to be integrated in order to develop a cohesive workforce while recognizing the unique challenges posed in some areas. This requires pro-active leadership by the human resources team. For example, the transportation team may commence operations much earlier than the catering team, yet both groups require induction training on commencement. Add to this a range of management training programs and the complexity of the training schedule is immediately evident. Just in time training is different for multiple teams at different stages of event implementation.

The main strategic focus in the event environment is organizational design and effectiveness. The unique life cycle of an event provides a completely new environment for the traditional human resources practitioner. In the areas of recruitment and staffing, training and development, employee relations, productivity management and reward and recognition there are similarities. However, the event workforce goes through several phases: ranging from a long planning period with relatively small numbers to a short operational and delivery period when potentially thousands of people are brought into the workforce. In this context, the human resource professional cannot afford to play a service and support role, but must instead act in a leadership and consultative role, outsourcing large sections of business activity (Boella and Goss-Turner, 2013). For optimal human performance in a dynamic and challenging project-oriented environment, human resource management must have a strategic focus. This is not only the case for mega events, but also for events such as those in the area of arts and entertainment. A creative focus requires innovative and flexible approach to human resource planning. This is particularly the case for an annual festival that needs to be sustainable over time.

Event purpose

In all event planning the vision, mission statement or purpose is the overriding statement that defines the event. Due to the competing interests of various stakeholders and the potential that there is to lose focus during planning, it is vital that the event organizer or committee has a clear and purposeful direction. In some cases, there is the undisguised motive of profit-making such as for a celebrity concert performance. In others, such as a not-for-profit arts festival, the aim may be to achieve social objectives. Many community festivals wish to retain their authenticity and to avoid commercialization at any cost. Decisions regarding the event purpose guide all decision-making, such as the source of funds, the design of event programme, marketing strategies and human resource strategies including the use of volunteers.

From the examples that follow, one can see how this can differ from one event to another:

> The Chelsea Flower Show is still viewed as the most important event in the horticultural calendar. Garden designers from around the world compete for space at the most famous of flower shows. With new trends constantly appearing – illustrated in the changing face of garden design – it is certain that the Chelsea Flower Show will continue to mark this country's ever-changing horticultural history.
>
> (RHS, 2007)

The Chelsea Flower Show is run by the Royal Horticultural Society:

> Established in 1804, the Royal Horticultural Society is now the UK's leading gardening charity dedicated to advancing horticulture and promoting good gardening. Our goal is to help people share a passion for plants, to encourage excellence in horticulture and inspire all those with an interest in gardening.
>
> (RHS, 2007)

From this short description one can immediately see that horticultural expertise and a passion for the industry would be selection criteria for anyone working on the frontline with exhibitors and visitors.

For events on a much larger scale consider the rationale to host major events:

> Qatar is using events as a way to reimage and position itself as a destination and increase its profile internationally in addition to gaining a competitive edge regionally. Other explanatory factors include: economic sustainability and diversification plans and tourism-related policies as well as social development strategies.
>
> (Khodr, 2012)

On a smaller scale, the Vancouver International Readers and Writers Festival is a registered non-profit charitable organization. Their objectives are:

- To advance literacy by introducing young readers to the wonder of books.
- To deliver the world's best writers to Festival audiences.

- To promote new and undiscovered British Columbian, Canadian and international writers.

(The Vancouver Writers Fest, 2014)

Finally, Special Olympics is an international organization dedicated to empowering individuals with intellectual disability to become physically fit, productive and respected members of society through sports training and competition. The mission of the Special Olympics is as follows:

> The global mission of Special Olympics is to provide year-round sports training and athletic competition in a variety of Olympic-type sports for children and adults with an intellectual disability, giving them continuing opportunities to develop physical fitness, demonstrate courage, experience joy and participate in a sharing of gifts, skills and friendship with their families, other Special Olympics athletes and the community.

(Special Olympics, 2014)

As these examples illustrate, the diversity of event type is matched by the diversity of purpose, goals and objectives. In order to ensure that the appropriate people are on board; are trained and motivated; and are provided with the means to perform at the highest level, the human resources team must be involved in the strategic development of the event concept and in all aspects of operational planning. It is only with this involvement that the customer service levels expected will be delivered and will sit consistently with the event purpose.

Integrating planning across functions

With this in mind, integrating planning across functions is vitally important. This is difficult because these functional areas (FAs) work at different rates in preparation for the event and generally want to conduct recruitment, training etc. just in time to meet their needs. This may be ahead of many others. For example, one area which may commence operations quite early is Technology. This functional area meets all information technology requirements in the lead up to the event such as building the event intranet and website. During the operational period their role could change to cover scoring and results reporting. In this project alone, one can see how a job analysis would reveal different phases, different staffing and training needs. This is replicated across a number of other functional areas such as Transport or Sponsorship.

Before going any further, it is essential to understand the concept of *functional area* which is widely used in event management. Functional areas are the divisions within the event organization that carry responsibility for delivering the key infrastructure and services. A number of functional areas (examples in Figure 2.1) work towards meeting the same final deadline but with different peak work periods. Along the way there are many 'which comes first?' questions of the chicken and the egg variety. Events organizations

Finance	Catering
Legal	Cleaning and waste
Programme management	Environment
Risk	Ticketing
Workforce planning	Marketing
Procurement and logistics	Media
Technology	Sponsorship
Transport	Merchandising
Security	Sport/entertainment/production
Accreditation	Medical
Ceremonies	Customer service

FIGURE 2.1 Functional areas for a major event

are extremely organic, shifting and changing as implications of one decision impact on others. For example, a change in sponsor might impact on uniform design, production and delivery. As a result, accreditation might be asked to delay their schedule to match uniform issue.

While these functional areas play a primary role during the early planning phase of an event, there comes a time when the sporting venues are nearing completion and the venue team needs to be established, generally including representatives of these functional areas. So for example, the stadium and the tennis centre would both need to provide catering services. At this point the organization structure of the event changes from a functional focus to a venue focus.

For most events, this change comes about as a shift to management of venues, zones, clusters or precincts, each of which operates almost autonomously. While the tradition of the Olympic Games is to call these *venue areas* (VAs) or precincts, this text will use the term *zone*. Not every event is so large that the incumbent venue management team is eclipsed by a team appointed by the organizing committee. In most cases, the event organization works with the incumbent venue management team, such as the full-time staff of a sporting complex.

When looking at much smaller events, even a fun run would operate on the basis of teams responsible at start, route and finish with a manager responsible for each. The geographical area is most commonly known as a zone, so that in this case one would have a Manager – Start; Manager – Route; and Manager – Finish and Ceremonies.

The shift to a matrix organization close to the time of event implementation/operation will be discussed in detail in the next chapter. In a matrix organization structure, a project manager has a dual role. According to Mahadevan 'such organization structure enables optimal utilisation of specialised resources in multiple areas. It also facilitates managing the interface areas identified through a WBS [work breakdown structure]' (2009: 413).

Figure 2.2 illustrates how a project manager responsible for risk and safety (a function) might be responsible for his or her team right up until shortly before the event, at which time staff are allocated to zones (or geographical areas) and report directly to the local manager while reporting only indirectly to the Manager – Risk and Safety for advice on

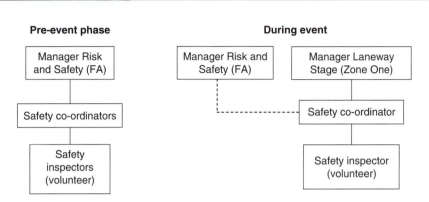

FIGURE 2.2 Evolution from functional area structure (left) to geographical area focus (right)

specific issues. Thus the Safety Co-ordinator no longer reports directly to the Manager – Risk and Safety but to the Manager of Zone One/Laneway Stage.

Evolution of the organization

All events undergo evolutionary development, either as single projects or as a series of smaller events, each with project characteristics. The Manchester Commonwealth Games project underwent several phases including:

- strategic planning (4 years)
- operational planning (1 year)
- operational stage (6 months)
- delivery (3 months)
- wind up (4 months).

At each stage of the project's development there is a different focus to planning and the structure of the organization can change. This is the case for events of all sizes and types. If the event is an annual event with a two year planning cycle, then the event team is doing several things concurrently for the two events, one in the strategic design phase

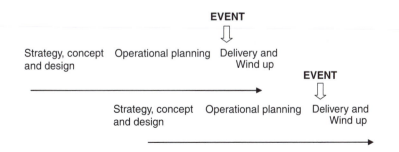

FIGURE 2.3 Timelines for multiple events at different stages

and the other in operational stage. This is illustrated in Figure 2.3 where for example, the 2016 event may be in the early design phase even before the 2015 event is wound up. For an annual music event for example, it may be needed to sign up acts more than a year out from the next event.

Toffler (1990) uses the term 'pulsating organization' to describe organizations that expand and contract. Hanlon and Cuskelly (2002) in their study of two major sporting events make recommendations for management induction which will be discussed in more detail in a later chapter. The point is well made that organizations such as these have a special character when compared with long-life organizations which are much more stable.

The organizing committee

Shone and Parry (2004) suggest the structure shown in Figure 2.4 for an event committee. Notable is the absence of anyone dedicated to the human resources role. This is quite common in the event environment in which there are seldom stand-alone human resources managers or officers for smaller events. In most cases, this function becomes part of the job of operations managers, venue managers, artistic directors and the like. Each hires the team and manages performance.

Shone and Parry suggest that in addition to the above, a range of stakeholders might be invited to meetings such as representatives from the venue, licence holders, sponsors, police, first aid, fire service and local council among others.

For larger events however, a human resources specialist is highly recommended with a role extending beyond that of the event organization's paid workforce to cover workforce planning, contractor management, volunteer management, recruitment and training, occupational health and safety, uniforms, meals and human resources policy.

1 Chair/President

2 Operations Officers

1 Finance Officer

1 Marketing Officer

1 Health, Safety and Legalities Officer

FIGURE 2.4 Organization structure for an event committee

Source: Shone and Parry (2004). Reproduced with permission Thomson Learning, London

Key roles or human resource management tasks

The following key roles for the human resources team or delegates are summarized in the pages that follow.

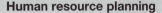

Workforce planning

Recruitment of paid staff has to be timed optimally. The workforce builds very rapidly close to event delivery. As Figure 2.5 shows, the majority of staff for the Manchester Commonwealth Games were appointed in the final stages (Manchester City Council, 2003). Where an event is running over budget the temptation is to delay some staff appointments for weeks or months. However, as one can imagine this has serious implications for the event's effective organization. While it is inconceivable that you would stop building the physical infrastructure of the event, it seems that human resources can be a soft target for cost savings.

CASE STUDY 2.2
Growth in workforce – Manchester Commonwealth Games

Figure 2.5 illustrates the cumulative employment of staff working for the Manchester 2002 Commonwealth Games. This provides a graphical illustration of the exponential growth of the workforce.

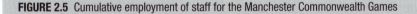

FIGURE 2.5 Cumulative employment of staff for the Manchester Commonwealth Games

Reflective practice 2.2

• Every new employee needs induction training. What are the implications for human resources of this workforce growth timeline?
• Compare the levels of team development and camaraderie with work colleagues for individuals at the two ends of the spectrum.

Organizational design

As mentioned previously, the organization's design is impacted by the project timeline with significant key points at which the organizational structure may change dramatically to a matrix organization. The involvement of a range of stakeholders is also significant and these need to be included in design of the structure and reporting relationships. This is also the case with contractors.

Contractor selection and management

For many events, contractors can make up almost half of the event workforce. This being the case, these contractors need to be selected with human resource considerations in mind such as labour force availability, expertise, training, recognition and retention. Contractors can include companies providing services such as equipment hire; lighting; sound; staging; catering and security.

Volunteer planning

Volunteers play a vital role in many events, ranging from sport to street parades. Their involvement needs to be planned and budgeted for. Motivational aspects are critical to the success of the event as the staff contribute in many ways to the ambience created. Industrial relations (union) issues can emerge if it is perceived that the volunteers are taking the potential place of skilled, paid and experienced staff.

Recruitment and selection

Many events conduct recruitment and selection online, and some are heavily oversubscribed by volunteers. By asking applicants to make early decisions about preferences for functional area, venue and shifts at this early stage, the organization of allocations can proceed more rapidly. Communication with staff and volunteers sets the tone for relationships with internal and external customers.

Training and development

Everyone working on the event site, whether front or back of house (behind the scenes), needs to be trained. This includes the entire workforce including, for example, sponsor employees and emergency services. Visitors are likely to ask questions of everyone in uniform and each person plays a customer relations role. Training can play a role in promoting the event and can become an event in its own right. As a motivating force it is unparalleled.

In the business event sector, long-term career development needs to be considered so that supervisory and management staff can achieve career progression. McCabe and Savery (2007) suggest a new career pattern in the convention and exhibition area in which individuals 'flutter' between sectors, calling this 'butterfly' progress. Given the short-term nature of many employment contracts in all sectors of the event industry most individuals on a development pathway would no doubt identify with this concept. Talent management is a particular challenge in industries in which stress, job burnout and unrealistic deadlines characterize the work and strategies for managing work-life conflict should be considered (Deery, 2008).

Health and safety

Concerns about safety dominate most current events, and an analysis of many induction sessions shows that the majority of time is spent on this topic (Van Der Wagen, 2007). It is a compulsory training component for everyone on site and needs to be documented. All employees need to be told about potential safety risks, about how to report incidents and how to respond in an emergency.

Uniforms, accreditation, meals and transportation

All staff require uniforms and accreditation passes as well as meals and transportation. These are sometimes the responsibility of other functional areas, but may be part of the human resources role.

Human resources policy

Policies and procedures need to be written for all aspects of staff management. This includes a code of conduct and disciplinary policy. Procedures need to be extremely detailed, such as incident reporting, shift allocation, redeployment, updating personal contact information, breaks and absence reporting.

Job analysis

Job analysis, otherwise known as work breakdown structure (WBS) in the field of project management, needs to be done for every element of the event down to its smallest detail. This can be done by a human resources team, most often in collaboration with each functional area or venue. From a strategic viewpoint, the point at which the venue 'owns' the staff and all their related human resources issues is a consideration. While Human Resources, as a functional area generally remains in a consulting capacity, this is a staff as opposed to a line function.

Leadership and motivation

Staff shortages, lack of motivation and attrition are the stuff of nightmares for the event organizer. A focus on organizational behaviour is essential with analysis of leadership and motivation in the context of the specific event, with programmes designed to reward and retain paid staff and volunteers.

PLATE 2.1 Professional catering service is essential

Risk analysis

Risk analysis and contingency planning is widely used in event management to anticipate issues of concern. Table 2.1 illustrates a risk analysis for the human resources planning of an event. The table shows identified risks which are then judged according to likelihood and consequence, thus determining the level of risk. Following this, consideration is given to potential preventative measures and contingencies that could be put in place should the risk become a reality. From this table it is evident that staff shortages in one form or another are a serious concern and that plans need to be developed for a redeployment team to fill any serious gaps. However, the highest risk in this analysis is mismanagement at senior level.

Looking at the risk table in detail, this example shows us the following analysis:

Mismanagement

This is listed as possible with major consequences. This can be prevented by effective planning and documented meetings. Contingency plans for when planning is derailed include negotiation, formal arbitration or appointment of a crisis management team.

TABLE 2.1 Human resources risk analysis

Identified risk	Likelihood	Consequence	Level of risk	Prevention	Contingency
Mismanagement or misdirection by committee or executive staff	possible	major	extreme	• clarity in event purpose and aims • documented meetings and actions • maintain media support	• negotiation • formal arbitration • restructure • crisis management team • press release
Unable to recruit critical staff with specific technical experience	possible	moderate	high	• workforce planning • international recruitment • database of applicants	• use agencies, network of contacts, head hunt • meet relocation expenses • provide incentives
Key staff member resigns or becomes ill shortly before the event	almost certain	major	extreme	• document policy and procedure • maintain records • work in teams • appoint assistants • provide incentives for staying until close down	• restructure • recover lost ground • reshape plans • reassign responsibility
Volunteer and staff attrition during the event	almost certain	moderate	extreme	• provide a reason to be there • reward attendance • acknowledge support	• ensure rosters allow for attrition (inevitable) • have a redeployment team
Contractor defaults on service immediately prior or during the event	possible	major	extreme	• appoint contractors based on selection criteria including past performance • contracts to have penalty clauses • work breakdown extremely detailed • monitor activities	• invoke penalties • hire another contractor • undertake work using own staff

(Continued)

TABLE 2.1 Continued

Identified risk	Likelihood	Consequence	Level of risk	Prevention	Contingency
Misconduct by staff member causes bad press	rare	major	high	• code of conduct • disciplinary policy • counselling and dismissal processes	• dismissal • press release
Fatal safety incident resulting from inadequate staff selection and training	unlikely	catastrophic	extreme	• job analysis • safety risk analysis • selection based on experience and in some cases, specific licenses • training in safety procedures • documented procedures and signed checklists • supervision	• incident reporting system • first aid services • communication system • crisis management team • press release
Non-compliance with industrial legislation	unlikely	minor	low	• assign responsibility for HR compliance • monitor compliance including contractors	• resolve with authorities

Staff shortages

This is listed as possible with moderate consequences. For some events the consequences could be more serious than here raising the risk to extreme level. Preventing staff shortages can be tackled by careful workforce planning and innovative recruitment strategies. Contingency plans include the use of employment agencies and the use of incentives for new applicants.

Loss of key personnel

Depending on the seniority of the person concerned and their role, this possibility must be taken very seriously. Many events have one person who carries an enormous amount of information 'in their head'. The loss of this person (through illness or accident) can be mitigated by the organization by documenting plans, policies and procedures and by working collaboratively. In the eventuality that this occurs, one would have to restructure and reshape plans.

Workforce attrition

Attrition or staff turnover is almost a certainty. For this reason plans need to be made to take this into account. This risk can be reduced by providing incentives and other motivational strategies. Many events plan for attrition by having a team specifically to fill the gaps, called the redeployment team. These people can be assigned to new roles at a moment's notice.

Contractor defaults

Unfortunately the event organizer is blamed for problems created by contractors or vendors. For example if food runs out, the organizer is regarded as 'at fault'. Careful selection and appointment of contractors is a preventative measure. Extremely detailed contracts with itemized specifications can be useful. Penalties can be included in the contract.

Staff misconduct

With a large workforce it is almost guaranteed that someone will behave badly, for example harassing athletes. Policies and training are essential. While dismissal is unpleasant there are occasions when it is quite appropriate to ask the person to leave the site as they risk their own safety and the safety of others.

Safety incident

This is an extreme risk, with potential fatal consequences. So while the likelihood is low, planning must be undertaken to prevent safety risks and to develop systems and procedures for dealing with near misses and serious incidents. This should include effective communication systems and detailed emergency planning.

CASE STUDY 2.3
Mega events support sustainable employment

The Games represented a one-off opportunity to provide workless people with a pathway to sustainable employment. An estimated 62,000 to 76,000 workless Londoners secured temporary or permanent employment as a result of the Games.

Source: Report 5: Post-Games Evaluation: Department for Culture Media and Sport (2013)

Reflective practice 2.3

Debate or discuss the potential for events of various types for increasing sustainable employment.

Chapter summary and key points

This chapter has examined human resource management for events at a strategic level and has made a case for developing the role so that it is included at executive level in the organization. For a successful event there are three major components: the programme of performance, the physical infrastructure and its operation; and the service provided to visitors in a vast number of ways. Professional human resources experts have a vital role to play in organizational development in the dynamic environment of event design, planning and delivery. In this chapter a number of key roles for human resources have been suggested and these will be elaborated in later chapters.

Risk management principles can be applied to the management of human resources and from a strategic view point, this is one of the most important early tasks. A risk assessment asks 'what could happen?' and looks at ways in which problems can be avoided and solved. These things can be negative (e.g. workplace accidents) or positive (e.g. too many volunteers). Each risk needs to be carefully evaluated in light of the external and internal event environment. Planning is put in place to deal with these staff related contingencies.

Revision questions

1   Explain five ways in which a strategic approach can be taken to HR planning for events.
2   Using an example, explain how the event purpose or mission drives planning for human resources implementation.
3   Integration of HR across a range of sub-projects is necessary. Explain how this comes about.
4   Where an event is small in scale the event manager might be responsible for HR functions. What would you list in the job description for this role to cover HR planning?

Industry voice by Kerrie Nash

HRM functions include recruitment, selection, remuneration and benefits. You will find in that last six months your organization, your paid workforce probably triples in size. That, in and of itself, is a challenge just from an attraction and recruitment point of view.

Organizational design is critically important in an event environment because that will grow and change over the years as the business changes and as people fall into place.

Employee relations and industrial relations are important, however not so much with the paid workforce, but with contractors where the industrial relations piece is particularly relevant.

Certainly engagement and communication to me is massively important because of the temporary nature of the workforce and also because of bringing the volunteers and contractors on board into one unified team. Diversity and inclusion too, whether that's included as one of the HRM functions or sits on its own.

They're the sort of typical corporate HRM functions, but in a very different way.

Then, on top of that you've got volunteer recruitment and volunteer training which is massive. We also lead the organization in workforce demand planning, and then scheduling and rostering the workforce for the Games period. Then at Games time, HR evolves into a workforce operations function which operates at all venues, managing things such as check-in, engagement and communications, and recognition programmes, particularly for the volunteers. Then, the other two functions that often sit within the HRM umbrella are uniforming and accreditation. These link back to the workforce planning numbers. Human Resources Director is sometimes a little misleading because people don't necessarily realize that there's much more to it than the traditional human resources function. That is why it is commonly known as Workforce Director, with a much wider scope of responsibility than that of a corporate HR role.

Discussion questions

1   How does Kerrie differentiate between HRM in conventional business environments to those of major and mega-events?
2   The scope of work of the Workforce Director is very wide, what does it include?
3   At what point in the planning process is the job of managing people performance shifted towards the managers of the different venues/zones?

References

Armstrong, M. (2012). *Armstrong's Handbook of Human Resource Management Practice*. London: Kogan Page.

Boella, M. and Goss-Turner, S. (2013). *Human Resource Management in the Hospitality Industry: A Guide to Best Practice*. Hokoben, New Jersey: Routledge.

Buller, P. F. and McEvoy, G. M. (2012). 'Strategy, human resource management and performance: sharpening line of sight', *Human Resource Management Review*, 22(1), 43–56.

Deery, M. (2008). 'Talent management, work-life balance and retention strategies', *International Journal of Contemporary Hospitality Management*, 20(7), 792–806.

Department for Culture Media and Sport (2013). *Post-Games Evaluation*. Available at: https://www.gov.uk/government/uploads/system/uploads/attachment_data/file/224181/1188-B_Meta_Evaluation.pdf; viewed 8 January 2014.

Hanlon, C. and Cuskelly, G. (2002). 'Pulsating major sport event organizations: a framework for inducting managerial personnel', *Event Management*, 7, 231–243.

Khodr, H. (2012). 'Exploring the driving factors behind the event strategy in Qatar: a case study of the 15th Asian Games', *International Journal of Event and Festival Management* 3(1), 81–100.

Mahadevan, B. (2009). *Operation Management: Theory and Practice*. New Delhi, India: Dorling Kindersley, licensee of Pearson Education in South Asia.

Manchester City Council (2003). *Manchester Commonwealth Games Post Games Report*. Available at: www.gameslegacy.com; viewed 17 May 2006.

McCabe, V. S. and Savery, L. K. (2007). '"Butterflying" a new career pattern for Australia? Empirical evidence', *Journal of Management Development*, 26(2), 103–116.

RHS (2007). *RHS Chelsea Flower Show*. Available at: http://www.rhs.org.uk/chelsea/history.asp; viewed 12 March 2012.

Shone, A. and Parry, B. (2004). *Successful Event Management*, 2nd edn, London: Thomson Learning.

Special Olympics (2014). *Special Olympics Mission*. Available at: www.specialolympics.org; viewed 2 January 2014.

The Vancouver Writers Fest (2014). Available at: http://www.writersfest.bc.ca/; viewed 10 June 2014.

Toffler, A. (1990). *Future Shock*. New York: Bantam Books.

Van Der Wagen, L. (2007). *Contexts for Customer Service*. Sydney: UTS (unpublished thesis).

Webb, T. (2001). *The Collaborative Games: The Story Behind the Spectacle*. Annandale, NSW: Pluto Press.

3

Event project planning

Learning objectives

After reading through this chapter you will be able to:

- Explain the reasons for application of project management principles to event management.
- Discuss the topic of scope management in project design.
- Analyse the evolutionary nature of the event organization.
- Describe the responsibilities of functional areas project teams.
- Describe the responsibilities of zone/venue project teams.

Introduction

The previous chapters have looked at some of the unique characteristics of the event environment that provide challenges for managing people in this dynamic and sometimes highly creative environment. This chapter will take a project management perspective, using some of the terminology widely used as part of the Project Management Body of Knowledge, PMBOK™.

There is some debate about the suitability of such a framework for event enterprises that are creative and organic (Goldblatt, 2005, 2012; O'Toole and Mikolaitis, 2002; Van Der Wagen, 2005), however this discussion can wait for the chapter on leadership. For the time being it is important to recognize that the methodology and terminology of PMBOK™ is widely used in the event industry. Tum et al. (2006) in their book on event operations management adopt a project management approach, the authors stating in the preface that 'each event is in fact a project, and the wealth of literature that is available on both operations and project management can be used to assist an event manager in the complex management of an event' (p. xxi).

Project management framework

A *project* is defined as a *temporary* endeavour undertaken to create a *unique* product or service (Project Management Institute, 2014). Temporary means that the project has a definite beginning and end, which is typical of most events. The finite end of the project drives most of the planning, and in this case the end is the culmination of the planning and comprises delivery of the event. In many other projects (such as engineering projects and software development projects) the activity can peak earlier. The second feature of projects is that they are unique. They may carry repetitive elements but this does not change the unique nature of the final product. For example, each golf masters championship is a unique event, and staging each contest is a project in its own right. Finally the project team often includes people who don't usually work together – a multidisciplinary team, often coming from different organizations.

From a human resources perspective it is well worth considering the role as that of Project HRM, with the emphasis on organizational planning, staff acquisition and team development that goes with every project. The terminology of PMBOK™ is useful, for example, one can use the concept of *scope* as the sum of the products and services provided as part of the project. If human resource management (or more commonly known as workforce planning) is a functional area providing specialized activities related to event staffing, a question of scope would be whether providing uniforms is part of the scope. In the hot house of event planning, there is often much debate about the scope covered by functional areas. People are constantly trying to shift, reduce or expand responsibility. Some men and women are heard wailing 'it wasn't in my scope' on the way to the crying room (more on stress management later).

Using mega events as an example, human resources/workforce planning is not responsible for developing every job description; these are within the scope of the functional area or venue team. In the same way that one has to delineate a project, one has to define the scope of each functional area in a logical way.

Most events, such as the Asian or Commonwealth Games, follow the precedent set by the Olympic Games and offer three levels of training to the workforce:

1   Orientation training – general information about the event, its history and the event programme. This training is generally delivered on a large scale.
2   Venue training – this training is run at the venue (competition or non-competition) and covers the layout of the site, emergency evacuation, incident reporting and the like.
3   Job specific training – this training is at small group or individual level providing detailed information about the tasks to be performed.

This work breakdown provides a good example of how the scope of the training sub-project is organized. In this case, Orientation Training is the responsibility of Human Resources (a key deliverable), while the Venue Management team (with advice from HR) plans and runs venue training. Finally, job specific training can come within the scope of a particular functional area within the venue, for example, the merchandising team at the stadium.

PLATE 3.1 The set up of an exhibition hall requires careful logistics planning

Design before detail

However, before project scope management can be started, the main focus needs to be on the event design. Figure 3.1 provides an overview of project management processes used widely in many industries and scope management helps to define the boundaries of the project. As Brown and James (2004: 59) point out,

> design is essential to an event's success because it leads to improvement of the event at every level … Event design is the critical component, underpinning every other aspect of the event, and central to the event design are the core values of the event.

They list the design principles as: scale, shape, focus, timing and build. In many ways this part of the design relies on theatrical concepts and anticipates the audience response. The authors argue that while it is important to be systematic in planning, event managers often concern themselves too much with logistics and budget, leading to a 'one-dimensional' event.

It is important to be mindful of this concern as project management principles are implemented. While the tools and techniques of project management are useful, they should not dominate to the extent that they compromise creativity and hinder change.

Project Management		
Project integration management • Project plan development • Project plan execution • Overall change control	**Project scope management** • Initiation • Scope planning • Scope definition • Scope verification • Scope change control	**Project time management** • Activity definition • Activity sequencing • Activity duration estimating • Schedule development • Schedule control
Project cost management • Resource planning • Cost estimating • Cost budgeting • Cost control	**Project quality management** • Quality planning • Quality assurance • Quality control	**Project human resource management** • Organizational planning • Staff acquisition • Team development
Project communications management • Communications planning • Information distribution • Performance reporting • Administrative closure	**Project risk management** • Risk identification • Risk qualification • Risk response development • Risk response control	**Project procurement management** • Procurement planning • Solicitation planning • Solicitation • Source selection • Contract administration • Contract close out

FIGURE 3.1 Overview of project management processes

Finally, before looking at project management phases and organization charts, it is well worth highlighting this point in relation to human resource management – people can contribute to the event's design. Shone and Parry (2004) describe this as ambience and service. The way people dress and behave will determine, to a large degree, the audience response. The most memorable event experiences are magical, and people create this magic.

Human resource management project

Following the logic of project management, once the event project is initiated then scope planning begins. Typically organizational planning follows several phases; in this case four stages have been illustrated: initiation, operations planning (functional), operations execution (venue/site) and performance (event delivery). There is of course the final wrap up stage (also known as close down or divestment) during which time reports are written, bills paid and contracts are acquitted, but this has not been illustrated here as there is usually only a small team remaining to complete these tasks. Evaluation of an event is vitally important including evaluating the success of human resources strategies. This will be covered in Chapters 12 and 15.

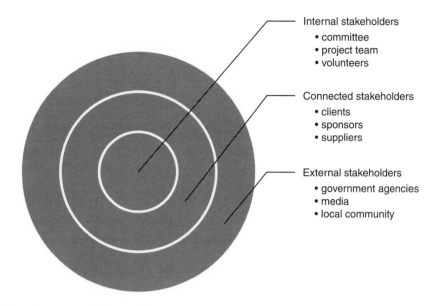

Internal stakeholders
- committee
- project team
- volunteers

Connected stakeholders
- clients
- sponsors
- suppliers

External stakeholders
- government agencies
- media
- local community

FIGURE 3.2 Stakeholder mapping

Stage 1 – Initiation: concept and feasibility

At this early stage of event concept development, when ideas are tested for feasibility, the organization (which is usually a committee) is generally quite organic. Flexibility and role sharing are important parts of this early phase when committee members are in a creative frame of mind, although this has to be tempered with reality. This being the case, the stakeholder mapping can take the form of a diagram such as that illustrated in Figure 3.2.

As mentioned in the previous chapter, this phase would also include evaluation of the external and internal environment. For human resource management this would include an analysis of labour forces statistics, community attitudes towards volunteering, industrial relations issues, affirmative action programmes and so on. In the case of the London Olympic Games, McDonald's (official sponsor) took on the role of selecting and training the volunteers. Before this could commence 1,800 volunteer interviewers were trained for the task of selecting 70,000 volunteers from the 240,000 applicants. McDonald's also delivered training to 12,000 LOCOG staff. In Beijing one of the biggest training initiatives was for food safety inspection using the HACCP methodology for food safety planning from source to user in the city, venues and athletes village (LV et al., 2006).

Stage 2 Operations planning: functional focus

During the next phase of event planning each of the functional areas begins to set up the infrastructure for the event. The manager responsible for security and risk management would, for example, look at the scope of work involved in providing security services for the event. These could include searches at entry points, patrols, observation of the field of play, use of CCTV, incident and reporting systems and the list goes on. This would

CASE STUDY 3.1
Crowd control

Training of stewards and security staff in crowd control should be implemented before an event in an effort to improve crowd safety and avoid panic should overcrowding occur. During a football match in Ellis Park South Africa, tear gas was thrown in to a crowd by event security in an effort to disperse intense overcrowding. This unfortunately served to incite panic and cause stampede.

Source: Soomaroo and Murray (2012)

Reflective practice 3.1

Crowd management is a shared responsibility of the venue (facility), event team and all health and safety support agencies or contractors. Every member of the workforce has a role to play.

How would you approach training in this area so that consistency in preparedness and practice is achieved?

require close liaison with a number of stakeholders such as police, first aid providers and emergency services. At this stage a decision would be made about outsourcing security services and a contractor would be selected by tender. In order to do this the scope of work has to be quite clear for the competitive tendering parties.

In the simplified chart shown in Figure 3.3, the functional area managers would report to the event manager. A more sophisticated chart would also show the key stakeholders (perhaps in a different colour) such as sponsors, emergency services etc. Relationship lines for stakeholders are just as important as reporting lines within the chart for paid staff. For example, sponsors can be vital to the success of the event and the event manager

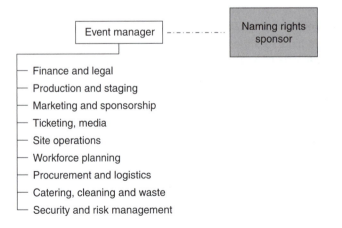

FIGURE 3.3 Functional area reporting

could decide that the naming rights sponsor has a direct relationship with him or her. The alternative would be for the marking manger to deal with all sponsorship arrangements. It is most helpful to add these stakeholders to the chart, using dotted lines to show *relationship* rather than reporting.

This stage is part of operational planning. Each functional unit must decide what needs to be done to meet the strategic plan. Where the strategic plan had a focus on *what* needed to be done, the operational plans deal with *how* this can be done. An operational plan:

- is a description of how objectives will be achieved;
- includes information about the resources that will be required;
- shows a timeline for project progress;
- provides the basis for action planning at the next level down.

While there are advantages of using a functional structure such as the one illustrated in Figure 3.3, there are pitfalls associated with a functional structure and these include functional managers losing sight of the big picture and the organization's objectives while they focus on their own specializations; staff have little understanding of other functions and this can lead to lack of co-operation or integration; and there is a heavy reliance on the event director to co-ordinate the activities of the functional areas. In lessons learned from the London Olympic Games, the IOC comments in the Final Report (2012: 96):

> On professional services, there is a need for reflection as seconded experts, in many cases, helped the planning and delivery of the Games, while in some functional areas, they were perceived as bringing too much unnecessary complexity – one reason being that this staff often has little Games expertise, but specific and advanced professional skills like project management.

In addition to co-ordinating the activities within the event organizing workforce, the event director or his/her delegate must co-ordinate activities with external stakeholders. The Chelsea Flower Show will be used as an example to illustrate the role and benefits accrued to stakeholders:

- Host organization – some events such as the Chelsea Flower Show are hosted by an association. In this case the Royal Horticultural Society (RHS) is a gardening charity. The RHS has a wide scope of operation and the Chelsea Flower Show is one of many events in their calendar of operations.
- Sponsors – most major events have several sponsors and these can range from naming rights sponsor through to various levels of sponsorship such as gold, silver and bronze. The sponsors generally expect media exposure, hospitality at the event and sales if their merchandise is available to purchase on site. This is done in return for financial support or value in kind support, where the sponsor provides for example, the motor fleet, telecommunications system or information technology services.
- Broadcast company – for many international events, the broadcast element is critical as many more viewers watch the event than attend it. Broadcast rights are sold before the event, and for mega events this is the main source of income after ticketing. The BBC is a sponsor and the official broadcaster for the Chelsea Flower Show.

- Beneficiaries – where the event contributes substantially to a charity, the design of the event must be compatible with the charity and values that it holds. For the Chelsea Flower Show the main beneficiary is the Royal Hospital Chelsea, a home for old soldiers.
- Exhibitors, concessions and other businesses – an event can involve numerous exhibitors and provide commercial outlets for catering and retail sales. At the Chelsea show there are 450 commercial exhibitors.
- Contractors – many event operational services are provided by contractors such as cleaning, waste management, lighting and sound. Hire companies provide temporary seating and many other elements of the event physical infrastructure.
- Government – approvals are required for all manner of things including arrangements for transport, parking and traffic management.
- Police, first aid and emergency services – working with these providers in the lead up to the event is vitally important as these people are the first point of call if there is a major accident or incident.
- Community – liaison with community is essential and some government authorities have specific procedures for notifying the local community and managing community relations.
- Customers – from a marketing viewpoint, analysis of consumer behaviour is part of the strategic marketing plan, this in turn leads to finalization of the event product which includes sales and customer service.

Stage 3 Operations planning – venue, zone or precinct focus

As the event draws near and it becomes possible to see the physical layout of the event, the structure of many events move to a geographical style, generally based on zones, venues or precincts. In the language of mega events this is known as 'venuization' or territorial deployment. Here a manager from the organizing committee 'takes over' the venue and installs the infrastructure for the upcoming event, also known as installing the 'event overlay'. If there is more than one sporting competition held at the venue, this overlay might be changed, from say gymnastics to basketball.

However this occurrence is rare and the terminology is not suitable for smaller events where the incumbent venue management team typically retains normal responsibilities for the physical infrastructure and services. For example, a music festival held in a park would see the event producer work with the park manager at every stage of planning. Figures 3.4 and 3.5 show the layout/map of the Good Vibrations Music Festival and corresponding organizational structure for the execution phase of the event. When planning the organizational structure, the Laundry Stage, Good Vibrations Stage and Roots Stage would each require a manager, as would the food services and amenities area. Thus a simplified organization chart would include the managers shown in Figure 3.5.

These project managers are responsible for specific areas. There are a number of reasons for this, the main one being that management of a physical area is logical from an operational and financial point of view. Imagine for example, that a show offers the following: a commercial exhibition area; competition area; entertainment area; and catering area. These areas are labelled as clusters, precincts or zones and they become

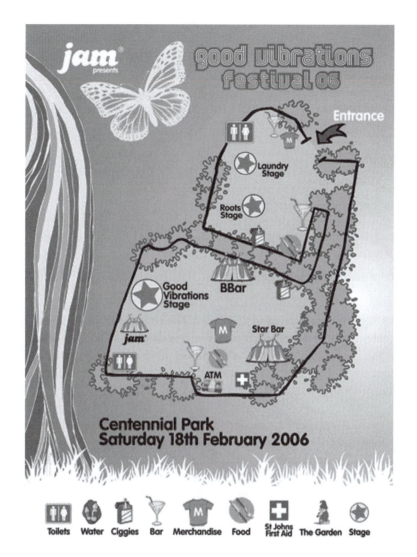

FIGURE 3.4 Map of Good Vibrations Festival

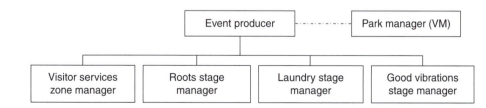

FIGURE 3.5 Managers reporting to the event producer

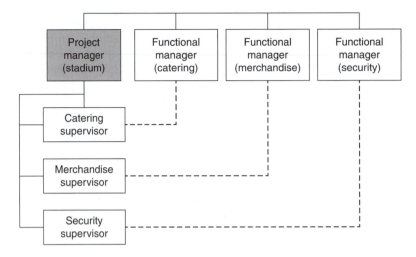

FIGURE 3.6 Matrix structure for cross functional teams

the responsibility of different managers. This simplifies decision making and also allows for the use of cost centres for financial purposes. In this way costs, such as staffing, security, and information technology, can be apportioned to the zone and their effectiveness evaluated post event. In project management terms this is now a *projectized* organization with projects comprising cross functional teams.

Figure 3.6 shows a matrix organization in which the dominant manager is the manager responsible for all events at the stadium. On his team he has supervisors representing functional areas such as catering, merchandise and security. While each of these people has a direct reporting relationship to the stadium manager, they do also have a secondary reporting relationship to their functional area (FA) manager. So for example, if a technical security-related issue were to arise, the supervisor might contact the functional area manager in charge of security for advice. This is similar to staff and line reporting relationships in traditional business environments.

These concepts don't only apply at the big end of the event business. The next illustration shows a very small event business, comprising of an owner/manager and four full-time members of staff, each a specialist in a particular functional area. This is also a matrix organization structure in that each person has dual roles. As can be seen from the chart, the dominant role for each person is that of project manager for one of the four events currently on the organization's agenda. These are a conference, and exhibition, a festival and a concert (these are used for illustrative purposes only as it would be unlikely that such a small business would diversify to this extent). As Figure 3.7 shows, while each member of the team has a project management role, each also contributes his or her specialist expertise to the other events. Thus for example, David is a marketing expert and provides this support across all events, while at the same time he has overall project management responsibility for the exhibition. Once again the solid and dotted lines show reporting relationships – one ignores the bit where one reports to oneself!

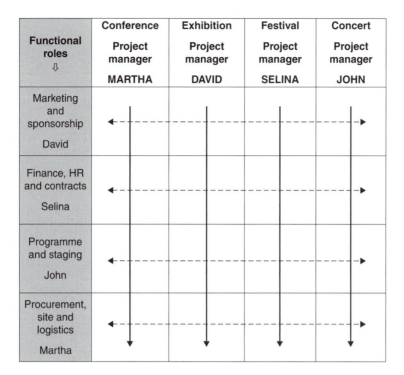

Functional roles ⇩	Conference Project manager MARTHA	Exhibition Project manager DAVID	Festival Project manager SELINA	Concert Project manager JOHN
Marketing and sponsorship David				
Finance, HR and contracts Selina				
Programme and staging John				
Procurement, site and logistics Martha				

FIGURE 3.7 Matrix organization for a small event management company

Stage 4 Execution – event delivery

Once the event is at the stage of implementation, a chart is needed to show everyone on site who is who. For this reason, every contractor needs to appear, as do all the on-site stakeholders, such as police. This chart, or a simplified parallel chart, also needs to show what to do when a minor incident or an emergency occurs. Generally there are shorter lines of communication if there is a crisis and this could be an insert in a corner of the diagram.

From a human resources perspective, the important feature of such a chart is its value to the internal customers, all the people included in the event workforce. The event chart is a communications device and needs to be comprehensive as well as user friendly. As with maps of the event layout, professional design will ensure that these inclusions in the training material will be valuable and useful.

Project deliverables for human resources functions

Looking at human resources from a project management perspective, there are a number of processes required to make the most of the people involved in the project. For a major, one-off event the following deliverables would be seen as part of the human resources function. Each of the following would be presented as a report or action plan.

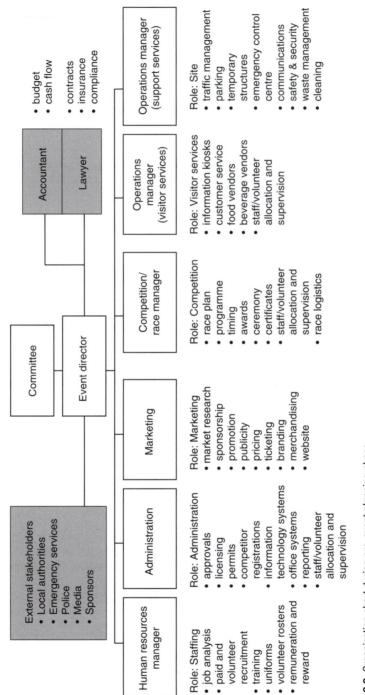

FIGURE 3.8 Organization chart during pre-event planning phase

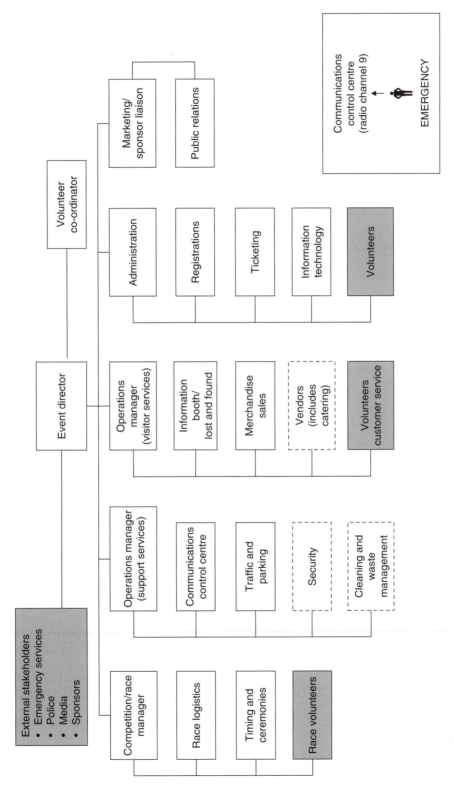

FIGURE 3.9 Organization chart on day of event

For the whole workforce:

- external labour force analysis to identify shortages and skills gaps;
- review of relevant industrial legislation and compliance issues, such as equal opportunity, diversity policy;
- job analysis based on work breakdown planning, including organization charts;
- job design and allocation of roles to paid and volunteer staff;
- training needs analysis ranging from general to specific knowledge;
- Health and Safety programme;
- workforce data base management and time recording system;
- workforce policies and procedures documentation;
- leadership and motivation, retention programme;
- internal communications plan;
- HR budget;
- post event evaluation report.

For paid event staff:

- recruitment plan;
- induction schedule;
- training materials and schedule for delivery;
- payroll system;
- performance management system;
- recognition and severance programme.

For volunteers:

- recruitment and selection plan;
- induction programme;
- training materials and schedule for delivery;
- recognition programme.

Optional involvement:

- uniforms, design, manufacture, distribution;
- meals including voucher system;
- accreditation system;
- transport plan for workforce.

In addition to the most obvious elements listed above, there are more demands on the event organization which may emerge over the course of the project.

Selection of contractors and monitoring of their staffing and training plans

As has already been mentioned, contract labour can form a large percentage of the workforce and for this reason this area needs close attention. Ultimately these people will need to deliver seamless service to the event audience and thus need to be fully integrated into human resources planning, which includes training and recognition programmes. There are significant costs associated with this.

Educational programmes

In response to successful event bids, many governments provide funds to meet training needs identified in a gap analysis. This may be as simple as providing event related information to transport employees working 'outside the tent' or it may involve a sophisticated programme of courses for upskilling. For example, training of apprentice chefs may be required or a plan may be necessary to import qualified people from overseas. Schools and universities are also keen to use major events in new curriculum initiatives and will approach the event organizer for assistance and support.

Involvement with sponsor human resources planning

Sponsors frequently have their employees working on site and therefore want to develop their own event related training. Moreover, some sponsors use the event to motivate staff, providing them with a range of tickets and hospitality options. These sponsor organizations may approach human resources for advice in this regard. Training and motivational programmes for sponsor employees may need approval and support.

Working with stakeholders

Influencing involves the ability to get things done. This means working with a range of stakeholders, the unions being the most obvious. It may however include fundraising committees, volunteering associations, parent committees and partners. This requires an understanding of power and politics, an ability to exert influence in the interest of successful project completion.

Standards

Standards are described by the International Organization for Standardization (ISO) as a series of guidelines that through widespread adoption become de facto regulations. Standards in their own right are not mandatory. There is current ongoing discussion on this topic; Julia Rutherford Silvers (2005) suggests that the event industry needs to adopt voluntary consensus standards for event management but admits that in the United States it is a tall order to expect agreement on federal standards much less international standards. This is the case in many countries. The EMBOK (Event Management Body of Knowledge) is an international initiative with the aim of developing a global curriculum framework for event management.

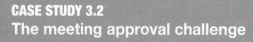

CASE STUDY 3.2
The meeting approval challenge

The American Express Meetings and Events Global Meetings Forecast explores several challenges meeting planners are facing and identifies four distinct trends that are common across all markets.

Budget challenges mean more local meetings

To maintain current levels of meetings activity in an environment where budgets are likely not growing in step with costs, many companies are transitioning from global to national or from national to regional locations for more meetings. Also, there is a trend of holding meetings in unique destinations such as restaurants or aquariums for potential additional savings.

Security and stability impacting destination choice

A continued emphasis on duty of care is translating to a focus on safety and security amidst potential political instability when planning a meeting in 2013. Suppliers indicated that this can sometimes be an advantage; for instance, some major hotel brands located in regions with political instability said they are often chosen based on the perception amongst meeting planners that they offer a more consistent, higher level of security.

Meetings approvals becoming more challenging

A significant portion of meeting planners in all regions indicated that gaining approvals for their meetings is becoming at least slightly more difficult. In addition, there is an emerging trend of meetings budgets not being approved until companies' latest financial data is available.

This dynamic is putting even more pressure on already reduced lead times and can negatively impact hotel negotiations, potentially leading to higher costs.

Increasing engagement via social media

Meeting planners are responding to the expectations of today's meeting attendees by employing social media to increase the value of events throughout their lifecycle. Leading up to events, planners are using social media to connect with attendees and to connect attendees to one another so they can maximize their time at an event. During events, social media is being used to drive even deeper connections and more immersive education sessions, presentation Q&A and other activities. After events, social media is also being used to extend event communities and foster connections made during events.

Source: American Express Meetings & Events 2013 Global Meetings Forecast, reproduced with permission

Reflective practice 3.2

1 Explain the following terms: procurement, preferred suppliers, lead times.
2 What are the cost implications of making last minute decisions to stage events?
3 How are suppliers impacted by last minute approvals or major changes to event plans?
4 Which of the trends do you see having the biggest impact from a workforce planning point of view?

Despite difficulties associated with international agreement on common standards to cover the full scope of event management, there are three areas in which common practice is emerging across the globe. These are risk management; crowd management and emergency planning; and environmental sustainability. Readers have already been introduced to a risk analysis in the previous chapter. Global concerns regarding crowd management are shared by the website www.crowdsafe.com with significant exchange between practitioners and researchers around the world. This website regularly features best practice legislation and guidelines. Planning for emergency evacuation in case of fire, for example, is increasingly consistent across the globe. The International Association of Emergency Managers provides the opportunity to become an accredited member. Finally, *Sustainable Events Management ISO 2012* provides guidelines for environmental sustainability. With this in mind, Minnaert (2012) points out that in her study of mega events 'the social aspect of sustainability was relatively neglected, particularly compared to the environmental aspect' (p. 367). When undertaking recruitment and training of event management personnel it is essential to be mindful of the requirements of these standards.

Chapter summary and key points

This chapter has introduced a number of project management concepts and has looked at the stages of an event project. Organizational design can vary for each of these phases ranging from strategic planning (project initiation) through to operational planning and event execution. For the small, more collaborative type of event, no doubt the small team is not conscious of these shifts in roles as the event draws near. However, even the smallest professional event company usually works on more than one project simultaneously and needs to use these planning tools. In this deadline driven environment the work breakdown structure can contribute to, or inhibit, event planning. These structures need to serve their purpose and assist with the designation of responsibility for operational planning and facilitate a possible shift towards a different implementation structure. Ultimately any diagram is a communication device and the human resources functional area contributes to and utilizes these diagrams for a range of purposes including induction and training. Human resources plays a vital role in managing transformation and change in the event environment.

CASE STUDY 3.3
Studio Festi

PLATE 3.2 Lighting and special effects   **PLATE 3.3** Artistic performance

Studio Festi is an artistic project and production centre bringing into being shows and grand installations, which have become internationally renowned for their poetry and aesthetics.

Founded in 1982 by Valerio Festi and Monica Maimone, Studio Festi operates from its main offices in Velate (Varese), its workshop in Venegono Superiore (Varese) and, in 2010, it set up a branch in Sao Paulo, Brazil.

Studio Festi's artistic activity covers four main areas:

- outdoor shows;
- installations of lights, also called architectures of light due to their unique features;
- video mapping and video projections;
- concerts for fireworks with live orchestra.

A common feature of all of its work is that it is specifically tailored to suit any type of celebration or occasion, from city festivals to commemorations, from exclusive private parties to the opening of sports events.

Studio Festi's spectacles are unequalled, due to their unique invention of stage machinery, their imaginative use of aerial dance, their introduction of video projections as scenic drama-turgical elements and their visionary revisitation of rituals such as the parade. Studio Festi has performed in more than 200 cities of the world: New York, Paris, Moscow, Milan, Madrid, Istanbul, Sydney, Tokyo, Hong Kong, Beijing, Lisbon, Bilbao, Damascus, Seongham, etc.

Source: www.studiofesti.it

Reflective practice 3.3

1   Why would you describe this company's work as highly artistic?
2   How do you see project management principles applying to the design and operations of these shows?
3   From a human resources point of view, identify five challenges associated with staffing these events which travel the globe.
4   Identify three key deliverables for the person responsible for the human resources scope of these projects.

Revision questions

1   How does an event (exhibition, conference, competition) meet the definition of a project?
2   List three types of training commonly delivered to the event workforce and explain who has responsibility for these.
3   Discuss the comment that 'using project management principles stifles creativity and limits flexibility, thus making events one-dimensional'.
4   Explain the concept of a matrix organization using an event example.
5   Provide examples of three standards relating to risk management or emergency planning.

Industry voice by Kerrie Nash

In terms of risk management in workforce planning I will list my top six risks.

1   Getting the discussions right with unions early is important so that you can achieve agreement that the Games are in everybody's interest to have industrial harmony, and get the plan right to ensure that can happen. I think if you don't get that agreement there's always a risk there that the Games can be used as a bit of a platform. That's the last thing you want.

2   The next thing I would say is achieving the mix of skills that are needed in an organizing committee and the lack perhaps in the local area of those skills. That can be everything from the specialist skills in the early days, which is why a lot of organizing committees end up with a population from around the world. It is because they have some very special skills that just aren't available in the local marketplace. Also then the volumes needed in certain areas as you get closer to the Games time, as I mentioned before, security and others if you don't de-risk that by having good employment and skills initiatives in place. Working with local government is very helpful in this area because it's a great opportunity, but it's also a great risk if you don't secure the volumes that you need.

3   The third one I would say is the risk is lack of integration or lack of good project management. I saw this happen with an event where the security contractor wasn't able to secure the numbers of staff they needed. It was because they didn't understand how to integrate every step of their process. They were recruiting people, but then couldn't get the names of the recruited people across to the training area; couldn't get the trained people into the accreditation system, etc. So integration and project management is a huge risk if it's not done well. You might not have everybody you need on day one of the Games in the right place at the right time.

4   Having a retention plan is important. If you don't proactively manage your communication engagement then attrition in the lead up to the event particularly on the volunteer side can be higher than you would want it to be. Ensuring that that is done well is important.

5   I mentioned before the budget pressures associated with growing too early. It is a huge risk that the organization gets nervous and starts kicking off things way too early and ends up doing the same planning three times, four times over. In the meantime a lot of cash has been burnt in the process and cash that you can't get back, so growing too early is a real risk.

6   Finally, it is to successfully blend the workforce on the ground so at Games time you have to have one seamless workforce, paid volunteer and contractor providing the best service to all your client groups. There is a real reputational risk if you don't do that successfully.

Discussion questions

1   Summarize these risks for HRM in the mega/major event area.
2   Explain how at least three of these risks are relevant to smaller events such as sporting events or conferences and how these risks might be mitigated (reduced).

References

Brown, S. and James, J. (2004). 'Event design and management: ritual sacrifice?' In I. Yeoman, M. Robertson, J. Ali-Knight, S. Drummond and U. McMahon-Beattie (eds), *Festival and Events Management: An International Arts and Culture Perspective*. Oxford: Elsevier Butterworth-Heinemann.

Goldblatt, J. (2005). 'An exploratory study of demand levels for EMBOK'. In *The Impacts of Events*. Sydney: University of Technology Sydney.

Goldblatt, J. (2012). *Professional Event Coordination* (Vol. 62). New York: Wiley.

International Olympic Committee (2012). *Final Report of the IOC Coordination Commission*. Available at: http://www.olympic.org/Documents/Games_London_2012/Final%20Cocom%20 Report%20London%202012%20EN.pdf; viewed 8 February 2014.

LV, Qing et al. (2006). 'Establishing HACCP system in catering sector, ensuring the food safety at the Olympic Games', *Food Science and Technology*, 11, 8–12.

Minnaert, L. (2012). 'An Olympic legacy for all? The non-infrastructural outcomes of the Olympic Games for socially excluded groups (Atlanta 1996–Beijing 2008)', *Tourism Management*, 33(2), 361–370.

O'Toole, W. and Mikolaitis, P. (2002). *Corporate Event Project Management*. The Wiley event management series. New York: Wiley.

Project Management Institute (2014). *What is Project Management?* Available at: http://www. pmi.org/About-Us/About-Us-What-is-Project-Management.aspx; viewed 1 February 2014.

Rutherford Silvers, J. (2005). *Standards: Fear or the Future?* Mark Sonder Productions. Available at: http://marksonderproductions.com/about/News/Feb05Standards.html; viewed 12 December 2005.

Shone, A. and Parry, B. (2004). *Successful Event Management*, 2nd edn. London: Thomson Learning.

Soomaroo, L. and Murray, V. (2012). 'Disasters at mass gatherings: lessons from history', *PLoS currents, 4*. Available at: http://www.ncbi.nlm.nih.gov/pmc/articles/PMC3271949/; viewed 12 January 2014.

Tum, J., Norton, P. and Wright, J. (2006). *Management of Event Operations*. Oxford: Elsevier Butterworth-Heinemann.

Van Der Wagen, L. (2005). 'Olympic Games event leadership course design'. In *The Impacts of Events*. Sydney: University of Technology Sydney.

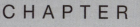

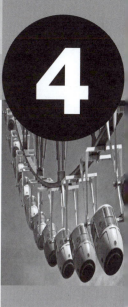

Volunteer management

4

Learning objectives

After reading through this chapter you will be able to:

*   Describe the roles played by volunteers in the event workforce.
*   Analyse the research on volunteer motivation.
*   Evaluate when the use of volunteers is appropriate.
*   Develop a code of conduct for managing volunteers.
*   Develop strategies for volunteer recruitment.
*   Provide a best practice example of volunteer management.

Introduction

While it would seem premature to introduce volunteering at this early stage of the text, best practice volunteer management is also best practice human resource management. Therefore, in order to create the appropriate context for activities such as recruitment, induction and training, this and the next chapter will deal briefly with two potential components of the event workforce: volunteers and contractors. Subsequent chapters on leadership, policy development, recognition and reward will thus apply to the combined workforce.

Incidentally, for mega events, the term 'inside the fence' is useful to identify the workforce as those people carrying event accreditation in the form of a badge or lanyard. For this type of event, therefore, the workforce might include paid staff, contractor employees, sponsor employees, volunteers, government officials and emergency services crews. All these people work within the event to make it successful, and it is the responsibility of the human resource department or the area managers to ensure that the workforce is cohesive and striving towards the same purpose: presenting flawless and integrated service to visitors (Byrne et al., 2002).

For a mega event, there are also many people working 'outside the fence' to support the programme. These include staff working in hotels, restaurants, train stations and information centres. This is a useful clarification, as human resource departments in the mega event environment often have a role to play in analysing workforce requirements in these sectors where the event has a significant impact. Even in the case of smaller events, such as hallmark events, the event organizers are similarly concerned with service levels 'outside the fence' as well as inside, since all form part of the consumer's event experience. Event organizers are often asked to provide or approve training materials issued to personnel working in these service areas. The Beijing Olympic Games Organizing Committee was pro-active to this end, releasing pre-Games training material on the internet three years before this event. This included an introduction to China, and Beijing in particular, an overview of the Olympic Games and materials relating to training sites by facilities and regions (Beijing Olympic Committee, 2005).

Scope of volunteering

Volunteers can form a significant part of the event workforce. At the Winter Olympics held at Torino, for example, there were 25,000 volunteers, 5,000 of whom were part of the ceremonies programme. Of these, 3,500 worked as dancers, actors, gymnasts, acrobats and musicians, while 1,500 worked behind the scenes as production assistants. For the Korean Jeonju International Film Festival (JIFF) 260 volunteers were divided into different teams, such as subtitles, ticket sales, information and traffic control. One of these volunteers, Kwak Wonhyeok, shares his experiences in Case Study 4.1 (Giammarco, 2005).

Before exploring some specific event volunteering issues, it is useful to look at the status of volunteering in world communities as the volunteering ethic varies from country to country, and this has important implications for organizers of social impact events such as fundraisers, arts festivals and the like.

In the United States about 64.5 million persons, or 26.5 per cent of the civilian population aged 16 and over, volunteered through or for an organization at least once during the period September 2011 to September 2012. Women volunteered at a higher rate than men across age groups, education levels and other major characteristics (United States Department of Labor, 2012). Interestingly, the rate of volunteering for employed persons was higher than for unemployed persons. Table 4.1 provides additional information on the characteristics of volunteers in the United States from September 2011 to September 2012.

In the United Kingdom, the Community Life Survey (2012) showed that in 2012–2013 44 per cent of adults volunteered formally (through a group, club or organization) at least once a year and 29 per cent did so at least once a month, increasing from 2010–2011 when the figures were 39 per cent and 25 per cent respectively. Volunteering for the London Olympic Games was popular, at the time of its launch in 2010, the Games Makers volunteer programme was substantially oversubscribed, with a quarter-of-a-million applicants.

According to the Centre for Volunteering in Australia, in 2010, 6.1 million people aged 18 years and more (36 per cent of the Australian population aged 18 years and over) had undertaken some form of voluntary work in the previous 12 months, up slightly from

CASE STUDY 4.1
Volunteers: a film festival's hidden strength

If you have ever attended a film festival in Korea, one of the things that may surprise you is the numbers of volunteer workers you will see. Of course, volunteers work at festivals around the world, but film festivals in Korea inspire thousands to apply for unpaid positions. At a recent film event in Europe, I asked a staff member if they could spare a volunteer to help me with something and he answered with a laugh, 'Sorry, but we don't have armies of volunteers like you have in Pusan'. So what is it that drives these people, usually students, to work at festivals for long hours and no pay? This year, one of my students, Kwak Won-hyeok, was working as a volunteer at the Jeonju International Film Festival so I took the opportunity to ask him about his experience.

Congratulations on being selected as a volunteer. I hear that the competition is pretty fierce.

Thanks, but actually, I wasn't selected at first. I was in China when the first round of selections was made so I was put on a waiting list. I was lucky because some people who were originally selected weren't able to make it. The application process begins very early. The deadline for applying as a volunteer is in December. On the application we can select what part we are interested in doing like ticketing or information … Then in early spring, we were interviewed. The interview lasted about 30 minutes. I had written on my application that I wanted to meet guests so part of my interview was in English and Chinese. I couldn't answer the questions in Chinese well – I have only studied the language since last winter.

What questions did they ask at the interview?

First they asked me about my experiences. I had mentioned that I was part of a leadership training programme and I am vice-president of my club at university. They also asked me why I had chosen to study English in England rather than another country. Finally, they asked me about what I thought of JIFF. I was worried about that question because, even though I am from Jeonju, I had never attended the films screened at JIFF. I would always enjoy the downtown atmosphere while JIFF was going on, but I had never thought that I would be interested in the kind of films they show. This experience has changed that. I have been very surprised at how excited people get about these independent and short films and I hope to have the chance to start watching more of them.

What do you do as a volunteer?

Well, I was part of the foreign support team so my job was to pick up guests from the bus terminal and bring them to the hotel. Or to meet them at the hotels and take them to the guest centre downtown. I also had to answer questions about Jeonju such as what to see or where and what to eat, manage the guests' interview schedules and take them to their appointments. JIFF had hired three taxis so we would call them whenever we needed.

It sounds like you got to meet many filmmakers

Well – not so many. Each of the volunteers in my team were in charge of seven or eight guests. I was in charge of some of the English speaking guests, but we had volunteers who could also speak Japanese, Chinese and French. Sosuke Ikematsu was probably the most popular out of all the guests among the volunteers. He was the little boy who appeared in *The Last Samurai*. He came with his mother and he was very bright and interested in everything. All the female volunteers wanted to show him around.

How many volunteers were there?

My team had twenty-six volunteers and five or six regular staff members. The whole festival had, I think, 260 volunteers divided into different teams like Subtitles, Ticket Sales, Information, and Traffic Control. I think I was lucky because some people on my team had to stay in the hotels or in the guest room just checking IDs. I was able to come and go if I was not needed, but we were on call constantly.

What hours did you work?

We began in the morning, usually about 10, and we were supposed to finish at 10 pm, but usually we were needed until about 12 midnight.

Those are long hours. What kind of benefits did JIFF provide for volunteers?

Well … they gave us W10,000 a day for lunch and dinner. (That's about US$10.) And we were able to go to the guest and press parties, I think there were five in all, but I was too tired by the end of the day to attend.

Well, you must have seen a lot of films

No! Volunteers can't watch the movies. Also, we weren't allowed to eat or drink with guests or press. They did have a special screening for volunteers of the short film *M* and a British animation called *The Magic Roundabout*. Those were the only movies I saw.

Wait. You don't get to see any movies, you work all day, and you can't spend much time with guests. What DO you get out of this experience?

I got to feel and experience the atmosphere of JIFF from a different perspective. It is a lot of fun but it's also a lot of work. I never realized what went into organizing and running a festival smoothly. Also, my team grew very close in the preparations before the festival and during our working days and I have made many valuable friendships. Also, the closer it got to the festival, the less important my reasons for joining became. I got caught up in the excitement of making this festival a success and I really didn't mind that I couldn't watch the films. I felt a sense of satisfaction with the way things were going and I really value this experience.

Is there anything that you would like to see improved or changed next year?

The only thing I would suggest is about organization. They need to give the volunteers in charge of guests a list of who is where. I was sometimes told to go to meet guests coming by shuttle bus from the airport, but I would have no idea who or how many people I was supposed to meet. I could only stand there with the JIFF sign and hope that they would find me.

Reproduced with permission; for further information see http://koreanfilm.org/jiffOS.html

Reflective practice 4.1

1   Summarize the feelings of this volunteer towards the volunteering experience.
2   Explain how the volunteer's expectations in this situation might not be met.
3   This volunteer had one suggestion – explain what he meant.
4   Interview someone who has volunteered for an event and find out about their experiences. Then develop five recommendations for volunteer management.

34 per cent in 2006. Volunteering was less common in capital cities (34 per cent) than outside capital cities (41 per cent).

Figure 4.1 illustrates variation in the relative size of the nonprofit workforce (paid and volunteer) as a share of local workforce, by country. In New Zealand and Norway the volunteer numbers were higher than the paid workforce in the nonprofit sector. Overall for the countries in the survey, the average paid and volunteer contributions were 5.20 per cent and 2.20 per cent respectively as a share of the workforce in all 13 countries (Lester

TABLE 4.1 Volunteerism by selected characteristics, September 2012 in the USA

Percentage of volunteerism in the US – demographic breakdown			
	Volunteer % of population	Men	Women
Age			
16–19	27.4	25.1	29.8
20–24	18.9	16.0	21.8
25–34	23.2	18.8	27.4
35–44	31.6	26.4	36.6
45–54	29.3	26.2	32.3
55–64	27.6	24.6	30.4
65 and over	24.4	22.9	25.6
Educational attainment			
Less than a high school diploma	8.8	7.8	9.8
High School graduates	17.3	14.8	19.8
College or associate degree	28.7	24.5	32.3
Bachelor's degree and higher	42.2	38.2	45.9
Employment status			
Full time	28.1	25.5	31.5
Part time	33.4	26.8	37.3
Unemployed	23.8	18.7	29.6

NOTE: Data on volunteers relate to persons who performed unpaid volunteer activities for an organization at any point from September 1, 2011, through the survey period in September 2012.
Source: Adapted from Bureau of Labour Statistics (2012)

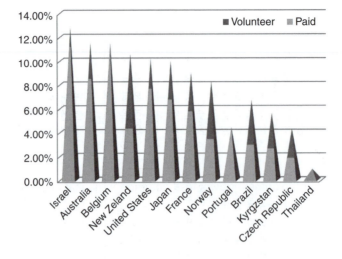

FIGURE 4.1 The nonprofit workforce, paid and volunteer, as a share of total workforce, by country

Source: Data from Lester et al. (2012): http://ccss.jhu.edu/publications-findings?did=393.

et al. 2012). While these numbers do not indicate the level of volunteering specifically for event, they are indicative of social and cultural trends.

Zhuang (2010) points to a paucity for studies concerning volunteerism in Chinese society and provides a historical framework of the evolution of volunteerism in Chinese society spanning three historic periods from ancient to modern China. While the ethos of volunteerism is shown to be prevalent in cultural values such as Confucian benevolence, the introduction of formal volunteerism in China began in 1989 when the first volunteer association was set up in Shenzhen. Zhuang's report provides an overview of the volunteer programme for the Beijing Olympic Games for which 70,000 Games volunteers were selected, predominantly university students from Beijing (90 per cent). The justification for this selection was the logistical ease with which this could be done, as well as the students' English language capability, deemed better than that of retired Chinese people for example. In terms of outcomes, the volunteers were able to improve their knowledge of world cultures, improve their English further and were able to enhance their employability as a result of their experience. According to Zhuang, 'though the younger generation of Chinese people seem keen on future participation, the older generation (i.e. the generation of the volunteers' parents) are limited by their professions and the lack of free time to contribute in such a way' (2010: 2855).

In 2009 the FIA sanctioned the first ever running of an F1 Grand Prix event in Abu Dhabi. Aside from being responsible for successful management of the race, the Automobile and Touring Club of the UAE (ATCUAE) also retained the responsibility of recruiting hundreds of volunteers to assist with this global event. The demographic profile of the volunteer workforce was one concern emerging from this research with very low numbers of Emerati people (only 8 per cent of the total), a workforce that was predominantly male, aged between 22 and 44. Only 17 per cent of volunteers were female and 82 per cent of all the volunteers were full-time employed, 2 per cent unemployed. The findings of the research are discussed in more detail in Case Study 4.2. One of the report's recommendations was that a dedicated commitment was necessary to actively recruit volunteers from those currently underrepresented demographic profiles, including females, students, those seeking enhanced employment prospects and elder members of society. It also recommended that the training programme needed adjustment and that this should include mandatory attendance requirements. It is recommended that readers access the full report which provides an excellent example of HR evaluation.

CASE STUDY 4.2
Profile and contributions of volunteers Abu Dhabi Formula 1 Grand Prix

A research study conducted between 2009 and 2013 by the Motorsport Knowledge Institute, a sub-division of ATCUAE, in association with the University of Ulster, UK, had the aim of developing an understanding of the profile and contribution of the volunteers who assisted with the Abu Dhabi Formula 1 Grand Prix.

A number of findings were uncovered upon completion of this study. These included:

* The majority of the volunteers working at the Abu Dhabi F1 Grand Prix were highly educated, young male professionals of Asian or European origin. The event, a landmark global sporting spectacle, also serves as an excellent example of the richness of Emirati society as it brings together members of the expatriate communities working alongside the indigenous Emirati people.
* The number of Emiratis working on their host F1 event stands at 8 per cent of the overall total, which is proportionally higher than might be expected, indicative of their willingness to volunteer at major sporting events staged in the country and which portray the host nation in a positive light.
* Displaying moderate to high levels of experience of working at Formula 1 events, the volunteers emerged from an array of professional backgrounds and fulfilled a wide range of duties at the event. Indeed most volunteers said the experiences they encountered whilst working at the F1 Grand Prix exercised a profound impact on their personal and professional lives, suggestive of the fact that volunteering in this way presents a unique opportunity to improve the career prospects of many UAE residents.
* The work of volunteers at the event further positively impacted on UAE society by generating an elevated awareness of the country as a preferred business and tourism destination, increasing civic and national pride in the achievements of the UAE, as well as assisting towards the creation of a more skilled labour force. Their work, engaging with spectators, the competing teams and helping to host visiting dignitaries, conveys a very positive image on those attending the event, and it is this legacy that often remains with visitors to the country long after the event and who are then encouraged to return in future years. So the volunteering 'legacy' is also a significant outcome of this process and worthy of closer inspection in the time ahead.

- Economic savings of over AED 6 million were realized through the recruitment and training of volunteers at the Abu Dhabi Grand Prix event by ATCUAE, with a number of additional direct and indirect economic outcomes also evident across other business sectors including leisure and tourism (p. 8).

Source: Economic Impact Report For Volunteers Of The 2012 Abu Dhabi F1 Grand Prix, Atcuae, Online: http://www.fia. com/sites/default/files/basicpage/file/ATCpercent20Unitedpercent20Arabpercent20Emiratespercent20Volunteers_0.pdf

Reflective practice 4.2

- What are some of the cultural factors that would contribute to the current workforce profile?
- Why do you think that the recommendation was made regarding the demographic profile of volunteers?
- This report points to positive social and economic impacts. Debate or discuss the need for volunteers at such an event.
- Why is an evaluation of HR practice for an event useful?

Hall et al. (2005: 11) suggest that nonprofit and voluntary organizations are not simply places of employment and the authors reinforce the concept of building social capital:

> What makes them significant are the functions they perform, and these functions are multiple. For one thing, these organizations deliver a variety of human services, from health care and education to social services and community development. Also important is the sector's advocacy role, its role in identifying unaddressed problems and bringing them to public attention, in protecting basic human rights, and in giving voice to a wide assortment of social, political, environmental and community interests and concerns. Beyond political and policy concerns, the nonprofit and voluntary sector also performs a broader expressive function, providing the vehicles through which an enormous variety of other sentiments and impulses – artistic, spiritual, cultural, occupational, social and recreational – also find expression. Opera companies, symphonies, soccer clubs, hobby associations, places of worship, fraternal societies, professional associations, book clubs and youth groups are just some of the manifestations of this expressive function. Finally, nonprofit and voluntary organizations have also been credited with contributing to what scholars are increasingly coming to call 'social capital', those bonds of trust and reciprocity that seem to be crucial for a democracy and a market economy to function effectively. By establishing connections among individuals, involvement in associations teaches norms of co-operation that carry over into political and economic life.

Clearly volunteer programmes can produce positive social impacts. However, Chapter 6 raises the issue of exploitation of volunteers and interns, particularly when the programme is driven by cost saving, as would be the case for a commercial as opposed to a nonprofit

PLATE 4.1 Volunteers are ready to help with information

community event. In many cases the difference between profit and nonprofit events is not clear, as is the case of arts festivals where some shows are ticketed and others are open to the public.

Volunteer motivation

Motivation is the one significant distinguishing difference between human resource management for volunteers and paid staff. Retention is a major issue for HR managers and needs to be addressed at all stages during recruitment, induction and training to ensure that volunteers have accurate expectations of the work and that the work will meet their needs. Volunteers generally have a much shorter commitment to the job and, in the case of a large event, it may not even be noticed if they leave before their allocated shift is over. While there would be repercussions for a paid employee who walked off the job, there are none for the volunteer. Ongoing communication at all stages, from recruitment to close of an event, is vitally important in ensuring that retention of volunteers does not become a problem for HR managers during the execution of an event (Byrne et al., 2002).

During a detailed study of event volunteers participating in a regional marathon, Strigas and Newton Jackson (2003) conducted a factor analysis which produced a five-factor model for explaining motivation of event volunteers at this type of event:

1   *Material factor*. This includes incentives where the volunteer calculates the expected utility gain, which can include material rewards (such as goods and services) or social status that carries a material value. This may be represented by complimentary items, for example.
2   *Purposive factor*. Here the motives of volunteers were compatible with those of the event and the community: 'volunteering creates a better society'.
3   *Leisure factor*. In some cases, volunteering was seen as a leisure choice, an escape from everyday life and an opportunity to develop new interests.
4   *Egoistic factor*. Social interaction, networking and building self-esteem were motivations where the individual sought social contact as an affective incentive.
5   *External factor.* These factors were outside the individual's immediate control and linked to family traditions or course completion requirements.

In an analysis of motives and their importance, Strigas and Newton Jackson (2003) found the highest and lowest ranking reasons as illustrated in Table 4.2.

It would seem that there are often almost as many reasons to volunteer as there are volunteers. Many attempts have been made to analyse motivations according to demographic characteristics, but in a study of the motivational needs of adolescent volunteers, Schondel and Boehm (2000) found that there were similarities between the motivations of adolescents and those of adults and college students. These included helping others, social interaction and recognition of contributions. There were also differences, indicating that developmental stages of identity formation may influence motivation of this age group. Callow (2004) argues that the senior citizen segment is far from homogenous in its motives for, and behaviour towards, volunteering, which may have an impact on the effectiveness of recruitment campaigns.

TABLE 4.2 Highest and lowest ranking motives for volunteering for a sporting event

Highest ranking reasons	Lowest ranking reasons
• Volunteering creates a better society • Wanting to help make the event a success • Fun in volunteering for a marathon event • Putting something back into the community • Volunteering enables the organizational committee to provide more services for less money	• Wanting to gain some practical experience • Extra bonus/credit for volunteering from employer/school • Receiving complimentary items • Volunteering will look good on résumé • Volunteering makes person feel less lonely • Wanting to be recognized for doing this volunteer work

(Adapted from Strigas and Newton Jackson, 2003: 117)

Research studies assist in clarifying and classifying the many and varied volunteer motivations (Monga 2006). Gordon and Erkut (2004) in their study of the Edmonton Folk Music Festival's 1,800 volunteers found that while people are usually enticed into volunteering for the folk fest by perks, such as free access to the entertainment, gourmet meals and T-shirts, their willingness to return year after year depends on an intangible degree of satisfaction. This study shows that the initial reasons for signing up as a volunteer are not necessarily the ones that contribute to satisfaction and retention. Indeed, in the author's experience, issuing designer jeans to volunteers a week before the fashion show will not ensure that all the volunteers will turn up on the day, quite the contrary!

A consistent theme appears to be the importance of volunteers understanding the strategic purpose of the event and the important role that they will play in its success. As discussed in the previous chapters, an event is a major project with multiple subprojects. Knowing that the project is temporal and finite is important both for volunteer and paid staff. If progress and tangible success are evident, then the whole team will be better motivated. This is illustrated in Case Study 4.1: the volunteer does not see any of the films shown at the film festival but feels that, despite the lack of tangible reward, he has played an important role in the successful outcome of the project.

Leadership and motivation will be covered in detail in later chapters of this book, and in the remainder of the text the workforce will be discussed in the context of 'one team, one fence' (Byrne et al., 2002), with occasional references to specific volunteer issues.

Deciding on the use of volunteers

Whether to involve volunteers in an event or not is a significant strategic decision. Volunteers are not 'free' as they need to be recruited, selected, trained, supervised, uniformed and fed. The total cost per volunteer, excluding management, for the Sydney 2000 Olympic Games was A$750 (Lockstone and Baum, 2009). There are many reasons why an event organization would recruit volunteers as a component of the workforce or, in some cases, as the complete workforce:

1   *Establishing the event.* Some events emerge as a result of the combined efforts of a group of individuals who have a cause-related reason to develop and run an event. These volunteers form a committee and the concept grows from there. Many music festivals start from small beginnings and grow over time, as do many historical celebrations.

2   *Expanding the workforce.* One of the most common reasons for involving volunteers is to expand the workforce in a cost-effective way. Without the contribution of volunteers many mega events and hallmark events would not be able to run in their present format as the contribution of volunteers is so significant in terms of the total hours contributed.

3   *Expanding the level of customer service.* Volunteers are primarily employed in customer contact roles and can contribute to the ambience of an event in important ways. At the Winter Olympics in Salt Lake City, for example, the level of service was so high that it attracted the interest of the media, including NBC's *Today Show* and the *Wall Street Journal*.

4 *Contributing to community spirit*. While it is true that events can contribute in important ways to developing community spirit, this is not typically the sole reason why an event is staffed by volunteers.

5 *Creating a social impact*. By using volunteers in a developmental role, thus improving their qualifications and employment prospects, events can have a long-term social impact. In South Africa, for example, events are widely regarded as part of 'capacity building'. The expectation of social impacts was also behind the bid for the FIFA World Cup.

6 *Contribution to diversity*. Event volunteers come from a remarkable range of backgrounds. This can be helpful in providing representative languages and cultures for sporting competitions or world music festivals. Volunteers with diverse backgrounds also bring new ideas to problem situations that can be enlightening.

7 *Expanding the network*. Volunteers are often co-opted by family and friends. In this way the volunteering network can grow, leading to contacts with new sponsors and contractors.

8 *Belief in the ethos of volunteerism*. Some organizations have a strong belief in volunteerism, exhibited by their taking on volunteers and also by providing volunteers to work at events. This can lead to enhanced learning and organizational development.

While many of the above reasons are altruistic, it is essential for an organization to be honest about their reasons for recruiting volunteers. The motive of reducing labour costs is generally quite apparent to volunteers, and this can be stressed in recruitment efforts along the theme of 'we can't do this without you'. It is also important to ensure that volunteers perform an 'expressive function' rather than a role better allocated to a paid staff member. The volunteers of successive Olympic Games have contributed enormously in their roles as country ambassadors.

Code of conduct for managing volunteers

Most professional event organizations have a code of conduct for managing volunteers and such guidelines are also provided by many volunteer associations. Following is a summary of the important elements of a code of conduct for organizations utilizing the services of volunteers.

The event organization will:

- meet all legal obligations such as anti-discrimination legislation;
- provide a healthy and safe workplace;
- plan and document safe work practices;
- provide insurance cover for volunteer staff;
- provide clear and accurate information about how volunteer expectations will be met;
- provide orientation and training;
- avoid placing volunteers in positions more suitable for paid staff;
- treat volunteers as an integral part of the team;
- avoid placing volunteers in situations that are difficult or dangerous;
- provide meals, drinks and breaks as required;

- provide protection from the sun and the elements;
- provide adequate levels of supervision and support;
- define jobs and issue job descriptions or checklists;
- develop human resources policies and make these available to volunteers, including procedures for grievance resolution;
- acknowledge the rights of volunteers;
- offer opportunities for learning and development where possible;
- meet out-of-pocket expenses such as transportation;
- keep volunteers up to date with important information;
- constantly acknowledge the contribution of volunteers on both an individual and a group basis.

Returning to Gordon and Erkut's (2004) analysis of the Edmonton Folk Music Festival, it appears that one of the key factors contributing to volunteer satisfaction at this event was the scheduling tool that enabled volunteers to state their limitations and preferences. Many volunteers wish to work with friends and prefer to go online to select appropriate shifts. The importance of volunteer productivity (and ensuring that volunteers are not underutilized) is reiterated in the quote from Kerrie Nash at the end of the chapter where she suggests that the HR manager needs to keep a brake on the number of volunteers so that they don't feel that their time is wasted. Kerrie makes the point that retention is more of an issue during the recruitment and training process than it is during the event's execution. Her benchmark for attrition in the lead up to a mega event is 20 per cent which means that during the recruitment, training and accreditation process it is likely that this percentage of applicants will drop out. She says that for an event such as the Olympic Games the attrition rate during the running of the event is minimal, and the remaining volunteers who become more efficient at their jobs over successive days are easily able to take up the extra work. This, however, may not be the case for other smaller events, particularly when there are issues with weather, transportation, organization, etc.

Long- and short-term volunteers

Volunteers contribute at various stages of an event project, including working on the organizing committee for many community events. In some event organizations this affiliation can last for years. For example, a Canadian, Al Ingram, was awarded the annual volunteer award from Sports Hall of Fame recognizing decades of loyal service in the community. He served as president and board member of minor hockey for 20 years and helped establish minor softball in the village of Bobcaygeon. He also acted as director of youth curling for several years.

For larger annual events or mega events such as an Olympic Games, some volunteers come on board very early and stay with the planning group for an extended period. In Manchester (at the Commonwealth Games) these volunteers were known as Long Term Volunteers (LTVs) while in Sydney they were known as Pioneer Volunteers, both groups working with the respective organizing committees for a year or more. For events such as the Grand Prix, there are many veteran volunteers who have worked every year over a long period. However, the majority of event volunteers work for a short time only, ranging from a few hours to a few days or weeks.

Interns work for event organizations for up to a year, sometimes in a voluntary capacity as a requirement of their study programmes, and in other cases they work in paid internship roles. This is a popular way to gain entry to the event industry and gain experience as well as networks.

Source of volunteers

While recruitment is the topic of Chapter 8, it is useful to point out here that there are several specific contact points for finding volunteers, particularly those with relevant expertise and experience. Many of these associations work with event organizers in a partnership arrangement to ensure the success of the volunteering programme.

Volunteering associations

There are volunteering associations at local, state and national levels in most countries. Organizations such as AVA (Association for Volunteer Administration) in the United States and CSV (Community Services Volunteers) in the United Kingdom provide guidelines for volunteer management, statistics, and other publications and services.

Related associations

Many associations in the sporting arena support events by supplying qualified officials and judges; similarly in the arts, where organizations provide expertise in supporting exhibitions, competitions and concerts. In fact, many such associations provide grants to support events and can provide advice in relation to volunteer programmes.

Sponsor organizations

Sponsor organizations are often keen to have their staff involved in an event for the purpose of professional development or simply for the incentive that this provides to their staff.

Universities and colleges

Internship programmes and work experience programmes that form a compulsory course component are an invaluable source of volunteers, providing students who are interested in a particular field with valuable hands-on experience. Some students work for the event organization for a long period, participating fully in the planning process; others work for just a week or so on several events in order to widen the scope of their experience.

Special interest groups

Event volunteering can form part of an affirmative action programme. For example, a youth concert may be organized by a group of unemployed youths involved in a special programme.

Typical roles for volunteers at events

The outline of a code of conduct above stressed that the roles allocated to volunteers should not be roles that are typically paid jobs. If this were the case, it would certainly get the unions and other employee associations agitated. Using volunteer workers in paid jobs such as cleaning is regarded as exploitation.

Cuskelly and Auld (2000) have produced a guide to volunteer management which, among other things, presents a summary of comments from the national and state winners of the National Australia Bank Community Link Awards (see Table 4.3). One of the strongest themes emerging from this summary is the importance of workforce integration. Volunteers want to be treated the same as paid workers, feel part of the team and have their services recognized. Most importantly, they do not want to be taken for granted.

PLATE 4.2 Volunteers are briefed before shifts start

TABLE 4.3 Good practice advice for volunteer management

	Good practice advice	
	DO	DON'T
National winner Bicycle South Australia	• Provide written job descriptions for volunteers • Ensure training sessions are relevant • Acknowledge their achievements	• Neglect the recruitment of new volunteers • Ignore their interests • Treat them differently from paid staff
State winner Queensland Q-Rapid	• Identify clear paths for volunteers • Value each person's qualities, skills and efforts • Provide real responsibilities for volunteers through training	• Take people for granted • Provide ineffective information • Ignore volunteer services
State winner NSW Coonamble Rodeo Association	• Use time efficiently • Delegate according to skills • Openly discuss all issues	• Neglect to guide new volunteers • Forget to acknowledge contributors
State winner Victoria Kilmany Family Care	• Respect the role of volunteers • Ensure they have access to debriefing • Ensure that fun is part of the work	• Put barriers up to communication • Assume volunteers have all the required knowledge • Take anyone for granted
State winner Tasmania Tasmanian Trail Association	• Accept volunteers for what they can do • Listen to all viewpoints, including those of paid officials	• Lose patience • Be inflexible • Take anyone for granted
State winner WA Recreation and Respite	• Include volunteers as part of the team • Listen to their ideas • Show appreciation of their efforts	• Overload volunteers with work • Isolate volunteers from staff • Put volunteers in difficult and dangerous situations
State winner ACT Australian Football International Youth Trophy	• Choose people according to their talents and desires • Involve those who can raise the group's profile • Make tasks enjoyable • Give positive feedback	• Give too few people too much work • Spring jobs on volunteers at the last minute • Assign jobs that are too difficult

(Reproduced with permission of the Australian Sports Commission)

Management of volunteer programmes

Volunteer programmes require careful planning and go well beyond recruitment and training. Volunteer management includes logistics: rosters, meals, uniforms, transportation, safety and sometimes accommodation. Added to this is the need to develop recognition and reward programmes. Problem solving and communication are key elements during the operational phase.

While the topic of job descriptions will follow in Chapter 8, the example of a job description for a human resource manager in Case Study 4.3 demonstrates the volunteer management role in detail.

CASE STUDY 4.3
Festival – volunteer co-ordinator position

Human Resources and Administration Manager

Duty statement and selection criteria

Position outline

Reports to: Festival Director
Position type: Full time
Duration: Two-year contract with scope for renewal

The Human Resources and Administration Manager reports to the Festival Director and is a key role within the management team. This is a key role both in the organization of the festival as an annual event, and in the ongoing running of the festival as a company. The Human Resources and Administration Manager has responsibility for the efficient day-to-day running of the festival office, management of a dedicated volunteer budget, and the recruitment, maintenance and deployment of volunteers. Some of these duties are shared with the Production Manager.

The success of the festival is built on its volunteer community. The volunteer team is one of the festival's most important resources and this position is crucial to the success of developing and maintaining volunteer morale. The successful applicant will be a strong advocate for volunteering in the community and will be expected to play a key advocacy role within the community on behalf of our festival volunteers.

Duties

Volunteer programme

- Manage volunteer recruitment, rostering, training and deployment, including the identification of some 70 co-ordinators (across 45 teams) of major areas during the festival.
- Manage on-site volunteer support services such as volunteer reception and the volunteer kitchen.
- Build morale and motivation within the volunteer team.
- Manage co-ordinator recruitment and support.
- Implement, enforce and revise volunteer policies, ensuring that all procedures are documented and comply with risk management/organizational policy.
- Prepare and manage a budget for volunteer services, including volunteer training, co-ordinator meetings, debriefings and documentation of volunteer activities.

- Facilitate and organize volunteer and co-ordinator meetings, debriefings and social functions.
- Manage the preparation, publication and distribution of quarterly newsletters to some 1,500 volunteers in conjunction with the Publications Manager.
- In areas where a co-ordinator has not been found, or is not functioning properly, act as contingency manager until a replacement is found.

Year-round administration

- In conjunction with the Festival Director, Production and Programme Manager, identify and develop timelines and checklists for the different streams of festival operations (i.e. performers, stalls, ticketing, marketing, etc.).
- As part of the management team be involved in the forward planning of the festival as a company and an annual event.
- Manage pre-festival volunteer teams, recruiting, training and deploying volunteers so as to meet projected timelines in any or all areas.
- Manage administration systems throughout the year, including large mail-outs, phones, fax, emails, stationery and volunteer staffing.
- Develop and improve advance purchase ticketing system.

Computing

- Assist in development of advance purchase ticketing database and systems.
- Assist in development of the master and volunteer databases.
- Assist in production of newsletters and forms.
- Manage data entry into all databases.

On-site (i.e. during the festival)

- Manage the reception and deployment of some 1,100 volunteers.
- Liaise with coordinators to ensure their volunteer staffing needs are being met.
- Manage 'top up' volunteers for unforeseen emergencies, and no-shows in other areas.
- Act as contingency manager as and when required during the festival.

General

- Secretariat services to the Festival Board, including record keeping, minute taking and meeting organization.
- Troubleshooting and problem solving, in any festival-related area, as necessary.
- Research, analysis and report preparation.
- As a team member attend regular staff meetings and follow up on requested actions.
- Manage the personnel functions for the festival, including worker's compensation, income tax and maintenance of personnel records.
- Other duties as requested by the Festival Director.

Selection criteria – essential

1 **Personal qualities.** The Human Resources and Administration Manager plays a critical role in the ongoing success of the festival. The Human Resources and Administration Manager needs to be adaptable and responsive to the needs of our volunteers and the strategic directions as set down by the Board.

2 **Communication skills.** The successful applicant will have well-developed communication skills, being required to communicate professionally, efficiently and respectfully with volunteers, professional colleagues/stakeholders, sponsors and staff. This role requires highly developed negotiation and interpersonal skills. This position requires the ability to work with an enormous variety of people. The successful applicant will be able to communicate effectively with people from differing cultural and educational backgrounds and age groups. The role requires patience, tolerance, compassion and the ability to assert boundaries where appropriate. The Human Resources and Administration Manager will, on occasion, be required to speak publicly at conferences and forums.

3 **High level of initiative and motivation**. The nature of the position is often deadline-driven. It is important that the Human Resources and Administration Manager has the ability to remain calm and clear-headed in busy times and is self-motivated and able to work unsupervised.

4 **Ability to work within budget**. The Human Resources and Administration Manager will be given an annual budget. It is essential that the Human Resources and Administration Manager has the ability to operate within this budget. Operational budgetary areas include volunteer training, onsite volunteer kitchen, overall volunteer needs/services (e.g. stationery equipment), volunteer activity documentation, newsletters and social functions.

5 **Demonstrated ability to work as a part of a team**. The success of the festival past and future is dependent upon the hard work, commitment, skills and cohesiveness of its operational team. This team includes both paid staff and a large number of volunteers. The Human Resources and Administration Manager must have the demonstrated ability to work well in a team environment. This environment is collaborative and productive.

6 **Computer skills**. The Human Resources and Administration Manager is required to manage and maintain the volunteer database and to use and train volunteers in the use of the operating systems within the festival office.

Reflective practice 4.3

1 Describe the primary purpose of this role in two sentences.

2 Compare this job description with another similar one found online.

3 Debate or discuss the following statement: 'The volunteer co-ordinator has to act as advocate for the volunteers in order to avoid them being exploited'.

4 Describe the planning activities that are undertaken by a volunteer co-ordinator.

Chapter summary and key points

This chapter has highlighted strategic decisions regarding the volunteer component of the event workforce. Volunteer motivations have been discussed in some detail with research studies indicating that there are diverse reasons why people volunteer. Demographic and other forms of analysis show few consistent trends and therefore the event organizer has to acknowledge that for any event there will be a wide range of different motivations and expectations to be met. Acknowledgement and recognition of the important role that volunteers play appear to be significant factors in volunteer management in most studies, as does the event organization's expressed purpose of the event. Integration of a cohesive workforce is a priority, with one team 'inside the fence'. Everyone wants to feel the buzz, the sense of involvement in something big, something exciting and something that is going to be good.

Revision questions

1 Compare the volunteering rates in your community or country with those in this chapter.
2 Investigate one mega event and discover the number of volunteers and the types of roles they have played.
3 List and explain five reasons why people volunteer for sporting events.
4 There have been several studies of event volunteers, mainly focused on motivation and retention. Review and discuss five studies.
5 Provide a rationale for including volunteers at a specific event.
6 List and describe three recruitment sources for volunteers.

Industry voice by Kerrie Nash

You know the good news story in every Games is the volunteers and they are the universally great story that always captures the media's attention and the general public's attention, which is fantastic. That's almost a given, providing you treat your volunteers well and they have a good experience.

Volunteers are not free and sometimes the organization is very good at saying, 'we've got lots and lots of volunteers' and then when it comes to supporting them, 'we've got to cut back here and cut back here and cut back here'. If you really expect people to turn up for day two, and week two, you do have to provide basic care, including good quality and variety in the food provided. That's an easy one to use as an example of where we sometimes misalign our thinking on things like that. Quality catering for volunteers is more than 'a nice to have', of course it's essential.

If you want to avoid attrition it is important to right size or even undersize your volunteer population. Of course after day three, or during day four, you can do more with less because people learn their jobs and become very skilled and very able. Even if you did have attrition you're likely going to be able to cover it with your existing workforce. The last thing you want to do is disrespect people's time by hiring and putting them through all of that training and then having them turn up and be told to sit there, and eight hours later they're still sitting there waiting to be told what to do.

Therefore one of the constant things that we have to challenge in the planning stage is the size of the workforce. This is done by asking functional area managers, 'why do you need all those volunteers? Tell me the jobs that they're going to be doing. How are they doing those jobs every day?' and trying to get people to skim back their numbers. I have to say that in the all years I have been doing it, and with the reduction in numbers that I've encouraged functional areas to settle for, never once has any manager turned to me at Games time and said 'I didn't have enough people'.

Discussion questions

1   Discuss the rationale for right sizing or undersizing the volunteer workforce. Should you plan for a certain attrition level? Use three events as specific examples and include your rationale.
2   Kerrie talks about getting the basics right, such as catering. What other things would you put in this category as being absolutely essential for volunteer wellbeing?
3   Volunteers can play an important PR role. Does HR have any responsibility in this regard?

References

Beijing Olympic Committee (2005). *The Pre-Games Training Guide*. Available at: http:/len. beijing-2008.org/71/76/column211637671.shtml; viewed 10 June 2005.

Bureau of Labour Statistics (2012). *Volunteerism by Selected Characteristics, September 2012 in the USA*. Available at: http://www.bls.gov/news.release/volun.t01.htm; viewed 2 February 2014.

Byrne, C., Houen, J. and Seaberg, M. (2002). 'One team', *Communication World*, 28–32.

Cabinet Office (2012). *Community Life Survey, August 2012–April 2013*. London: Cabinet Office. Available at: http://communitylife.cabinetoffice.gov.uk/assets/q4-2012-13/Community percent20Lifepercent20Surveypercent20Q4percent202012-13percent20Bulletin.pdf; viewed 2 January 2014.

Callow, M. (2004). 'Identifying promotional appeals for targeting potential volunteers: an exploratory study on volunteering motives among retirees', *International Journal of Nonprofit and Voluntary Sector Marketing*, 9(3), 261–274.

Cuskelly, G. and Auld, C. (2000). *Volunteer Management: A Guide to Good Practice*. Australian Sports Commission: Active Australia.

Giammarco, T. (2005). *2005 Teonju International Film Festival Report*. Available at: http://koreanfilm.org/jiff05.html; viewed 1 October 2005.

Gordon, L. and Erkut, E. (2004). 'Improving volunteer scheduling for the Edmonton Folk Festival', *Interfaces*, 34(5), 367–376.

Hall, M., Barr, W., Easwaramoothy, M., Sololowski, S. and Salamon, L. (2005). *The Canadian Nonprofit and Voluntary Sector in Comparative Perspective*. Toronto, Ontario: Imagine Canada.

Lester, M., Salamon, S., Sokolowski, W., Haddock, M. A. and Tice, H. S. (2012). *The State of Global Civil Society and Volunteering: Latest Findings from the Implementation of the UN Nonprofit Handbook*. Comparative Nonprofit Sector Working Paper No. 49. Baltimore: Johns Hopkins Center for Civil Society Studies.

Lockstone, L. and Baum, T. (2009). '2006 Melbourne Commonwealth Games Australia: recruiting, training and managing a volunteer program at a sporting mega event'. In K. Holmes and K. Smith (eds), *Managing Volunteers in Tourism: Attractions, Destinations and Events*. Oxford: Elsevier, pp. 215–223.

Monga, M. (2006). 'Measuring motivation to volunteer for special events', *Event Management*, 10(1), 47–61.

Schondel, C. and Boehm, K. (2000). 'Motivational needs of adolescent volunteers', *Adolescence*, 25(138), 335–344.

Strigas, A. and Newton Jackson, E. (2003). 'Motivation: volunteers to serve and succeed', *International Sports Journal*, 7(1), 111–123.

United States Department of Labor (2012). *Volunteers by Selected Characteristics, September 2012 in the USA*. Available at: http://data.bls.gov/cgi-bin/print.pl/news.release/volun.t01.htm; viewed 30 December 2013.

Zhuang, J. (2010). 'Beijing 2008: volunteerism in Chinese culture and its Olympic interpretation and influence', *International Journal Of The History Of Sport*, 27,16–18.

5

Contractor management

After reading through this chapter you will be able to:

- Explain the roles played by contractors in the event organization.
- Discuss the role of human resource specialists in contractor management.
- Identify some of the industrial relations issues emerging from the use of contractors.
- Describe best practice in contractor management.

Introduction

Contractors make up a significant part of the labour force for most events, providing services such as staging, entertainment, technical production, ticketing, registration, catering, security, cleaning and waste management. For this reason, this component of the workforce is a major concern from a human resource perspective, necessitating the development of integrated internal and external customer relations. In the USA the contractors are referred to as vendors and in other countries also as suppliers of goods and services.

There are numerous and varied issues to consider here, including the different working conditions under which these contractors are employed, their health and safety on site, insurance and provision of meals. In the event environment, integrating the efforts of these service teams is challenging, and for this reason it is essential that they are involved in event training, particularly induction or orientation training. From the consumer's perspective, everyone on site who is working has a customer service role to play and is a target for questions and complaints.

If the decision is made to take on volunteers, organizing committees can experience some backlash from potential contractor organizations and unions because they believe that the volunteers will take the place of paid staff. These organizations also argue that the

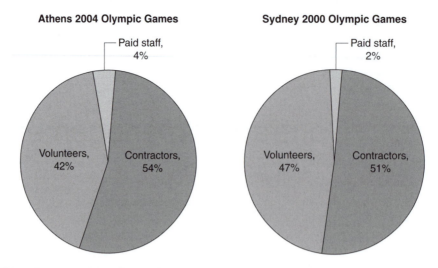

Athens 2004 Olympic Games

Paid staff, 4%
Volunteers, 42%
Contractors, 54%

Sydney 2000 Olympic Games

Paid staff, 2%
Volunteers, 47%
Contractors, 51%

FIGURE 5.1 Sydney and Athens Olympic Games workforce composition

volunteers are not appropriately trained or qualified for the work they are required to do. Ongoing and productive communication is therefore essential with these stakeholders.

Strategic decisions are generally made early as to which event services will be outsourced and which provided internally because there are many legislative considerations, such as appropriate licensing of riggers, forklift drivers, electricians and security staff. Insurance against workplace accidents is another important consideration with responsibility cascading downwards from the organizer to the smallest contractor. Contracts for event services are often renegotiated due to changing conditions in the event environment and this also needs to be taken into account in the planning stage (Allen et al., 2010).

As Figure 5.1 illustrates, contractor staff comprises the biggest segment of the mega-event workforce – at the Sydney 2000 Olympic Games, 51 per cent, and at Athens 54 per cent.

Figure 5.2 provides a more detailed breakdown of contractor numbers for the London Olympic Games and these ratios may be useful for managers planning smaller events. In this figure, 'Games Accredited Contractor Workforce' is only those individuals at a 'live accredited' status. The total number quoted here does not represent the entire Games

Games accredited contractor workforce*							
Sectors	Catering and hospitality	Cleaning and waste	Events and security	Retail	Logistics	Traffic mgt	Totals
Contractors	23	4	11	8	7	3	56
Total WKF	26,684	5,254	23,111	3,953	2,246	2,864	64,112

*Games accredited contractor workforce is only those individuals at a 'live accredited' status.

FIGURE 5.2 Games accredited contractor workforce
Source: http://static.squarespace.com/static/50b4ab77e4b0214dc1f631e9/t/5135c657e4b0ce79dfabd391/1362478679066/Annex%202%20-%20Games%20Time%20Jobs%206HB%20Statistics%20%28Nov%2012%29.pdf

accredited contractor workforce, which numbered circa 100,000 people. This is just the Accredited Contractor Workforce within sectors where LOCOG's Employment and Skills team acted to support Games time recruitment through the Employment and Skills jobs brokerage partnership.

Common types of contractor services

The following services are most frequently contracted out to event services companies or suppliers. The list is not comprehensive, nor does it include suppliers of rental equipment or a multitude of different products. As mentioned previously this group is described variously as contractors, vendors or suppliers, in this text we refer to them as contractors.

Event design

Specialists in event design are briefed in the specifications required by an organization for a conference, awards ceremony, incentive or product launch, for example, develop the concept and cost it for the client.

Production

In a general sense, production means putting on the event – from concept through to implementation and evaluation. Sometimes production refers more narrowly to the performance component of the event.

Entertainment

Speakers, singers, dancers and musicians are just a few of the entertainers who might be contracted for an event. For a concert or music festival this is the core component of the event product and may involve promoters and agents. Entertainment contracts are complex and mostly include a 'rider', an attachment to the contract requiring additional payments by the event organizer (Allen et al., 2010).

Lighting, sound, audiovisual and multimedia

All multimedia services can be outsourced, including the highly technical requirements of a sophisticated multimedia presentation. These services are often referred to as technical production.

Logistics

Organizing event operations may involve a logistics expert to transport and install all equipment and organize event elements such as crowd flow, communications, amenities, computer systems, sound and lighting systems, perimeter fencing, etc., particularly in relation to temporary outdoor sites. Logistics may also be responsible for the transportation of performers and VIPs, as well as their equipment.

Registration

Large exhibitions generally use the services of a professional organization to take registrations online using specialized software and to take remaining registrations at the entry to the exhibition.

Decor

Decor requirements may include props, chair coverings, balloon art and flower arranging. In some cases, a themed event will require a complete design and build.

Printing

Printing requirements range from tickets to programmes, training materials and signs. Some events develop a 'look', which includes the colour scheme, logo, type font, etc., and this is used consistently across all printed material and signs.

Photography and video

Specialist photography and video services are common, with the results available in different formats and online after the event.

Staging

Preparing the performance space is a vitally important role and may include, for example, specific lighting effects and other stage design features. Staging can range from a simple stage and set to a state-of-the-art, highly technical grand opening ceremony.

Catering

Most events require catering and there are numerous companies which provide these services, including menu planning, initiating appropriate food safety guidelines and providing qualified and experienced staff. Catering can range from fast food to fine dining. In some cases, catering is allocated to concessions or stalls, in which case a separate contract is needed for each.

Cleaning and waste

Cleaning and waste management is a specialized service, particularly in the event environment where a waste management plan is almost compulsory for outdoor events. The waste output from Manchester is illustrated in Table 5.1.

PLATE 5.1 Cleaners sorting waste streams at a festival

Security

Searching bags and premises and providing supervision of people (crowd management) and property are some of the roles of security staff, many of whom are trained for emergency management as well. The role of the security contractor hit the headlines prior to (and following) the London Olympic Games. According to the Public Accounts Committee (2013) the contractor G4S struggled to meet staffing deadlines:

> First, the company did not stand back and rethink its approach to project management when in light of the contract being scaled up significantly [from 2,000 to 10,400 personnel] in December 2011, and its project management was not fleet of foot enough to deal with the complexities and risks of the revised contract. Second, there was a critical failure with the management information about candidate tracking; with the result that it only emerged very late in the day that insufficient numbers had passed through all the necessary stages of recruitment, training and screening.

This example illustrates the importance of project planning from an HR perspective for both the organizing committee and the contractor. This is reinforced in this analysis of stakeholder perspectives (Fussey, 2014: 10):

> Particular disparities existed between LOCOG and private venue and private security providers. Security managers at the ExCel Exhibition Centre, the largest venue

Venue	Residual	Cardboard	Plastic	Glass	Paper	Ferrous	Aluminium	Total
Sportcity	175.24	0.3	1	5.8	2.6			184.94
Velodrome	24	1.2		2.6	0.4			28.2
Belle Vue	28							28
Salford Quays	6							6
G-Mex	20			1.2	2.6			23.8
Aquatics	33.6							33.6
MEN Arena	16			1.5		31.09	3.11	17.5
Rivington	6.4							6.4
Bolton Arena	30.3			1.5				31.8
Wythenshawe Forum	11.2							11.2
Heaton Park	28							28
Athletes' Village	135.22	17.86	1	4.7	3.4			162.18
Bessemer Street	48.8	22.48	0.42	1.2				72.9
Town Hall	2							2
IBC Other	56.8				7.5			64.3
Total	621.56	41.84	2.42	18.5	16.5	31.09	3.11	701.12

TABLE 5.1 Waste streams and tonnages by venue – Manchester Commonwealth Games 2002 (11 July–6 August 2002)

Source: Manchester City Council (2003)

outside of the Olympic Park, repeatedly criticised LOCOG for excluding them from security planning until the very late stages (interview with security planner January 2012). Moreover, LOCOG had previously insisted that private security provider (and Games sponsor) G4S should replace individual venue's in-house officers. Not only does such insistence contradict established best practices of security provision (e.g. the value afforded to tacit and experiential knowledge of a given environment), once it was clear that G4S would spectacularly fail to meet their obligations and hubristic assessment of their capabilities, LOCOG were forced to backtrack and allow existing security officers and the military to staff these venues.

Recruitment

For the larger event, a recruitment company might be used to manage the process of recruitment of paid staff, including headhunting locally and overseas for appropriately experienced event professionals.

Training

Training is sometimes outsourced to a training organization. For example, Holmesglen TAFE in Victoria provided training for the Melbourne 2006 Commonwealth Games. London

2012 volunteers were recruited and trained by McDonald's staff as part of a multi-million pound sponsorship deal.

Responsibility for appointing contractors

For a small event, the organizer would find contractors (vendors/suppliers) on the internet or through a recommendation. At the next level up in size, an expression of interest may be circulated by the organizers, for example, for the provision of catering services at a venue. This could lead to the appointment of preferred providers, thus excluding all other caterers from that venue, regardless of the type of event. Finally, the service can be put out to tender, leading to a formal selection process. In European Union (EU) countries there are rules about invitations to tender for event services, covering the amount awarded in the contract specifications and the process of selecting contractors.

Stages in contract management for event services

The process of contract negotiation through to service delivery and evaluation is outlined below, mainly from a human resource perspective:

1   Project scope and work breakdown:
    - Scope project, conduct job analysis.
    - Develop project specifications.
    - Conduct labour risk management analysis.
    - Review external labour force issues, numbers and expertise.
    - Develop human resource specifications, such as staffing guarantees and service level indicators.
2   Tendering and evaluating proposals:
    - Evaluate tenders against criteria and weighting system.
    - Check references of applicants.
    - Evaluate tenderers' understanding of external and internal HR constraints on meeting service requirements.
    - Check compliance with industrial legislation and awards.
    - Determine ways to handle potential termination.
    - Negotiate outcomes and sign contracts.
    - Prepare for variations.
3   Lead-up phase:
    - Develop and distribute operational manuals, procedures and checklists.
    - Organize participation in induction/orientation training.
    - Monitor delivery of job specific training by contractor.
    - Check roster planning.
    - Organize accreditation and uniforms.
    - Organize contractor staff meal requirements.
    - Check transport arrangements (this can be problematic for staff who need to travel extremely early or late).

4   Event delivery phase:
- Implement operational planning.
- Monitor service delivery.
- Solve problems by trouble-shooting.
- Communicate and motivate.
- Monitor attrition.
- Involve contractors in reward and recognition programmes.

5   Evaluate service provision:
- Check incident reports.
- Evaluate service levels provided.
- Develop recommendations.
- Close out contract.
- Send thank you letters and commendations.

While human resource departments are generally not responsible for contract management, there is a need for HR input when outsourcing event services since contract employees are often the bulk of the labour force.

Industrial relations issues

One of the more complex aspects of contractor management is the problem of different working conditions under different industrial/labour agreements. While it is the responsibility of the contractor organization, and not the event organizer, to manage this, it can nonetheless be problematic. In order to deliver seamless service at the Sydney Olympic Games, an industrial agreement (award) was developed that covered everyone employed on site ('inside the fence'). This had the advantage of enabling staff to cross over from one function to another and for all staff to be paid loyalty bonuses on completion of their allocated shifts. With all paid staff on the same wage scale, contractors were able to budget more accurately too.

Few events are able to create such agreement across the board. This leaves most event organizers and services suppliers with the headache of having to work with multiple workplace agreements. The following extract from the Cleaning and Building Services Contractors (NSW) Award (Australia) illustrates specific roles, rates of pay and a wide range of other conditions not shown here (40 other clauses) for cleaning employees (Office of Industrial Relations, 2006). One allowance is for cleaning offensive substances, which is quite understandable. From this it is immediately obvious that a more generic role description would lead to greater flexibility.

Event cleaning stream

(a)   Event cleaning means all work in or in connection with or incidental to the industries or industrial pursuits of cleaning, repair and maintenance services in or in connection with the staging of sporting, cultural, scientific, technological, agricultural or entertainment events and exhibitions of any nature. Event cleaning shall not include regular maintenance cleaning and shall be for a specific event and limited in duration to not more than three weeks.

(b) 'Event Services Employee Grade 1' means a casual employee who performs general cleaning duties before, during and after an event (as defined above), and shall include, but not be limited to, duties such as: operating hand-held powered equipment such as blowers, vacuum cleaners and polishers, wiping of seats, cleaning toilets used by the general public, picking up rubbish, vacuuming around and under seats, sweeping under and around seats, vacuuming and cleaning table tops, and other work of a manual nature and is subject to direct supervision.

(c) 'Event Services Employee Grade 2' means a casual employee who performs cleaning duties before, during and after an event (as defined above) and who, in addition to performing, when required, all of the duties of a Grade 1 employee, drives/operates ride-on powered sweeping and scrubbing machines, mobile compaction units, vehicular rubbish collection; operates steam cleaning and pressure washing equipment; is responsible for the distribution and ordering of stores and supplies; is responsible for the supervision of Grade 1 employees in the performance of their duties; delivers on-the-job training and is subject to general supervision.

(d) 'Event Services Employee Grade 3' means a casual employee who, in addition to performing, when required, all of the duties of a Grade 1 or Grade 2 employee, is an operations trainer/work co-ordinator …

As this labour agreement illustrates, a base level cleaner can do only manual cleaning and cannot operate cleaning equipment apart from blowers, vacuum cleaners and polishers. These classifications are extremely limiting, particularly when cleaning needs to be done between sessions, which means all hands on deck, including the supervisor.

Further, this award makes specific reference to the principal contractor contracting out to subcontractors who in turn must comply with these conditions. As mentioned previously, this is an important risk consideration. The event organization sits at the top of a pyramid of contractors, and thus carries responsibility right down the line. For this reason, contracts must include up-to-date insurance certificates for public liability and workers compensation.

During the Sydney Olympic Games there was close co-operation between the contractors/services providers, human resource department (workforce planning), the unions and the venue managers, with union representatives on site to resolve immediate issues. This level of co-operation was unprecedented for an event of this scale. As Webb points out, 'the Games organizers brought together the public and private sectors and the trade unions to create a unique set of industrial agreements that, over time, built mutual respect, trust, honesty and openness in the personal relationships between many of the key players'. He goes on to recommend that the following questions should be asked of contractors:

- Where is your information on workforce numbers and skills coming from?
- Your casuals, how will you hold onto them when they are also being recruited by others?

- How will you get people to work if travel time is longer?
- How many of your regular people won't be available?

(Webb, 2001: 78)

In addition, we might ask what level of attrition is expected, as on any given day some staff will not turn up due to illness or other reasons. Collaborative planning in partnership with suppliers is vitally important. This sounds easy in principle but, in practice, it is often the case that contractor organizations are appointed too late for this level of collaboration to occur.

Recruitment and training of contractor employees

Event organizers explain the problems associated with large events in tangible operational terms such as 'We had to hire every piece of technical equipment in the country and even had to fly in some components from overseas'. Human resource issues are similar. Very often the city does not have the required labour pool to meet the needs of a short-term event.

Catering contractor Spotless Services describes the problems of recruiting 8,000 staff from a very shallow employment pool and the strategies used to meet labour shortages:

1   Borrowing competence. This includes borrowing staff from their other international operations, and specific event placements for staff and students from colleges who may be on holidays during the event.
2   Buying competence. This involves recruiting people without experience and providing certified and government-funded training.
3   Building competence. Staff are seconded from other projects and provided with training to meet the needs of the new project.

(Webb, 2001)

Recommendations from previous events also indicate that contractors gain considerable benefit from attending the same orientation and venue training as paid staff and volunteers. This is more likely to lead to a more cohesive workforce and seamless customer service. However, following the Commonwealth Games in Manchester some contractors expressed a need to have specific programme material to meet their needs: 'there was a bit of a sense of being "bolted-on" rather than "rusted-on"' (Tourism Training Victoria, 2002).

In their study of major sporting event organizations, Hanlon and Cuskelly (2002) point out that contractor employee participation in generic event training needs to be spelled out within the tender brief, as this can add to labour costs for contractor organizations: 'in doing so, outsourcers would be more prepared for the high expectations and amount of induction time required' (p. 237). These authors also stress the importance of induction and onsite operational manuals as training resources in the event environment. Most events have an operational manual and these are frequently underutilized as a training resource.

Contract supervision

Goods and services specified in the contracts need to be monitored during the event by functional area managers. For example, the functional area manager for cleaning and waste management (a paid staff position) would have ongoing responsibility for cleaning contract management, including fine tuning as the event draws near.

Volunteers carrying checklists can be utilized to monitor levels of service by, for example, checking the cleanliness of event venues. If, as a result, the functional area manager has nothing to do during the event except monitor quality, this is an indication of good contract negotiation during the lead-up period. However, as Maund (2001) points out, it is important to acknowledge that contractor employees are not employees of the event organization; otherwise this can lead to uncertainty and confusion about reporting relationships. Issues relating to service standards need to be raised with the contracting organization (management and supervisors) and not directly with their staff on the ground.

Contract specifications and service standards

Writing the tender specification for an event supplier requires a detailed understanding of the service standards expected. In the catering area, for example, the types of meals and the number required are minimum requirements in the catering brief. There are different styles of food service (fast food to silver service) and vastly different levels of quality (ranging from a hot dog to an à la carte meal). The determination of service quality, in specific terms, is essential. Depending on the size of the event, and the degree to which planning has to occur prior to calls for tender, the level of work required in preparing the specifications will differ. For the smaller event, without formal tendering, the process of negotiating menus and services levels can be undertaken collaboratively. This, however, is one area in which misunderstandings can occur very easily. Is the menu to be à la carte or is it to be banquet style, i.e. two choices served to alternate guests? How many courses will there be? Is the food prepared from scratch or pre-prepared in frozen commercial quantities? Is a buffet a consideration? Is there provision for vegetarians? Is the alcohol billed on consumption or is it a fixed price? Can guests order spirits? Is the coffee filter or espresso?

Taylor (2005) suggests that the effect of tender procedures for catering in the public sector is to limit choices, leading to bidders coming in with low-cost and low-quality bids. Quality and cost configuration need to be evaluated in detail. For this reason, he suggests that this type of bid should be conducted in two rounds. This would certainly be recommended for the type of event at which food is an important feature, expensive and linked to the theme. A gala dinner is an example of an event at which the quality of the catering is vitally important. Where food is not central to an event, such as the provision of informal fast food, a contract containing specifications is still required, the most important being food hygiene planning if the event is to be held outdoors.

A catering contract for a food vendor at an outdoor site could include any of the following specifications:

- menus and prices
- staffing levels
- food safety plans
- waste management plans (recyclable cutlery and plates)
- infrastructure requirements (water and power)
- equipment brought on site.

Contract management is highly problematic if standards are not met. Therefore the more detailed the specification, the less likely that a misunderstanding will occur. For a one-off event, if the contractor does not deliver, then it is too late to find another! Menus should be tested and quantities discussed prior to the event.

The following detail should be included when drawing up contracts:

- *Written*. All agreements must be in writing. With most organizations this occurs as a matter of course in the early days of the negotiation. However, as the event draws near, small requests are added and things change. Contract variations must be clearly noted and agreed in writing.
- *Specifications*. The contract should clarify expectations on both sides so that products and services are clearly defined. As an event organizer you don't want to be embarrassed by a contract caterer who runs out of food. People will blame you! Furthermore, the event organization wants to hold the vendor fully responsible for the standard of product or service provided, which may include entertainment, decor, floral arrangements, seating, audiovisual, etc.
- *Insurances and licences*. As mentioned above, the contractor must carry the appropriate licences or permits and must have insurance. Verbal agreement on these matters is not sufficient; copies of workers compensation and public liability insurance policies should be provided by the contractor before contracts are signed.
- *Indemnification for damages*. The event organization needs to be indemnified against loss or damage caused by the contractor. For example, organizations responsible for outdoor parklands can issue severe fines for damage to grass and trees, and these fines will be passed on to the offending contractor. This should be made clear in the original specifications.
- *Payment terms*. Agreement on payment terms must be negotiated, including upfront payments prior to the event and completion payments after the event. Payments can take the form of commissions or percentages, such as a percentage of gross sales of merchandise. Rent may be charged to a vendor using space for a stall. Deposits may be required, refundable when the event is over, equipment has been removed and the site returned to pristine condition.
- *Regular meetings*. Ongoing positive negotiations conducted in good faith can lead to long-term business relationships. When problems emerge, they need to be resolved quickly. Positive working relationships in the lead-up to an event can reap rewards when extra commitment is needed.

McCabe et al. (2000) in their text on convention management suggest the following four ways in which service quality can differ:

1 Technical quality – what is delivered? This can include food, lighting and other technology.
2 Functional quality – how is it delivered? Are the staff trained and competent? Do the systems and procedures work?
3 Process quality – judged during service. Is every element integrated for seamless service from the customer perspective?
4 Output quality – after service is performed. This is the post-service customer evaluation, very often conducted by using questionnaires.

In summary, the management of contractors involves careful selection of suppliers, vendors, etc. Following this, contracts need to be negotiated, with clear specifications included. Ongoing positive relationships in the build-up to an event will have a payoff if problems occur, as integration and effort are often required from everyone on site in the last frantic moments. Case Study 5.1 presents some of the issues from the contractor point of view. However, from the customer perspective, there is only one contact, the event organizer, who is responsible for all aspects of service provision. Besides, the customer is generally unaware that the operation is supported by a number of contractors harnessed for the duration of the event.

CASE STUDY 5.1
Best practice in contractor training

What is a Health and Safety training passport?

A health and safety training passport is similar to any other passport. It allows the holder access to a passport-controlled work environment. The passport is a robust and secure card – similar to a UK driving licence – that displays a tamper-proof photograph of the successful trainee. The photo card features a special ultra-secure 'holocote' finish to prevent fraud.

Who should attend the live event safety passport course?

The particular training course has been designed specifically for event technical production services, including general crew, production, stage hands, lighting and sound crew, stage builders, backline technicians, electricians, safety stewards and drivers.

Why we offer the SPA Passport Scheme?

This is the leading multi-industry health and safety training passport scheme. Safety Pass Alliance is an organisation providing a safety passport scheme to many industrial sectors.

This industry-led, nationally recognised scheme reflects Health and Safety (HSE) syllabus guidance.

Contract workers and their employees who successfully complete the training course can prove their awareness of basic principles of health and safety in the workplace by showing their safety passport. There is a high level of demand for the SPA Passport programme. The scheme represents a UK-wide commercial opportunity, giving you a chance to open up new markets for your business.

Source: http://www.festivalorganisers.org/news/safety-passport-scheme-live-events-industry. With permission Association of Festival Organisers and Pinnacle Crew

Reflective practice 5.1

1   What are the advantages of using an agency that supplies ready trained staff in the area of safety?
2   List five other areas in which training and licensing is necessary for event staff.
3   What are the benefits of developing a long-standing relationship with an employment agency?

PLATE 5.2   Briefing for vendors

Chapter summary and key points

This chapter has looked at the role of contractors, or suppliers, in the event environment and has stressed that it is quite common for the number of contractors on site to exceed the number of staff employed by the event organization. An exhibition company, for example, is highly reliant on contractors to build the exhibition and manage registrations. In the process of appointing contractors there needs to be discussion about whether they have a reliable source of skilled labour. Contractor employees also require event specific training in order to fit comfortably into the event environment and answer questions from the general public. Cleaning staff, it could be argued, play a more important customer service role than many other staff on site. For this reason, in order to provide optimal service, everyone on site (including contractor employees) should undertake event-related training such as orientation training and venue training.

Revision questions

1   List and explain five examples of contractors/suppliers and the services they provide.
2   There are several phases in the management of contracts. Explain these briefly.
3   'The planning, selection and management of contractors is the role of the venue manager'. Discuss this statement in light of this chapter's suggestion that there is a role for human resources to play where multiple contractors are appointed and that their staff form a significant part of the workforce.
4   Explain how a risk management approach could be used to manage the contractors supporting an event.

Industry voice by Kerrie Nash

We do have an opportunity, and I believe a responsibility, in that HR intervention environment to contribute to the local economy from a skills and employment opportunity perspective. Now, that largely comes through your contractor population because that's where the big numbers of recruits come from.

It is about planning from the early days, even before you have your contractor companies on board, about doing your labour market analysis. What's available in the local market in terms of caterers, cleaners, security staff, bus drivers, etc.? What do we need to do therefore to build skills in readiness of the Games? What opportunities does that create for unemployed, underemployed, new graduates, apprenticeship schemes? All sorts of things that you can do. There's a lot of construction going on; there are opportunities in construction.

In London they did that very well. They had some really, really great schemes involved in skilling people in the construction industry. That creates I think some really good news stories for the media and for the general public as well as leaving a definable legacy.

Your contractor workforce is actually double or triple the size of your combined volunteer and paid workforce at most events. When you put it that way, they are the people who actually, by design or not, have a lot of contact with the general public, athletes and other client groups. To think that you can kind of leave them to one side and not include them and get the best result for your event I think is rather naive because they will have an impact. That's the first thing. Contractor management is a priority for you in terms of the success of the event.

Of all of the contractor groups, security is big numbers. They need specific qualifications and that takes time to build in the community. If you don't engage with those contractors early and get them educated about the size and scale of what they're taking on, then the problem of supply winds up back with the organizing committee as it has done at some recent events. People sometimes think in the event that if I've outsourced something I can walk away and everything's going to be fine. If the contractor turns around several months before the Games and says 'look, I can't find enough people to fulfil my contract' it still becomes the organizing committee's problem. The timeline on recruitment, training, accreditation, uniforms and rosters is also months, not weeks.

I think one of things that we did in Sydney which we've done in a few different events now which has been quite successful is having someone in the HR team whose sole job is that contractor integration piece. This is a person or team who works really closely with the contractor organizations once they're on board to inform, share information, give them access to policies and procedures, and offer training modules including orientation. It provides contractors with a 'one stop shop' into the organization.

Discussion questions

1   Kerrie points out that contractor workforce is often double or triple the size of your combined volunteer and paid workforce at most events. What are the implications for the HR manager?
2   Who carries responsibility for the training of contractor employees, particularly in the service areas? For example, cleaners are usually the first point of call for event information.
3   What was the organizational response to the shortage of security staff at the London Olympic Games?

References

Allen, L., O'Toole, W., Harris, R. and McDonnell, I. (2010). *Festival and Special Event Management*, 5th edn. Brisbane: John Wiley & Sons.

Fussey, P. (2013). 'Command, control and contestation: negotiating security at the London 2012 Olympics', *The Geographical Journal*. doi: 10.1111/geoj.12058.

Hanlon, C. and Cuskelly, G. (2002). 'Pulsating major sport event organizations: a framework for inducting managerial personnel', *Event Management*, 7, 231–243.

Manchester City Council (2003). *Manchester Commonwealth Games Post Games Report*. Available at: www.gameslegacy.com; viewed 17 May 2006.

Maund, L. (2001). *An Introduction to Human Resource Management*. New York: Palgrave.

McCabe, V., Poole, D., Weeks, N. and Leiper, N. (2000). *The Business and Management of Conventions*. Brisbane: John Wiley & Sons.

Office of Industrial Relations, NSW Department of Commerce (2006). *Cleaning and Building Services Contractors (NSW) Award*, award code 116, serial C3860. Available at: www.industrialrelations.nsw.gov.au/awards/pathways/results.jsp?contentlist=true&contentlistresults=false&award_code=116; viewed 4 May 2006.

Public Accounts Committee (2013). *The London 2012 Olympic Games and Paralympic Games: post-Games review – Public Accounts Committee*. Available at: http://www.publications.parliament.uk/pa/cm201213/cmselect/cmpubacc/812/81205.htm; viewed 12 February 2014.

Taylor, P. (2005). 'Do public sector contract catering tender procedures result in an auction for "lemons"?', *International Journal of Public Sector Management*, 18(6), 484–497.

Tourism Training Victoria (2002). *Strategic Training Issues for the 2006 Commonwealth Games*. Melbourne: Arts and Training Victoria.

Webb, T. (2001). *The Collaborative Games: The Story Behind the Spectacle*. Sydney: Pluto Press.

Employment law and duty of care

After reading through this chapter you will be able to:

- Explain why a basic understanding of essential employment legislation is important.
- Discuss the statement 'a little knowledge is a dangerous thing' in this context.
- List and describe key employment laws and regulations.
- Explain the concept 'duty of care'.
- Apply knowledge of occupational health and safety legislation to the event workplace.
- Differentiate between the roles and entitlements of volunteers and interns.

Introduction

This chapter will deal with employment or labour legislation rather briefly for the potential scope of this subject. Employment laws, awards and regulations differ from country to country and from state to state. For this reason, general principles will be covered, with a cautionary recommendation that these issues be explored by managers locally and in depth. Event organizers, regardless of the size of their events, need to pay close attention to the working conditions of everyone on site, with safety being the highest priority. A compulsory pre-event briefing is increasingly commonplace at today's events where safety issues are discussed and procedures for incident reporting and emergency evacuation are explained. For most, compulsory attendance (and in some cases the answering of a safety quiz) is required for all workers, including contract workers. This is the cornerstone of a risk management approach and essential for insurance purposes.

Duty of care is everyone's responsibility at every level as there are many examples of event fatalities at football matches and rock concerts. At least 11 people died and 72 were injured in a crowd trampling incident in South Korea in October 2005, reminiscent of the

PLATE 6.1 Fatigue is a serious health and safety risk in the event environment

1979 The Who concert tragedy in Cincinnati, Ohio, in which 11 people died. Eight of those killed in South Korea were senior citizens or children, including one 12 year old and a 76-year-old woman. People were waiting to enter a stadium in Sangju City for an evening concert when the doors did not open on time.

In Australia, in 1999 a race marshal was killed at the Melbourne Grand Prix. In the USA, Daniel Fair, who volunteered as a spotter at the annual World Champion Punkin Chunkin festival, allegedly suffered spinal fractures after he was thrown from an all-terrain vehicle (ATV) that hit a depression in the ground and landed on top of him. Fair sued the event organizer, asserting negligence and premises liability for conditions at the Punkin Chunkin field. Mukherji (2013) suggests that even if Fair signed a waiver assuming liability, such waivers don't protect against injuries or death caused by the organizers' gross negligence, 'from a premises liability standpoint, Fair may try to argue that event organizers should have leveled the pumpkin landing zone for the spotters. After all, volunteer spotters race back and forth at high speeds on ATVs to verify the distance each pumpkin traveled'.

Safety is important for both spectators and staff who could be caught up in crowd incidents such as fires and acts of terrorism. The lead-up to an event, called bump-in or build, is a time when risk is highest as there is always pressure to meet deadlines. Thirteen immigrant workers lost their lives on Athens' Olympic facilities, prompting outraged Greek unionists to draw comparisons with Sydney preparations that cost the life of only one building worker. 'What's happened is criminal in the truest sense of the word and it's been done in the name of profit', said Giorgos Philiousis, president of the construction workers' union at the Athens 2004 Olympic Village. 'As the time got pressured with contractors chasing bonuses, and without serious health and safety measures, the number of accidents increased' (Workers Online, 2004: 216). According to unions there was also a high number of injuries. In contrast, Sydney's involvement of the unions in 2000 is illustrated in Case Study 6.2 at the end of the chapter and is now regarded as a benchmark.

Thus, from a human resource perspective, a priority is the development of workforce safety policies and procedures and for this reason workplace health and safety will be discussed in the chapter in some detail. Event organizers carry responsibility not only for their own workers (and volunteers) but for all workers on site. Also covered in this chapter are the employment conditions of those on employment contracts with the event organization, as opposed to those on service contracts. These include equal employment opportunity (EEO), minimum wages and leave. Policies to deal with performance management, dismissal and grievance resolution will be covered in more detail in Chapters 11 and 13.

The role of unions is another topic for this chapter. In Sydney in 2000 there were 10,000 union members on site ('inside the fence') and 30 union organizers. A collaborative group of unions (calling themselves Union 2000) negotiated a special award for the Games which gave Olympic workers, on average, pay 15 per cent above normal conditions. In addition, they received free transport, free meals and an attendance bonus of $1.50 for every hour worked, as was mentioned in the last chapter. The support of the unions is crucial to the success of mega events. The London Organising Committee of the Olympic Games and Paralympic Games (LOCOG) went further still to develop an agreement regarding working conditions right through the entire global supply chain. In this agreement, made between LOCOG and the Trades Union Congress on behalf of the Playfair Campaign (LOCOG, 2012), a sustainable sourcing code was developed. Included within it were contracts with licensees and suppliers, as well as the ETI base code for ethical trading and compliance with internationally recognized labour standards. This would be particularly relevant to the production of souvenirs for example. Playfair called for LOCOG to ensure that workers in their supply chains knew their rights and how to use a complaint system.

Legal context of employment

Event and human resource managers must be familiar with the legal context of employment. Common law is the law created by judges in their court decisions and is based on precedent. Statute law is law made in parliaments, sometimes at various levels. Statute laws cover issues such as anti-discrimination, occupational health and safety, and minimum wages.

Common law

Two aspects of common law are most relevant to employment. Contract law covers all contractual relationships, specifically here, the contract of employment. When an employee accepts an offer of employment (oral or written), a contract of employment has been established. Under this contract, both the employer and the employee have certain rights and obligations. If there is a breach of contract, this must be taken up with the courts as common law is the jurisdiction of the court system. Under common law an employer must:

- pay correct wages (including national minimum wage);
- reimburse employees for work-related expenses;
- ensure a safe working environment suitable for the performance of the employee's duties;
- not act in a way that may seriously damage an employee's reputation or cause mental distress or humiliation;
- not act in a way that will damage the trust and confidence necessary for an employment relationship.

Some terms of a contract of employment may not be written down, but are implied by law or by custom and practice in the workplace. For example, the employer's duty to provide a safe, secure and healthy environment is implied by law into all contracts of employment. An employee must:

- obey the lawful and reasonable instructions of the employer;
- exercise due care in the performance of the work and do it competently;
- account to the employer for all moneys and property received while employed;
- make available to the employer any process or product invented by the employee in the course of employment;
- disclose to the employer information received by the employee relevant to the employer's business;
- be faithful to the employer's interests; for example, by not passing on to a competitor information about the employer's business or denigrating the employer's products and services.

The last of these is particularly relevant to ambush marketing in the event environment. This is where a competitor tries to ambush the marketing efforts of official sponsors and gain advantage without the expense of a sponsorship arrangement. For example, if 20 event staff were paid by a competitor to wear a t-shirt or other item with the competitor brand slogan this would work against the employer's interest.

The second important aspect of common law is that of negligence, under which employers owe their employees a duty of care. This involves providing a safe place of work and safe systems of work. If an employee is seriously injured he can make a common law claim for compensation, although this may be limited by statute in some countries. In doing so it must be shown that the employer did not take reasonable precautions to prevent such an accident.

Employment/labour legislation: statute law

As mentioned above, legislation is created by parliamentary processes. There are many acts which cover such conditions as parental leave, mechanisms for dealing with industrial disputes, legitimacy of unions, provision of collective agreements or awards, workers' compensation and occupational health and safety. Some of these will be dealt with rather briefly, particularly the field of discrimination in which many countries have multiple acts.

Workplace health and safety

Workplace health and safety is a matter dealt with by statute law. While under common law, an employer has a duty of care, these acts go further requiring, for example, the appointment of safety committees and reporting of workplace accidents. Breaches can lead to investigation and fines. In the United Kingdom, the Health and Safety at Work Act (HASAWA) requires all employers to protect the health, safety and welfare of their employees. Most countries, including the United States, Australia, New Zealand and South Africa, have legislation with similar provisions. This legislation covers all work practices.

Employers must make every effort to prevent injury or ill health at work, and generally, health and safety legislation also places duties on employers to protect the public whilst on their premises, as well as temporary staff and contract workers.

An employer should provide:

- a safe system of work;
- a safe place of work;
- safe equipment, plant and machinery;
- safe and competent workers, because employers are also liable for the conduct of their staff and managers.

An employer should carry out risk assessments and take steps to eliminate or control any risks. Employees should be informed about all potential hazards associated with any work process, chemical substance or activity. Instruction, training and supervision are key elements of workplace safety. Note that employers' safety obligations extend to other workers on site (e.g. contractors and members of the public). There are some specific risks in the event industry which require particular attention. As Figure 6.1 shows, at the Manchester Commonwealth Games, injuries were the most common incident. These can occur because of use of incorrect equipment, because people are tired or because people are working in a highly pressured, unfamiliar environment.

PLATE 6.2 Safety is everyone's responsibility

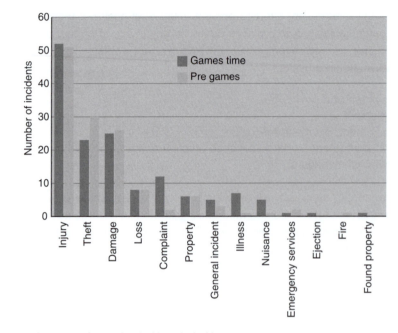

FIGURE 6.1 Pre Games and Games time incidents by incident type

One common injury which can occur is through manual handling where a risk assessment is needed, based on the load and the person's capability. Personal protective clothing is required in some cases. Instructions and material data sheets should be provided for workers handling chemicals and equipment. Where employees require licensing, it should be checked that their licences are up to date and relevant to the job at hand – this relates to the requirement that employees must be working with competent others.

In the event industry there are two critical times when safety is often compromised, at bump-in and at bump-out. At bump-in the organizer is usually pressed for time and it is not uncommon for installers to work around the clock. At the end of the show or exhibition, bump-out carries an even higher risk as everyone is exhausted. Special attention should be given to working hours and breaks because fatigue is a significant risk factor. In the European Community there are directives governing working times and these provide useful guidelines in any context:

- forty-eight-hour maximum working week;
- four weeks' paid holiday;
- minimum daily rest periods of 11 hours;
- twenty-minute daily rest breaks after six hours' work, with young workers entitled to 45 minutes if more than four and a half hours are worked;
- a weekly rest period of 24 hours every seven days.

A risk analysis specifically for workplace health and safety should be conducted. This includes the following steps: establish the context; identify the risk; analyse the risk; evaluate the risk; and treat the risk. Most countries have a standard for risk analysis that should be applied, including British Standard BS ISO 31000. This topic is too detailed to be covered here but an example of a simplified risk analysis is included in Table 6.1.

As with the assessment in Chapter 2, risks here have been assessed in terms of likelihood and consequence, with a subsequent evaluation of the level of risk. In this

TABLE 6.1 Sample workplace health and safety risk analysis

Type of risk	Level of risk	Prevention/treatment	Contingency
Incompetent or unqualified staff, e.g. driving forklift or skylarking	Major	Ensure job specifications are accurate, including licensing requirements for specific roles Conduct job-specific training based on job description and specifications Conduct safety briefing before shift Supervise and monitor workforce	Remove worker or volunteer from task immediately Investigate incident Report incident Implement disciplinary procedures if necessary
Inadequate procedures and instructions for crowd control	Catastrophic	Fully document crowd measures Assign responsibilities Conduct training using scenarios Brief staff Conduct drills and simulations	First aid treatment if required Advise venue communications centre and enlist support Investigate and report incidents
Hold-up during cash transfer	Catastrophic	Prepare hold-up procedures Copy instructions and post in key locations Train staff in procedures	Follow procedures to the letter Investigate incident and report
Manual handling injury	Major	Provide appropriate equipment Ensure supervisors trained Provide instructions during job-specific training regarding manual handling Put up posters in staff areas	First aid treatment Investigate and report incident Submit claim if necessary
Injury caused by antisocial spectators	Major	Roster adequate security personnel Limit alcohol consumption Involve police	First aid treatment Contact police and security Complete incident report
Bomb threat, fire or act of terrorism	Catastrophic	Prepare procedures according to national standards Train supervisors and staff Rehearse procedures Conduct searches	Follow established emergency procedures, alerting venue communications centre
Exposure to extreme heat – dehydration	Moderate	Provide water, hats and sunscreen Warn staff and volunteers and ensure that they take necessary breaks Explain symptoms of dehydration	First aid treatment Water and rest

risk analysis the situations with the highest level of risk are fire, armed hold-up and bomb threat since both carry the possibility of injuries and fatalities. Other identified risks include crowd control issues, incompetent staff, manual handling injuries, injuries caused by antisocial spectators and illness caused by heat and dehydration. In each case preventative measures have been suggested, followed by contingency responses should this type of risk eventuate.

During workforce induction training, the following workplace health and safety related information should be covered:

- the layout of the venue;
- the command structure at the event, particularly for reporting serious and minor incidents;
- examples of event-specific risks likely to be encountered;
- prohibited items at the event (such as bottles and flares);
- access control;
- bomb inspections and suspicious articles;
- evacuation procedures;
- potential hazards and personal risks;
- first aid treatment;
- personal accidents and injuries;
- accidents and injuries involving the public;
- duty of care and insurance.

As mentioned previously, some event organizations ask participants to complete a questionnaire to check their comprehension of safety information. If this is not done, at least an attendance register is essential to monitor who has and who has not done this training. Those who do not attend need to be provided with this information via email or a similar system. All the above information can be summarized in the form of a pocket guide. There are numerous books and research papers on events and event safety covering risk management in more detail and providing guidelines for workplace health and safety risk management: Anderton (2009), Bowdin et al. (2012), Reid and Ritchie (2011), Tarlow (2002), Taylor and Toohey (2006).

Workers' compensation

Closely allied to workplace health and safety is workers' compensation. Under this legislation, employers are required to compensate employees for workplace accidents. In the United Kingdom, the United States and Australia, for example, as well as in other countries, this is no-fault legislation (also known as strict liability). The employee is compensated regardless of whether they have adequately taken care of themselves. Some acts specify specific sums for particular types of injury. In the past, an employee could claim negligence under common law as well and make a claim in the courts. In some countries efforts are underway to limit common law liability claims by setting limits or excluding the possibility entirely. In the United States, for example, the employee receives money and medical benefits in exchange for forfeiting the common law right to sue the employer. The employer benefits by receiving immunity from court actions against them by the employee in exchange for accepting liability that is limited and determined (see Case Study 6.1).

The general purpose of this legislation is to compensate for workplace accidents, injuries or fatalities. The acts that cover workers' compensation can vary and undergo frequent updates. Note that volunteers by definition are not workers and therefore generally do not come under the scope of workers' compensation insurance. They would be covered by the event organizer's public liability insurance or insurance taken out specifically to cover volunteers.

CASE STUDY 6.1
Health and safety

Every employer has a legal duty to ensure the health and safety of its employees. In the United Kingdom these duties are set out in *The Health and Safety at Work Act* and *The Management of Health and Safety at Work Regulations* (see http://www.hse.gov.uk/legislation/hswa.htm).

In the USA the *Occupational Safety and Health Act (OSH Act)* assigns two regulatory functions to the authority: setting standards and conducting inspections to ensure that employers are providing safe and healthful workplaces. OSHA standards may require that employers adopt certain practices, means, methods or processes reasonably necessary and appropriate to protect workers on the job. Employers must become familiar with the standards applicable to their establishments and eliminate hazards.

In all countries, organizations have a duty of care to ensure that employees and any other person who may be affected remains safe at all times. In Australia this includes for example, visiting contractors and volunteers.

Previously health and safety acts were highly prescriptive, identifying, for example, the maximum weight that an adult male/female should lift. These days a risk assessment approach is taken at a macro and micro level. For example, when lifting it is necessary to take many variables into account including the shape and size of the object being lifted, and the capacity of the individual to lift the item. There are differences in the work health and safety acts in the various countries, but the central aim is to protect the safety, health and welfare of people engaged in work or employment.

Reflective practice 6.1

1 Investigate health and safety laws and regulations in your country, describing the key responsibilities of employers and employees.
2 Why is it vitally important that provision is made for volunteer safety?

Conditions of employment

Industrial relations legislation can set up a framework for negotiating conditions of employment, which can vary widely from country to country and job to job. While some employees' conditions are extensively covered (particularly if their industry is unionized), other employees remain largely unprotected except, for example, by minimum wage rates and core statute legislation. In the case of union-negotiated contracts, awards and agreements, conditions of employment are spelled out in remarkable detail, covering special allowances, hours of work, casual and full-time rates of pay, etc. In Australia, there are moves afoot to reduce the number of conditions that form the minimum requirements for an Australian Workplace Agreement (AWA) in order to increase workforce 'flexibility'.

Equal opportunity and anti-discrimination legislation

Under most countries' laws, an employer cannot base employment, training and promotion decisions on personal characteristics that are not job related. These characteristics generally include:

- age
- race
- sex
- marital status
- religion
- country of origin
- disability.

An interviewer isn't allowed to ask questions relating to these characteristics. Interview questions that aren't allowed include:

- Are you married? Are you planning to get married?
- Do you have children? Are you planning to have children?
- Will your children restrict your flexibility and availability?
- Where were you born?

This applies to volunteers as well. The reasons for rejecting an applicant must be job related.

Minimum wages and working time

The concept of minimum wage has already been mentioned. In the United States, the Fair Labor Standards Act (FLSA) sets minimum rates at federal level. This Act is very specific about working hours for young people (child labour). The Wage and Hour Division is responsible for administering and enforcing the minimum wage, overtime and child labour provisions of the Fair Labor Standards Act and the Family and Medical Leave Act

(FMLA). The FLSA requires that employees must receive at least the minimum wage and may not be employed for more than forty hours in a week without receiving at least one and a half times their regular rates of pay for the overtime hours.

Working hours for the United Kingdom were covered earlier, including break and rest times. From an event management perspective, working hours' rules provide challenges, as this can be a crisis environment in which people are working above and beyond expectations to stage the event and generally they do this quite willingly. An employer must acknowledge, however, that this is not only a breach of guidelines but a serious risk. By allowing workers and enthusiastic teams to work unacceptable hours the employer is not displaying proper duty of care.

Leave

There are many different leave provisions: annual leave, parental leave, bereavement leave, etc. These may be covered by statute law or by employment contract and variations from country to country are extensive.

Unions

The potential role of the unions has already been mentioned. Again, there are significant differences between countries such as the United States and the United Kingdom in the way in which unions and government work. Asian countries are less likely to be unionized and labour laws may vary widely. For this reason, event companies that work in a global environment are likely to use contracted labour as much as possible in order to manage these obligations appropriately for the country in question.

Discipline and dismissal

Disciplinary issues are more common than one would think in the event environment. Perhaps this is because there is less routine and control in terms of supervision. Workers and volunteers might harass athletes, celebrities or each other. Stories of major equipment disappearing are legendary. Many items are removed from the athletes' villages during closing ceremonies: taking home 'souvenirs' such as flags and other decorative items is commonplace. Many volunteers also feel the urge to take home memorabilia. One Sydney volunteer working in accreditation made himself a badge that would allow him into the athletes' village, but unfortunately he made it in the name of a popular and famous athlete and his identity was immediately questioned. Policies in relation to misconduct and dismissal will be covered in Chapter 11.

In the majority of states in the United States, employees not working under an employment contract are deemed to be 'at will'. At-will employees may be terminated for any reason, so long as it's not illegal. There are numerous illegal reasons for termination. Typically such reasons fall into one of two large categories: illegal discrimination or illegal termination in violation of a public policy. Generally, employees who work under an employment contract can only be terminated for reasons specified in the contract.

Registering attendance

One of the most problematic issues for event organizers and contractors is registering attendance of their staff and volunteers. This is particularly the case for people who may work across a number of precincts, signing on at one location and signing off at another. Clearly, a sophisticated, barcoded or RF tagged accreditation badge that can be scanned on entry and exit would solve this problem. Generally, however, most event budgets cannot accommodate such systems for temporary venues. The issue of signing on and off duty must be solved, however, as it is incumbent upon the event organizer to account for all personnel on site. Attendance registration for volunteers would form part of the procedural guidelines for managing volunteers. As mentioned previously, insurance for volunteers is recommended.

Validating suitability

In the process of assessing an individual's suitability for employment, there are a number of checks that might be done such as:

- visa and other requirements for official employability status;
- licences and permits (e.g. to drive a forklift);
- educational and other qualifications (e.g. responsible service of alcohol certificate, food safety training, first aid certificate). All of these need to be checked for currency;
- police check, mainly for mega events;
- working with children, training and register of child offenders;
- references from past employers.

In all cases, the individual has to provide consent for the check to take place. This is commonly done by including a statement to this effect at the end of the application form, which the prospective employee or volunteer signs. This is also an important consideration when accepting applications online.

Offer letter

As mentioned previously, the employment offer is a contract like any other. Some important details need to be included such as:

- position offered;
- compensation/pay;
- benefits;
- trial period;
- start and finish date (if project or temporary);
- reference to the attached job description for duties and responsibilities;
- reference to the attached employee handbook for policies and rules;
- signatures of both parties.

In the case of volunteers, it is equally important to highlight the position as a voluntary position and include clear expectations of both sides.

Record keeping

Employee record keeping requires that the following information is maintained for auditing purposes (by the taxation department in particular). The period of time required for storing these records differs from region to region; however, seven years is a good guideline.

- name
- address
- position held
- hours or time card details
- gross pay or earnings
- deductions such as tax
- record of leave due and taken.

It is also highly recommended that records of interview, training, evaluation and timekeeping are maintained for volunteers.

Labour exploitation

From some perspectives the use of volunteer labour at commercial events is exploitative. However, many arts and cultural events are staffed by volunteers or interns and these organizations argue that they are not sustainable without this effort. As Lyn Gardner (2013) reports, unpaid work has become an accepted route into the creative professions. But she asks, 'but when does opportunity become exploitation?' She points out that 40 per cent of graduates entering the cultural sector do so through unpaid work. This discriminates against anyone who cannot afford to work unpaid, as well as anyone who cannot afford to travel for this opportunity. An unpaid role is also likely to be out of reach for anyone who is unemployed and who needs to show job seeking activity and might risk loss of benefits. Macdonald (2012) suggests that today the Edinburgh Fringe is a professional organization, yet many of the venues are still paying their staff well below minimum wage. The result is that semi-voluntary roles (with free accommodation and a small stipend) are available only to the middle class, 'those with financially supportive parents' and out of reach of the unemployed.

Arts Council England in their guide to internships provides several useful suggestions for building high quality internships. First they provide definitions:

> Volunteering – volunteers are not entitled to payment or benefits in kind, and are not classified as workers. There should be no contractual obligations between the volunteer and the organisation.
>
> Voluntary work – voluntary workers are specifically defined in legislation and are not entitled to the minimum wage. They work for a charity, voluntary organisation, associated fundraising body or statutory body. They receive no monetary payments and only limited and specified payments.
>
> Student placement – unpaid work undertaken by someone in education as a required part of their course, with reasonable expenses paid.
>
> (Arts Council England, 2011)

The guidelines define internship in the following ways:

- it is short term, ideally two weeks to six months
- where the intern fulfils 'worker status' through the activities they undertake and their contractual relationship with their employer, it is a paid position
- the internship should be either their first experience of a particular sector or role, or the next step on from, for example, a volunteering role
- the intern is expected to contribute to the work of the organisation, rather than taking on a purely shadowing role
- the intern should be provided with a defined role and job title.

(Arts Council England, 2011)

As such the majority of interns would most likely be classified as a 'worker' for the purposes of the National Minimum Wage Act and its associated regulations.

These guidelines provide a useful way to differentiate between volunteering, student placement (student internship) and other internship roles, and they emphasize the importance of mutual benefit to both employer and intern, thus avoiding any suggestion of exploitation.

CASE STUDY 6.2
Rings of confidence

In his study of the Sydney Olympic Games, Tony Webb (2001) showed that the government and the unions reached a new level of co-operation, and goes on to explore a number of the lessons in more detail.

Industrial relations at the Games – how it worked on the ground

'It got to the point where we almost forgot sport was involved we were so caught up in dealing with the problems on the site'.

(Paul Howes, Unions 2000)

What the unions also learned was that for all of the planning some of the arrangements for the Games workforce would be found wanting during the Games operation. Two weeks before the Games the unions were given accreditation for an official at each venue, allowing direct contact with the workforce, and thirty-two union officials from five unions were rostered to provide coverage throughout the Games. In addition, members could access union support through a general call-centre number linked to a Unions 2000 office on site in the OCA building at Olympic Park. The plan was that unions would be in touch with the workforce and on call to identify and deal with any workplace or industrial relations problems that arose during the Games. In order to ensure efficient handling of disputes all officials involved went through a three-day training programme organized by the Labor Council and SOCOG. On site the rostered union officials had status on a par with venue staffing managers. The industrial structure envisaged by SOCOG was that each venue management would supervise the Games venue staff and volunteers allocated to that site. Contractor companies in the venue would have their own management and supervise their workers but report to the venue manager.

Fortunately a range of disputes in the twelve months leading up to the Games had helped in the building of trust between the unions, SOCOG and the companies. There had been:

- changes to the awards;
- issues over paid and volunteer workers for the Ceremonies;
- the question of bonuses for bus drivers;
- a major dispute over young people, some as young as fourteen, employed as vendors who were being defined as 'contractors' with full responsibility for self-employment;
- the problem of New Zealand security workers recruited without licences or job guarantees;
- underpayment of wages at Bondi Beach Stadium.

And a number of others.

All had been resolved satisfactorily and a large reservoir of trust and respect had been established. But nothing like the problems encountered during the Games had been anticipated.

Even before the Games some problems were apparent. The opening of the Games villages in June 2000 exposed a lack of understanding among staff of the systems, particularly payroll for workers. The unions assisted with presentations to supervisors and helped with the interpretation of the award. Within a few days of the Games Opening Ceremony, caterers struck problems. People were simply not purchasing food on the scale anticipated and the contractors proposed to lay off 1000 staff. Using the award provisions for flexible working the unions negotiated redeployment of some to other Games work. SOCOG staff used email networks to contact a number of industry groups, letting them know that there were people willing, keen and available, and asking if they needed any staff. These industry groups sent the message on to their members and within minutes SOCOG had emails from all over town saying they had openings for this or that number, skill etc. and a hotline of positions found many people work. For the remainder, the unions and caterers negotiated an across the board reduction of hours rather than layoffs so that no one was without a job.

But above all the problem was with the payroll. Day in, day out there were problems with people not being paid, in some cases for weeks. It was not that these were unusual, complicated or difficult to resolve. It was the sheer unremitting volume and the knowledge that the problem was a generic one – that the systems were simply inadequate and could not be reorganized during the course of the Games.

In all the unions negotiated twelve major disputes, eight with 'real strike-potential', during the Games period that required intervention from SOCOG at a senior level and dealt with over 2500 individual problems mainly over pay. The official procedure for dealing with issues through the venue manager was largely bypassed. Most problems were resolved directly with the companies involved. Many employers had people in place who were committed to resolving issues as they arose and networks of personal relations between the unions and these companies had been established. Some problems the unions stepped back from – judging that employers were acting with goodwill and working to deal with the issues.

One example might illustrate the nature of the collaboration. As part of the major problem we discussed earlier where caterers were laying off staff early in the Games, twenty workers in four bars in the Stadium threatened to walk out because three of their workmates had been laid off by the catering contractor Sodexho. Chris Christodoulou says:

> It took three meetings, at 10 pm, 12 midnight and 5 am, along with help from John Quayle, from SOCOG – along with a few drinks in the bar near the Novotel with the key workers in the dispute to fix it.

Paul Howes describes another:

> There were just two food halls for some of our people to take their meal breaks. We had employers saying the meal break starts when they leave work and they would have to get back in twenty minutes. As you know everything was jam packed on the site so it could take that long just to get between the buildings. SOCOG overruled the companies, saying that it starts when they get to the food hall but, during the Games, there were long lines in the halls – it could take ten minutes to get served – so it was changed again – based on the principle that workers deserved a real break – they had to be fed properly – we gave flexibility on meal times and short breaks – and the companies gave back within a human relations principled framework. Nobody abused the system and morale stayed high.

Overall the Games were a success, 'the best Games ever'. In the face of this the problems, large and small, pale into significance – unless that is, we wish to learn from both our successes and our failures in order to better understand:

- What are the underlying components of the human relations framework that made this success possible?
- Which aspects were not in place in those 'near-disaster' areas and did their absence contribute to the problems?
- Why did these areas nevertheless succeed in spite of the problems?
- Whether any of these lessons might be useful in planning other major events or projects requiring collaboration between large groups of people in the future?

(Extract from Webb, 2001: 88–91. Reproduced with permission)

Reflective practice 6.2

Answer the above questions for this case study.

Chapter summary and key points

While labour or employment laws and regulations differ widely from country to country and state to state, effective human resource management requires close attention to these matters. The most important issues are working time and wages, followed by workplace health and safety on the event worksite. Events carry significant risks and a visit to www.crowdsafe.com will convince anyone that crowd management and safety are essential components of induction training, on-the-job training, briefings and debriefings. Duty of care requires responsible management of everyone on site, including visiting workers and volunteers. Duty of care also extends to the public.

A risk management analysis needs to be done on the issue of legal compliance as it applies to human resource management, covering all pertinent laws and regulations. This should be extended still further to cover the topic of workplace health and safety in detail as this is the one issue that dominates the minds of organizers and supervisors responsible for a temporary and often unskilled workforce.

Revision questions

1   Who has a contract of employment?
2   Is a volunteer covered by workers' compensation insurance?
3   What is duty of care?
4   What are the responsibilities of employers under workplace health and safety laws?
5   Referring to discrimination in employment, which characteristics are causes for complaint?
6   Give five recommendations for managing an internship programme.

Industry voice by Kerrie Nash

The sort of things that I think about are getting the employment contracts right with the right flex in them because you'll find that just about 80 per cent of your paid workforce will do a different job at Games time than what they've done in the lead up to the Games, in the planning stages. Ensuring that the contracts are written in a way that enables you to move people around into different roles is important.

The date by which you want them to finish their contract is problematic. You may not know what that date is when you recruit them particularly at the early stage. This is because depending on what job they end up doing at Games time you might want them to leave straightaway, or you might want them to come back to the office to help with contract closure, dissolution or transfer of knowledge. So again, you need to have the right flex in the employment contract to enable you to do what you need to do in consultation with the employee.

One of the other challenges from a legal point of view is a product of the different skills of the management population that you have. You can never rest on your laurels that a manager has the right experience to the right things in terms of equal employment opportunity or discrimination or just good recruitment practice. I've heard some horror stories of people saying entirely inappropriate things in recruitment interviews because they didn't know any better and no one ever trained them. The next thing you have a legal challenge on your hands.

On occasion, someone may not work out and plans will need to be put in place to help the employee be successful. Some managers don't have the experience to do this. You may end up with a constructive dismissal case or similar because the manager they're working for hasn't managed things in the right way. You can be quite busy as an HR person dealing with that kind of stuff.

I think depending on the environment, depending on the country, the industrial relations piece particularly around contractors may require careful management.

Discussion questions

1   A job description is generally used by the HR department to outline roles and responsibilities. Discuss the importance of 'flex' raised in Kerrie's quote in terms of the employment contract, and presumably the job description, for an event manager who is going to be working in a changing environment.
2   Kerrie suggests that managers need training regarding EEO as well as performance management and dismissal. While this may be essential for a mega event, do you think this type of training is important for a smaller, community based event?

References

Anderton, C. (2009). 'Commercializing the carnivalesque: the V Festival and image/risk management', *Event Management*, 12(1), 39–51.

Arts Council England (2011). *Internships in the Arts: A Guide for Arts Organisations*. Available at: http://www.artscouncil.org.uk/media/uploads/internships_in_the_arts_final.pdf; viewed 12 February 2014.

Bowdin, G., Allen, J., Harris, R., McDonnell, I. and O'Toole, W. (2012). *Events Management*. Abingdon: Routledge.

Gardner, L. (2013). *Arts Internships: Chance of a Lifetime or Cut-price Labour?* Available at: http://www.theguardian.com/stage/theatreblog/2010/feb/23/arts-unpaid-interns-exploitation; viewed 28 December 2013.

LOCOG (2012). *LOCOG: Taking Action to Ensure Respect for Workers' Rights in Global Supply Chains*. Available at: http://www.playfair2012.org.uk/wp-content/uploads/2012/02/LOCOG_TUC_Playfair2012_agreement.pdf; viewed 28 December 2013.

Macdonald, A. (2012). *Cheap Labour and the Edinburgh Fringe*. Available at: http://brightgreenscotland.org/index.php/2012/08/cheap-labour-and-the-edinburgh-fringe/; viewed 27 December 2013.

Manchester City Council (2003). *Manchester Commonwealth Games Post Games Report*. Available at: www.gameslegacy.com; viewed 17 May 2006.

Mukherji, Aditi (2013). *'Punkin Chunkin' Volunteer Sues Over Injuries*. Available at: http://blogs.findlaw.com/injured/2013/11/punkin-chunkin-volunteer-sues-over-injuries.html; viewed 28 December 2013.

O'Toole, W. and Mikolaitis, P. (2002). *Corporate Event Project Management*. Brisbane: Wiley.

Reid, S. and Ritchie, B. (2011). 'Risk management: event managers' attitudes, beliefs, and perceived constraints'. *Event Management*, 15(4), 329–341.

Tarlow, P. E. (2002). *Event Risk Management and Safety* (Vol. 16). Brisbane: Wiley.

Taylor, T. and Toohey, K. (2006). 'Impacts of terrorism-related safety and security measures at a major sport event'. *Event Management*, 9(4), 199–209.

Webb, T. (2001). *The Collaborative Games: The Story Behind the Spectacle*. Sydney: Pluto Press.

Workers Online (2004). *Athens Update: Dying Games*. Available at: http://workers.labor.net.au/216/news85_athens.html; viewed 12 October 2005.

Job analysis

Learning objectives

After reading this chapter you will be able to:

- Explain the process of job analysis.
- Evaluate the most appropriate ways in which to approach job analysis.
- Develop job descriptions and person specifications.
- Differentiate between different conditions of employment.
- Explain why job descriptions are key elements of human resource planning.

Introduction

Job analysis is the process of collecting information in order to develop a comprehensive awareness about specific jobs, including job descriptions and person specifications. As this and the next chapter will show, job descriptions form the basis for recruitment and selection, as well as training and performance management. While some small event organizations are cavalier about their lack of human resource planning and have no written job descriptions, those event organizations that operate in professional and complex environments find that job descriptions are an invaluable part of planning. A job description can form the basis for recruitment of the most appropriate staff, provide guidelines to the individual accepting the position, form the basis for training plans and provide a foundation for performance management. For most individuals and organizations, job descriptions are invaluable – in the event business, job descriptions (like checklists) are part of the micro level planning that contributes to flawless performance.

What is job analysis?

Job analysis is the process of discovering the nature of jobs (Brannick and Levine, 2002) and for this to occur a systematic process is necessary. The outcomes of job analysis are primarily the job description and person specification for each role, including volunteers.

A job description is an outline of reporting relationships, tasks to be performed, job outcomes expected and working conditions. A person specification (also referred to as 'job requirements') provides details of the ideal candidate, including knowledge, skills and other attributes required to perform the above tasks. In conjunction with project planning, the following questions might be asked as the job analysis process evolves:

*   What is the primary purpose of the job?
*   Is this job going to be performed by a paid staff member, a volunteer or a contractor?
*   What are the tasks that need to be performed?
*   What are the skills, knowledge and other attributes required?
*   Are there any legislative considerations, such as requisite licences?
*   When and where are the tasks performed?
*   What are the reporting relationships?
*   Which environmental factors need to be considered?
*   Are specific job outcomes expected?
*   Is the job likely to change during the course of the project?

As Figure 7.1 illustrates, the human resources strategic plan leads to the development of work breakdown structures, chunking the major project into smaller subprojects. These are then illustrated on charts and timelines. A labour force analysis is necessary to identify any gaps in supply or training and this in turn leads to identification of roles assigned to paid staff, volunteers and contractors. At this stage organizational charts can be developed.

The human resources operational plan has the objective of ensuring that all tasks are assigned and performed at the highest possible level. This involves recruitment, selection, training, workforce logistics management, performance management and recognition. All of these stages are supported by the foundation pillars of the human resources risk analysis; the human resources budget; policies and procedures; and detailed, systematic job analysis at every stage of the project.

Simple approaches to job analysis

There are whole textbooks on this topic and it is difficult to do it justice in a short space. The following approaches are simple ways in which job analysis can be done, resulting in person specifications and job descriptions. In the process, some thought must be given to job design, which takes into account the features of a job that make it rewarding, interesting and satisfying to the incumbent. For example, job rotation is one way in which volunteers' roles can be made more interesting, particularly if some are placed near the

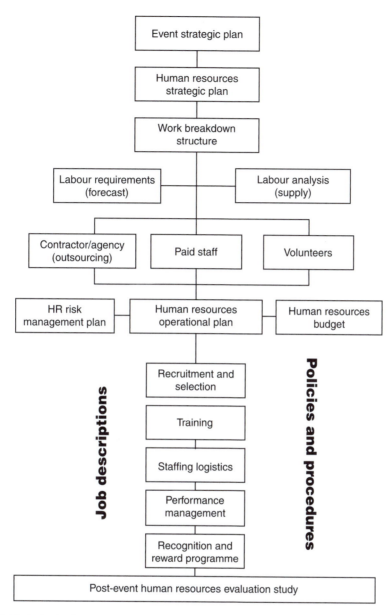

FIGURE 7.1 Strategic plan for human resource management

field of play and others not. However, job design is not a major consideration for any except paid roles in the event business. Even there, the short-term and varied nature of the work tends to ensure that jobs provide sufficient challenge. In most cases, the nature of the project (exhibition, festival, street parade, conference) tends to determine the tasks required, with little room to apply the job design principles evident in jobs for large, stable organizations in which motivation and career planning considerations are quite different.

Methods of job analysis are outlined in brief below.

Project management processes

Chapter 3 looked at project management principles in some detail. This is one of the most common ways in which event organizations analyse the human resource requirements necessary to execute the overall plan. By breaking down the work into smaller and smaller subprojects it can ultimately be decided which tasks need to be performed in order to achieve the project outcomes. This is colloquially known as 'drilling down'.

Focus groups

Most event organizations are comprised of a group of experienced individuals at management level. Using their experience, a series of focus groups can be conducted which may abbreviate the detailed project planning identified above. This group can contribute something vital – they can identify the things that have worked and haven't worked in the past. Also, the members of the group have experience with employing their own staff, contractual arrangements with suppliers and volunteer management. Tapping into this experience, which may be local or international, is an essential part of job analysis.

Interviews

Individuals may have a wealth of ideas to contribute. As with the above approach, it is best to structure the sessions, using questions such as those described in the previous section to ensure that the discussion doesn't go off track.

Questionnaires

A simple format for job analysis is useful once the high-level planning has been completed. An example of a template for creating job descriptions in functional areas is shown in Figure 7.2.

Research

Industry research is another component of job analysis. Similar occupations and events may have similar roles. Legislative requirements, such as certification to serve alcohol, may be part of the person specification. Knowledge of food safety systems and procedures would be essential for catering supervisors.

Job title, job summary, reporting relationships
Duties/responsibilities and job outcomes
Job environment/context, special requirements, equipment
Conditions of employment (paid, volunteer, term)

FIGURE 7.2 Template for developing job descriptions

Critical incidents

There is nothing more powerful than a critical incident analysis to point to planning deficiencies. Using this approach, the following questions would need to be asked:

- What went wrong/right?
- What were the contributing factors?
- How did people performance contribute to the incident (in a positive or negative way)?
- How was this reflected in human resource management plans, policies and procedures (or not, as the case may be)?

For example, it may be found that an access control monitor has allowed people into an area who should not be there, leading to a security scare and bomb search. This could point to insufficient training for the access monitor and in turn should lead to a review of training materials and possibly the development of an assessment task to check volunteers' comprehension of the various codes on accreditation passes. More serious incidents such as injuries and accidents could result in more emphasis on control measures and thus more volunteers assigned to safety monitoring roles.

As Sanchez and Levine (2000) point out, job analysis is far from an exact science, regardless of the approach taken. Researchers of job analysis often evaluate the accuracy of the outcomes by analysing rater agreement. However, Sanchez and Levine propose that consequential validity is another way in which the outcomes of job analysis can be reviewed. Figure 7.1 shows the final stage of human resource management for an event as the evaluation report and it is here, post-event, that consequential validity of many elements of the human resources plan can be evaluated. By analysing critical incidents (and many of the not so critical ones) any deficiencies in job analysis, job design, recruitment and training can be highlighted.

Success factors are another consideration. The question asked could be 'How does this critical incident illustrate the success of our human resource programme?' If we take an incident, such as a volunteer going beyond the call of duty to assist a spectator who is feeling ill, or the part played by a security officer in providing information to visitors (one of whom turns out to be a visiting journalist), it is necessary to look back at their selection, training and motivation programmes to see how these members of the workforce were empowered to provide exceptional service.

Sanchez and Levine make the point that very detailed job analysis sometimes fails to lead to relevant selection procedures. Thus, while the process should be systematic, in the event environment heuristics (a little informed guesswork) has a role to play in the dynamic process of project planning. Indeed, the project management environment is often characterized by rapid change, competing demands and incomplete information (McCray et al., 2002). However, when using heuristics it is important to acknowledge potential biases and apply appropriate measures to offset them.

Establishing conditions of employment

Part of job analysis involves establishing conditions of employment. In the event environment there are many different arrangements, with few staff working traditional jobs as full-time permanent employees. These conditions may include any or all of the following.

Paid employee

A person is an employee if a number of criteria are met. Essentially an employee agrees to 'serve': he or she agrees to follow directions. Control is therefore one of the primary criteria of the employment relationship. Another is the organization test whereby the employee works on the premises and uses all the tools and equipment of the employer. The employee is thus assimilated into the organization (Maund, 2001). Finally, 'consideration' is the payment of the employee for the hours worked so that money changes hands.

Full-time employee

Full-time staff work a full week, normally an eight-hour day over five days. However, legislation of a particular country or region, and industrial agreements, have an impact on this arrangement. Where such agreements exist, employees must be paid overtime if they exceed these hours. In practice, many event employees are very flexible and are responsive to the pressure and demands of the 'hot action', working long hours during set-up and running of an event.

Part-time employee

Part-time is where a person works a percentage of a full-time position, with associated benefits such as pay and leave on a pro-rata basis. Thus someone who works half the week is paid 50 per cent of the full-time wage for the same position and is entitled to half the annual leave and sick leave.

Permanent employee

A permanent employee has an open-ended relationship with the employer.

Temporary

Temporary positions are common in the event industry. For example, a paid volunteer co-ordinator might be employed for three months.

Casual

A casual employee works on an hourly basis. The pay rate reflects this, carrying loadings to compensate for the lack of sick leave or other leave. The hourly rate is thus higher than that for a permanent or temporary employee.

There are also other ways in which people might be employed to work on site.

Agency staff

Agency staff are somewhat complex as their employer is technically the agency that has hired them and is paying them. However, they do work in much the same way as employees, taking direction and participating fully in the organization. Despite this, they remain the employees of the agency.

Volunteers

Volunteers are not employees. They are not paid and are not able to access the benefits of employees. They are not covered by workers compensation. Where the position is unpaid this should be clearly stated on the job description and in all correspondence with the volunteer.

Contractors

An independent contractor does not fall within the definition of an employment relationship since he or she has control of an independent business and decides where, when and by whom the work should be done. The business is separate and runs the risk of profit or loss. Tools and equipment belong to the contractor company. People employed by the independent contractor are answerable to their employer even if working on the event site.

   While collectively everyone on site is described as being part of the 'event workforce', only a portion of these people are paid staff. Clarity about the basis for employment is essential for legal reasons. Anyone working as an employee of the event organization should be issued with an offer letter, which is essentially an employment contract.

Applying job analysis to human resource programmes

Many organizations see job descriptions as a formality, a paperwork requirement of the human resource department. Once completed, they are then disregarded. In the event business, job descriptions are vitally important and can contribute in many ways to the project's design and implementation. Managing the entire scope of people performance is the aim of the human resources operational plan, an example of which is illustrated in Figure 7.3. As Plekhanova (1998: 116) points out,

> most traditional approaches to process modelling do not provide an analysis of critical human resources and their impact(s) on project performance and output quality ... because they are concerned with resource availability and utilization, and do not provide study, analysis and management of resource capabilities and compatibilities.

While this author is discussing this topic in the context of software design, what he says could not be more pertinent to event management where 'people and their capabilities

Job descriptions
The main feature is a list of duties and outcomes

⇩

Person specifications
Allow for the identification of the knowledge, skills and other
attributes of the ideal employee or volunteer

⇩

Training programmes
Gaps between the skills and knowledge of the appointee and the
requirements of the job role form part of a training plan

⇩

Performance appraisals
Performance can be measured against the duties and outcomes
listed in the job description

⇩

Disciplinary processes
Deficiencies in performance can be clearly identified in relation to clearly
set out duties and responsibilities

⇩

Post-event evaluation
Planning can be evaluated by asking selected individuals to identify
shortcomings in the original design of their position, roles and responsibilities

FIGURE 7.3 Developing a human resources operational plan

have a major impact on project performance and its quality' (Plekhanova, 1998: 116). Johnson (2012) points out that outside of the core team, the nature of an event organization often precludes precise HR planning such as would occur in a traditional organization, instead structures and plans may need to adapt around the skills that emerge in the wider workforce, including 'peripheral' contractors and volunteers. Drummond and Anderson (2004) point out that staff need to be flexible and responsive because change is inevitable in this environment. Managing change requires a clear focus on the event strategic plan and specific objectives, otherwise flexibility can be taken too far. As the time of the event draws near and new people are brought on board, they are often keen to make their mark, arriving with fresh ideas that sometimes aren't welcomed by the core team that has been working on the project from inception. This is one of the challenges of the pulsating organization (Hanlon and Cuskelly, 2002).

The job description

A job description is a summary of the most important features of a job, including the general nature of the work performed (i.e. duties and responsibilities) and level of the work performed (i.e. skill, effort, responsibility and working conditions) (see Case Study 7.1). A job description should describe and focus on the job itself and not on any specific individual who might fill the job.

There are four parts to a job description:

1   Identifies where the job fits within the organization and includes reporting relationships.
2   Describes the work performed, generally in the form of a list of duties or tasks. In many cases these duties can be clustered into groups of related items.
3   Describes the environment in which the person will work and any special requirements or limitations, including licensing and other mandatory requirements. Machines, tools and equipment are also described here. And this part may describe the context, such as outdoor work or shift work.
4   Describes the conditions of employment, including pay rate and period of employment.

These are illustrated in the job description for an events co-ordinator in Figure 7.4.

Job Description – Events Co-ordinator

Reports to: Executive Director

Summary

Plans, oversees and administers all aspects of events (conferences, workshops, board meetings, presentations and social events). Maintains the master calendar of events. Co-ordinates activities with administrative staff, and works with other staff members on events as appropriate.

Job responsibilities/tasks

1. Administers and oversees planning and execution of all organizational conferences, meetings and social events, both on site and off site
2. Identifies venues and suppliers of event services
3. Oversees and approves master calendar of events
4. Maintains a current, accurate and detailed project task timeline
5. Negotiates rates and contracts with venues and suppliers/vendors for a variety of services
6. Prepares budget and submits it for approval to Executive Committee
7. Monitors services to ensure contract terms are satisfied
8. Attends events to oversee activities and ensure details are handled as arranged
9. Issues invitations, monitors and co-ordinates replies
10. Arranges for travel and accommodation for event participants
11. Generates data reports on event activities as required
12. Co-ordinates in-house catering/hospitality

Job context

Extended hours and weekend hours may be required when running events.
Driving is necessary for occasional pick up and transportation of speakers and conference participants.

Conditions of employment

Full-time permanent (37.5 hours per week)
Salary level: Administrative staff, level three.

FIGURE 7.4 Job description – Events Co-ordinator

The person specification

The person/job specification describes the ideal person for the job in terms of competencies relevant to the job description. In the sample job description in Figure 7.4 it is clear that the person is required to have experience in a similar event context, to have developed budgets and to have used project-planning software such as Microsoft Project. All of these are directly relevant to the job role.

Charges of discrimination are unlikely to occur if the person specification includes requirements that are not relevant to the job role as outlined in the job description. If it can be seen that equal employment opportunity (EEO) principles have been applied, the recruitment and selection processes will survive scrutiny.

Most people writing person specifications have little difficulty with the sections on knowledge and skills (competencies) required. The difficulty is usually with the section called 'other attributes'. It is in this section that an inexperienced person is likely to list things like 'outgoing personality', 'organized and confident' or 'non-smoker'. First, these attributes are hard to judge objectively and, second, they are often hard to justify in relation to the specific job requirements. Certainly the criterion, non-smoker, cannot be supported. While there may be office or venue areas in which there is no smoking, there is no reason that a person should be asked whether they smoke in other places or on other occasions. This section is the one where the law is most likely to be broken. Some unusual requirements seen by the author include: 'must be petit to fit into our uniform'; 'under 35'; 'good for public relations'; 'attractive'; 'muscular'; and 'fit looking'. Even a criterion 'interested in sport' may not be relevant to a volunteer working at a sporting event if they are working back of house and nowhere near the field of play. Likewise, requirement of a driver's licence should not be included unless driving is an essential part of the job.

Examples of more appropriate 'other attributes' are shown in the sample person specification in Figure 7.5.

One final comment on the selection criteria included in the person specification: if it can be clearly shown that the event is themed and that the food and beverage staff are part of the theme, then selection of staff to fit the theme can be justified. For example, if the event included a Chinese banquet, decor and entertainment, it would be legal to select staff of Chinese appearance, with ability to speak this language, as would be done if hiring actors for a performance.

The People 1st Labour Market Review of the business event sector provides an overview of the wide range of roles available in this important sector of the economy. The business event sector comprises:

- *Corporate in-house organizers.* Large organization that run in-house events on a regular basis will have their own experienced events team to stage events such as company conferences and awards nights.
- *Associations.* Many professional associations in fields such as accounting and engineering regularly stage events for their members.

Person specification – Events Co-ordinator

Knowledge and experience

- Experience with event/meeting planning and co-ordination required at the same level
- Knowledge of event suppliers/vendors in the tourism and hospitality industry in the region, including venues, hotels, and food and beverage facilities
- Ability to organize travel, accommodation and hospitality for groups of 50 or more
- Experience negotiating contracts, primarily with hotels and event venues
- Experience in preparing budgets and allocating resources
- Proven ability to manage community volunteers, including recruitment and training
- Basic knowledge of audiovisual systems

Skills

- Computer programs: all Microsoft office products, including Excel and Project
- Knowledge of special event planning software such as EventPro an advantage
- Driver's licence

Other attributes

- Able to handle multiple tasks simultaneously
- Attention to detail
- Ability to work under pressure and meet timelines
- Team player, ability to work with different people, flexible
- Able to work with minimal direction or supervision, highly motivated

FIGURE 7.5 Person/job specification – Events Co-ordinator

- *Professional organizers.* In the conference area these professionals are known as PCOs, professional conference organizer. However there are now professional event organizers that have the capacity to stage a wide variety of events, including incentive travel or educational tours. These organizers act as intermediaries between the client and the suppliers.
- *Entrepreneurs* – develop events and market themselves. For this to be successful the entrepreneur needs to market the event successfully so that the event is profitable.

There are also numerous event industry suppliers including the contractors mentioned in the previous chapter. Suppliers include hotels and convention centres, specialist event venues, audiovisual experts, equipment hire companies etc. There is considerable overlap with roles in tourism and hospitality, particularly for hotels.

Table 7.1 illustrates three key roles in the business event sector, the skills shortage areas in the UK and the skills gaps identified in the People 1st Labour Market Review (2010a).

Using job descriptions as training and monitoring aids

Job descriptions can be used as the basis for employee and volunteer training. In fact, the volunteer job description can double as a checklist and control measure (see Figure 7.6), providing the volunteer with clear expectations of what the job entails and the supervisor

TABLE 7.1 Skills, recruitment and retention: event organizers

Occupation	Entry requirements	Ease of filling vacancies	Skill shortage vacancies	Skills gaps
Accounts director	• Prior experience of event industry • Solid understanding of suppliers • Strategy management • Relationship building • Negotiation and persuasion skills • Budget management • People management	Tends to be recruited internally and relatively easy to fill	Technical knowledge such as health and safety, sustainability	Technical knowledge such as health and safety, sustainability
Account manager	• Budget management • People management • Multi-tasking • Understanding of suppliers • Project management	Relatively easy to fill, especially since redundancies have been made by some event agencies	• Basic operational and logistic side of event management • All round hands on experience at event management	• An understanding of the client's industry • Customer service • Managing clients and suppliers • Crowd management
Event executive	• Excellent verbal and written communication • Time management • Articulate and approachable • Customer focused	These roles tend to be quite easy to fill because those applying tend to be either graduates or individuals with an administrative background	Graduates may not have the right attitude to go above and beyond to do a good job	• Attention to detail • Customer service • Interpreting and understanding messages

People 1st (2010b: 51)

Tasks	Times to be carried out	Record of daily inspection
Check access to electrical control box, in particular any blockages or obstructions	Hourly	
Check clearways/pathways, with particular attention to stairways to ensure that they aren't blocked	Twice per day	
Monitor cleanliness of staff areas, including canteen and change rooms	Twice per day	
Monitor use of recycling bins and report to kitchen supervisor if waste streams are contaminated	Hourly	
Monitor incident reporting system:	Three per day	

- Check that sufficient incident forms are provided for staff at staff entrance and staff canteen area
- Clear incident report form submission box and take forms to control centre
- Check signage for reporting major incidents or emergency evacuation

FIGURE 7.6 Job description used as training aid and control measure

with an outline for on-the-job training and measurement. Each task specified can be explained by the trainer and practised by the volunteer to ensure that the person knows what to do and feels confident.

Using job descriptions as performance management tools

Some organizations use performance appraisal forms that are more general than specific. For example, the criteria by which the person is appraised may include 'quality of work' or 'ability to work in a team'. Consider instead how useful it would be to judge the individual's performance against the duties listed in the job description. For example, using the event co-ordinator's job description illustrated in Figure 7.4, the evaluation would look something like that illustrated in Figure 7.7.

Task: Maintains current, accurate and detailed project task timelines; reviews the timelines regularly with staff to determine completed tasks, pending tasks and task changes
Rating:
Comment:

Task: Negotiates rates and contracts with venues and suppliers/vendors for a variety of services
Rating:
Comment:

FIGURE 7.7 Appraisal of performance against job description

PLATE 7.1 A volunteer protects stilt walkers from sabotage

CASE STUDY 7.1
Writing job descriptions

Job title: Staging Assistant Bump-in and Bump-out

Job summary

The volunteer will work with a team to put up tents, install seating, build stages and display kiosks. At the end of the festival the volunteer will work with a team to dismantle and remove all built items.

Reports to

Production Manager

Tasks

- Lifting and carrying equipment.
- Moving heavy items.
- Setting up tents and kiosks.
- Building the stage.
- Minor handyman tasks.
- Putting up signage.
- Other manual labour tasks.

Shifts

Very early start on bump-in day of 4 am, working until 2 pm.
Festival days 8 am to 4 pm.
Bump-out 10 am to 4 pm.

Conditions

Volunteer unpaid.
Uniform and meals provided.

Person specification/requirements

- Previous experience with this level of manual handling.
- Handyman skills, mainly carpentry.
- Basic occupational health and safety training.

Experience in a festival environment would be an advantage.

Reflective practice 7.1

Develop similar job descriptions for two of the volunteer roles for the 2015 FIFA World Cup™ (see box) by expanding the list of duties and being specific about the job requirements and conditions of employment.

Volunteer roles for 2015 FIFA Women's World Cup™

Accreditation

Accreditation is a primary security service. Measures to ensure appropriate and comprehensive accreditation and access are crucial to the successful operation of the FIFA U-20 Women's World Cup Canada 2014. Accreditation will be provided to staff, volunteers, media representatives, sponsors, VIP guests and other groups with approved access beyond the spectator areas. Volunteers will support the controlled access to the stadium and adjacent areas by working in the accreditation centre where they will greet guests, check their credentials and issue personalized identity documents.

Administrative services

The Administrative Services team is ideal for those looking to gain experience behind the scenes of a career in Sports Administration. An Administrative Services volunteer will have a unique opportunity to gain insight into how operational plans are executed to deliver a competition. They will interact closely with all the different sectors involved in the delivery of a FIFA competition. Key tasks may include, but are not limited to, photocopying, scanning, filing, collating of documents and working as a runner. Computer literacy would be advantageous.

Competition services

Competition Services volunteers have the opportunity to be involved in ensuring that a wide variety of activities run smoothly. From working as part of the match set up and maintaining team dressing rooms, to fulfilling the role of an operations runner, these volunteers often work at the heart of the action. On non-match days, these volunteers will assist the Local Organizing Committee in various aspects of team services including but not limited to team training sessions, assisting with team requests and working with the respective departments for on-going changes in schedules.

Guest services

Guest Services volunteers welcome and assist each spectator to ensure the guest experience is incredible. Volunteers will provide information and directional support as required.

Hospitality and protocol

The Hospitality and Protocol volunteer team will assist the Welcome and Information Desk at venues such as the airports, hotels and stadiums. Among their responsibilities is the dissemination of information to guests, such as the transport routes, event schedules and other general information. Onsite, these volunteers will assist with implementing the seating plans for the VIP tribune, greeting and ushering guests to their seats, and making them feel welcome. The ability to speak more than one language, as well as an understanding in respect of hospitality and protocol, will be an added advantage.

Information technology

To provide an optimal working environment for National Organizing Committee staff, broadcast and media representatives, we require a reliable and extensive IT and telecommunication network. Volunteers will assist in setting up and operating this network. Duties will include IT service and support.

Logistics

Logistics volunteers form the core implementation team for the operations department. Volunteers are responsible for the smooth and efficient delivery, storage and distribution of the equipment and materials. Volunteers will assist in coordinating and organizing deliveries, set-up and strike of temporary structures and decor, and loading and unloading of goods. Some roles will include physical activities and heavy lifting up to 50 pounds.

Marketing

Marketing volunteers will assist with promotions during the competition as well as monitoring and protecting the exclusive advertising around the stadium. Volunteers will be required to be friendly, outgoing, professional, have strong people skills and the ability to follow direction.

Media and communications

A Stadium Media Centre will be established at each of the four FIFA U-20 Women's World Cup Canada 2014 stadiums as a base for media representatives to file their reports and photos around the world. Volunteers will be the first contact point for media representatives, passing on the latest information, helping to organize and coordinate news conferences and assisting reporters in the media centre and press tribune.

Medical services

Medical Services volunteers fulfil a number of important roles ranging from stretcher bearers and doping control aides, to administrative support of the medical specialists looking after the health and safety of the various constituent groups. Some of the roles within the Medical Services will be gender specific due to the nature of the competition. Experience in the medical field would be considered an asset but not necessary. Candidates who apply must be able to lift 50 pounds.

Ticketing

Volunteers are required to support the venue ticketing staff with game-day operations and assist ticket holders as required. Ticketing volunteers will be working in a customer-facing role with the opportunity to interact with spectators from all over the world who have come to watch the competition and support their team.

Transportation

The Transportation team is responsible for providing safe, efficient and punctual services for staff, FIFA guests, partners and the National Organizing Committee ensuring they are in the right place at the right time. Transportation volunteers must be friendly and cordial because, in many cases, they are the first point of contact with delegate guests. Volunteers will work as drivers and will coordinate the transportation between various venues including airports, hotels and stadiums. Those with relevant experience will help maintain the vehicle fleet, aid in dispatch, or act as assistants to professional transport managers.

Volunteer management

The Volunteer Management team will support the Volunteer Co-ordinators in ensuring a smooth and efficient operation of the volunteer centres. These volunteers will assist in implementing the volunteer training sessions ahead of the tournament, provide assistance in the distribution of uniforms prior to the tournament and support the management of the volunteer centres during the tournament.

Youth programme

The Youth Programme for the competition encompasses the activities of the ball crew, player escorts and the flag bearers for the FIFA, FIFA Fair Play and national flags. Volunteers for the Youth Programme will be working with the venue team to ensure that the accreditation for the Youth Programme is received on match days, food and snack services for the children is delivered, uniforms are distributed to participants, assist in pre-match ceremonies and be responsible for the escort of children to the appropriate place and time. Experience in working with children between the ages of 6–18 would be an asset. A criminal background check is mandatory for these positions.

Source: FIFA Women's World Cup Canada 2015™ Edmonton – Volunteer opportunities Online: http://app.volunteer2.com/Public/Umbrella/844c2415-aa17-4a19-8baa-39be45865c28#. Reproduced with permission of 2015 FIFA World Cup™

Chapter summary and key points

This chapter has looked at the process of job analysis, the outcomes of which are the job descriptions and person specifications for paid and volunteer roles for an event. This process needs to be systematic but flexible since an event project generally evolves over time, with new priorities and even perhaps a new artistic direction. While the human resource department or event manager needs to oversee the process of job analysis, it is usually the direct manager (functional or zone manager) who develops the detail for each of the job descriptions. The Sydney 2000 Olympic Games plan resulted in 3,500 job descriptions; however, smaller events would produce just a few. Job descriptions contribute in many ways to the next operational phases of recruitment, selection, training and performance management, which are covered in the following chapters.

Revision questions

1   What is job analysis?
2   What is a job description?
3   Explain the four parts of a job description using an example.
4   What is a person/job specification?
5   Discuss the statement 'job analysis is a waste of time if event plans are constantly changing'.
6   Explain why it is important to differentiate between paid, volunteer and contractor working conditions.

Industry voice by Kerrie Nash

With regard to attracting and selecting the right people, two elements spring to mind. Firstly, what are the qualities that will help a person be successful in an event environment? Things such as flexibility, robustness, comfort with ambiguity and change, team player – as an HR director it is worth taking the time to work with the Leadership team to establish what these qualities are.

Secondly, what are the channels of supply? Events require a mix of highly specialized event-specific roles (e.g. sport management, venue management, press operations), other specialist skills such as technology, finance, HR, as well as more generalist coordination and administrative roles. On top of this, some roles start many years out from the event and some start a matter of weeks out from the event. A sound attraction and recruitment (and retention!) plan is needed, particularly for the short-term roles where it won't be possible to attract candidates through the usual recruitment channels. Secondments, students, employment and skills programmes come to the fore.

Discussion questions

1   Conduct your own research to find out the most common attributes that appear in 20 event management advertisements.
2   Discuss the statement event experience is not necessary if the person has the right attributes.
3   The timing of the various appointments is key. Discuss the issues associated with rolling recruitment in the pulsating organization in detail.

References and further reading

Brannick, M. and Levine, E. (2002). *Job Analysis*. London: Sage Publications.

Drummond, S. and Anderson, H. (2004). 'Service quality and managing your people', *Festival and Events Management*, 80–96.

Hanlon, C. and Cuskelly, G. (2002). 'Pulsating major sport event organizations: a framework for inducting managerial personnel', *Event Management*, 7(4), 231–243.

Johnson, B. (2012). 'Building an events team', *Events Management: An International Approach*, 94.

Maund, L. (2001). *An Introduction to Human Resource Management*. New York: Palgrave.

McCray, G., Purvis, R. and McCray, C. (2002). 'Project management under uncertainty: the impact of heuristics and biases', *Project Management Journal*, 33(1), 49–57.

Plekhanova, V. (1998). 'On project management scheduling where human resource is a critical variable'. In 6th European Workshop on Software Process Technology. London: Springer-Verlag.

People 1st. (2010a). *Labour Market Review of the Events Industry*, January. Available at: www.businesstourismpartnership.com/research-and-publications/publications/category/9-publications?download=70:labour-market-review-of-the-events-industry, viewed 1 January 2014.

People 1st. (2010b). *Labour Market Review of the Events Industry*. Available at: www.people1st.co.uk/research-policy/research-reports/

Sanchez, J. and Levine, E. (2000). 'Accuracy or consequential validity: which is the better standard for job analysis data?', *Journal of Organizational Behaviour*, 21, 809–818.

Human resource operations
Building the team

Part II of this book looks at the operational elements of the human resources plan. For practitioners working on smaller events this is the part where things get done! Here we look at recruitment and selection, finding and choosing the right people, and then the major task of training is covered as three distinct components.

In this section we will also look at workforce logistics: feeding and clothing people, getting enough of them there on time, providing essential staff services and registering attendance. The later chapters in Part II will cover two key elements of the human resources plan, leadership and motivation, the aim of which is to inspire and retain staff – even when the going gets tough. And last but not least we'll look at recognition, reward and internal communications, which is an essential part of any workforce management strategy.

Unfortunately, we can't have a party at the end of the book but that is often how the human resources operational plan folds up! Hugs and tears, plans for staff to stay in touch, a fine rosy glow, are the anticipated outcomes of every event, despite any crises and hardships that might occur along the way.

8

Recruitment and selection

Learning objectives

After reading through this chapter you will be able to:

- Define human resource needs.
- Source applicants.
- Select staff and volunteers.
- Maintain records of recruitment and selection.
- Ensure compliance with relevant legislation.

Introduction

This chapter will cover the processes of recruiting and selecting paid staff and volunteers, which are often fraught with difficulty. Some events are so popular that everyone wants to work there, the London Olympic Games attracting over 240,000 applications. It is an enormous processing task for an organization looking for 70,000 volunteers. And of these, many thousands of people want to be on the field of play during an opening ceremony. For one such event there was one individual who called the organizing committee every day for over 1,000 days to speak to anyone who would listen to him about his desire to be in this opening ceremony! For other event organizations it is quite the opposite: it is a real struggle to attract enough volunteers to sustain the event, particularly if it is a fundraiser.

Employing full-time temporary staff is another challenge, simply because the work is temporary. While event work has its intrinsic attraction, the event organization seldom offers permanency or a career path as would most traditional organizations. A convention centre is clearly able to sustain a group of permanent people at management level, but at the service end the staff cohort is almost always casual. Attracting volunteers to a concert is the easiest task in the world; it generally takes only one phone call and word spreads instantly. To advertise for volunteers would be insane, as the phones would ring around the clock for days.

Thus, an understanding of labour market forces, people's motivation and their interest level can assist a great deal when deciding how to approach recruitment.

Definitions of recruitment and selection

The terms recruitment and selection are often assumed to mean the same thing when in fact they do not. Recruitment is the process of attracting potential candidates to the organization. A successful recruitment campaign attracts a pool of candidates that is just large enough to handle. A campaign that is too successful is a disaster as each individual needs to be considered against the selection criteria. For example, a local council advertised an events manager's position and attracted 1,000 applicants. Unfortunately, they were not specific about their requirements in terms of knowledge, skills and experience, and other pertinent criteria were missing. Therefore, they had to work through all the applications, some from people who had experience arranging school fetes and charity balls and others from council employees who had worked on the approvals process and had qualifications in this area only.

It is therefore essential to establish the appropriate criteria before advertising. How demanding the advertised requirements should be is a question of judgement; if too demanding it could result in too small a pool of applicants. Selection is the process of choosing the most suitable candidates. It is here that an equal employment opportunity and diversity policy comes into full effect. The criteria by which candidates are chosen must be directly related to the position in question. A person must be offered the position on merit. The person specification is the document that supports the selection decisions.

Selection of volunteers is very difficult when jobs are fairly generic and there aren't many specific criteria, particularly if the interest level is high. If this is the case, the criteria should be expanded to include communications and customer service skills, experience in similar roles, knowledge of the city and region etc. All of these would support a spectator services role in an event environment. However, a volunteer cannot be discriminated against if they do not live in the area in which the event is held. As with all job requirements, the volunteer (or paid employee) must make his or her own decisions about transportation and accommodation.

Managing expectations is essential. If the job is routine, requires moving equipment or is away from the action, this needs to be explained beforehand. Some people will then remove themselves from the selection process because the position does not meet their expectations.

Defining human resource needs

The previous chapter on job analysis described the development of the master human resources plan, involving consideration of the number and type of people to be appointed and their start dates. In the event environment this is determined not only by need but also by the budget. It is not uncommon for appointments to be delayed until the last possible minute (or beyond it) in order to stay within budget. The commencement of recruitment thus needs to be approved by the responsible manager. This person will decide whether each position is necessary and whether it is in line with earlier planning. Specific requirements will be identified and the recruitment method and advertisements will be approved.

The process of recruitment and selection is illustrated in Figure 8.1. As this shows, once candidates have been sourced, they are selected against the criteria established in the person specification in a competitive process which identifies the best person or people for the job. Interviews are conducted, often by human resources personnel, and then by the direct supervisor. For very senior critical roles, such as artistic director, there is often a panel interview. Following this, references are checked and, for some events, a police check is done for accreditation purposes. Finally, the successful candidate is sent an offer letter which spells out the terms and conditions of their employment. It is also essential that unsuccessful candidates are advised in a timely manner.

In their study Arcodia and Axelson (2005) found that the top five skills mentioned in Australian advertisements for events managers were organizational/planning skills; general communication skills; team skills; customer service skills; and computer skills. These were closely followed by skill in building internal and external relationships. The top five attribute categories emerging from the study were motivated, flexible, positive,

PLATE 8.1 Issuing uniforms to volunteers

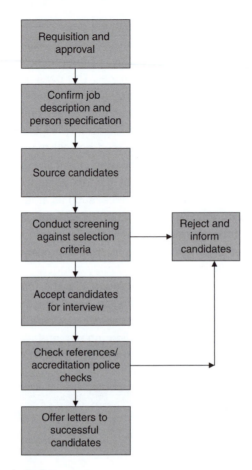

FIGURE 8.1 Recruitment and selection process

friendly and committed/dedicated. One of the most interesting features of this study was the cataloguing of 355 job titles related to event management out of an analysis of 1,002 job advertisements, some of which did not initially appear to have an association with event management. The *Labour Market Review of the Events Industry* (People 1st, 2010) provides a useful overview of the key roles in business events, these being account director, account manager and event executive. For account managers the key skills required are people management, project management, supplier management and the ability to liaise with and build relationships with clients (p. 6). This report provides an overview of the business events labour market, skill needs workforce development, as does the report by Bowdin and McPherson (2006).

Sourcing candidates

There are many ways in which people can be invited to apply for jobs, although success rates and costs differ markedly.

Referral by other employees

The most popular and cost-effective method of recruitment is to invite employees to make referrals (see Case Study 8.1). It appears that their judgement of who might be a good prospective employee and their explanation of the duties involved in the position lead to realistic expectations and higher than average success rates. In some cases, there are incentives associated with this practice. This is a core component of the recruitment practice of Cleanevent, a fast-growing international cleaning and waste management company that has provided cleaning services for four Olympic Games, the 2010 Vancouver Winter Olympics, two Commonwealth Games, the 2007 World Cup Cricket in the West Indies and the 2006 Asian Games to name just a few. Their human resources profile is exemplary and their website well worth visiting.

In their review of changing recruitment practices, Sinha and Thaly (2013) highlight the use of social media for recruitment; this is illustrated with the following sourcing channels as follows:

- job sites/portals 28 per cent
- social media (including LinkedIn, FB, etc.) 23 per cent

CASE STUDY 8.1
Recruitment channels

Which recruiting channels should be used depends on the job position, on the company's employer brand, on the resources the company has on its recruiting team, on how much recruiting budget the company has, etc. One can use them all and find out which suits the best. Every recruiting channel offers different benefits and limitations and works better for certain situations and companies. The key is collecting real-time recruitment metrics on these recruiting channels to figure out what works best for the company in different situations. The recruiting experience of each company is different and the best way to figure out what works best is to analyse metrics based on the past recruiting efforts, not the efforts of everybody else. Once the company has its recruiting metrics solution in place, it is time to start using the recruiting channels that the company thinks will work for it.

Source: Sinha and Thaly (2013: 148).

Reflective practice 8.1

1　Why do companies prefer referrals to other recruitment methods, particularly for volunteers and event industry experts?
2　Given the challenge of finding the best major event logistics person in the world, how would you approach the task of recruitment?
3　What are the shortcomings of using social media for recruitment?
4　There is always the risk that the best person for the job is not applying. Discuss this statement in the context of recruitment.

- campus recruitment 22 per cent
- employee referral 11 per cent
- agencies 7 per cent
- company website 5 per cent
- advertising 4 per cent.

While this study is based on high profile, global organizations, it does show the shift in practice towards social media.

Internet advertising on event or organization's website

Almost every major event advertises positions on their own website to encourage direct applications. Such sites are generally popular with consumers and cover all aspects of the event, including the programme and the organization. Events such as the Edinburgh Festival, Toronto Film Festival, Rio Carnival and the Volvo Ocean Yacht Race are all examples of events that would attract potential candidates by virtue of their reputation. Conversely, recruitment is much more of a challenge for the smaller event for which it may be necessary to look for staff and volunteers among the local community.

Employment agencies and recruitment consultants

As Case Study 8.1 illustrates, employment agencies are seldom used but for the most difficult positions. However, there is an exception. Many world-class events appoint an employment agency as a service provider and sometimes sponsor, enabling them to meet staffing needs across a range of areas. For example, Adecco recruited and trained 20,000 volunteers for the 2006 Torino Winter Olympics following their success at the Hanover EXPO, Manchester Commonwealth Games and Sydney 2000 Olympic Games. Working with LOCOG in 2012, the organization recruited 8,000 people, both permanent staff and people for the time of the Games, and in doing so processed 218,000 applications.

Listing on job sites/portals

There are many different job search websites including seek.com and mycareer.com. Placement on this type of website is cost effective and easy to organize. The sites often provide a template for the candidate to enter key information, making it easier to find relevant data. Others provide the applicant with the opportunity to attach letters and resumes to the application. These websites are categorized as monster job boards or niche job boards. The latter is a board maintained by an event industry association, which is a much more targeted approach than placement on a monster job board. Figure 8.2 provides an example of a website advertisement.

Associations and clubs

Volunteer associations are a first rate source of people and advice. Many sporting and music events are supported by associations and clubs, which play a vital role in their planning

---

Logistics & Operations Manager

Events & Logistics Management

Brilliant career opportunity

Prestigious sporting icon

Outstanding career opportunity to join the functions and events division of a well-known sporting institution. Reporting to the Food & Beverage Operations Manager, you will be responsible for the daily planning, purchasing, inventory control and distribution of food and beverage operations within this dynamic organization.

Click here to apply ⇨

FIGURE 8.2 Example of a website advertisement

and organization. Qualified umpires and officials are essential for sporting events and they can be co-opted from such clubs. Networking with clubs and associations is the best and quickest way to find specialists in fields such as basketball, golf, blues music, etc.

Colleges and universities

These institutions are an exceptionally good source of volunteers and interns. If the event organization works closely with a university, the relationship can reap benefits for all parties. For example, the BA (Hons) Event Management students within the Tourism, Hospitality and Events (THE) School at Leeds Metropolitan University have a placement year in industry (Williamson, 2005). With this length of internship, there is no doubt that the intern is well placed to make a valuable contribution, applying theoretical knowledge in a practical and fast paced environment.

Advertising positions

When developing an advertisement, whether it is to be used online or on a college notice board, the purpose is the same: to attract the best candidates and reject those who are unsuitable. This requires a fine balance between selling the position in the most positive light and being quite clear about requirements and expectations. In the advertisement in Figure 8.3, there are two parts: one explains and sells the job in a positive light and the other states the selection criteria. If these are stated clearly, the individual can self-select by deciding whether or not they meet the minimum criteria.

Many event-specific websites include online magazines which also carry this type of advertisement (see www.specialevents.com.au).

Following are some tips for employment advertising:

1   Make sure that the main heading identifies the job.
2   Include the company name and contact details.
3   Explain and sell the paid or volunteer position.
4   Be clear about the selection criteria.

> **Event Sponsorship Co-ordinator**
>
> We are a government agency with a brief to deliver high-profile events in the harbour area. We are looking for an exceptional person to drive our sponsorship programme, look after marketing and manage our ongoing relationships with business organizations. The position is challenging and requires someone with a strong track record in a competitive market.
>
> Job details
>
> - Deliver new sponsorship deals for our events
> - Maintain and effectively manage current sponsor arrangements
> - Manage marketing initiatives for current and new events
> - Negotiate with other government agencies where required
> - Manage and develop business and industry contacts
>
> Selection criteria
>
> - Previous demonstrated experience in sponsorship development and management in Arts and Entertainment
> - Previous experience in negotiating and managing contractual relationships with key clients
> - Project management skills, ability to meet tight deadlines
> - Established relationships with key players in government and business
> - Degree qualifications in Marketing, Business or Events Management
> - Understanding of main legislative compliance issues for events

FIGURE 8.3 Example of a balanced advertisement

5   Describe the job context and conditions of employment.
6   Make sure that the wording meets equal opportunity guidelines.

Using the internet for recruitment

There are several excellent guides to recruiting on the internet, some with particular focus on specific demographics such as Gen Y and Z. With Gen Z predicted to make up at least a third of the workforce by 2020 it is essential to understand how best to target this group. When developing an online recruitment option on an event website, a facility for applicants to enter their data should be provided. This is absolutely essential for volunteers otherwise someone has to enter data for every written application.

Questions asked by the Athens Organizing Committee for the Olympic Games included:

- name and contact details
- educational background
- occupation
- field of studies (for students)
- medical conditions (for consideration)
- disability (in order to facilitate placement)
- availability
- languages (verbal and written).

The application then asks for experience and interests according to functional areas:

- spectator services
- security
- doping control
- venue staffing
- transport
- accreditation
- village operations
- press operations
- technology
- ticketing
- venue management
- medical services
- sports (applicants could choose up to three sports, identifying their capacity: athlete, referee, instructor, club member).

For such positions the framework is quite rigid, giving the applicant little opportunity to go off track. For more senior positions, however, it is essential to allow for more free text or for submission of a resume. The resumes are then stored in a digital database. From here they can be retrieved by using key search words. Text strings such as 'risk management', 'staging', 'Microsoft Project', 'conference planning' and 'crowd management' can be used to find applicants on the database. An automatic note of thanks should be generated for every application or resume submission. The organization needs to think about the public relations role played out during a recruitment campaign. The biggest campaigns, generally both media and internet based, generate a significant amount of interest in the event, which may also result in ticket sales. The profile of the organization, and the goodwill it generates, is a significant consideration in human resource planning and operations.

To ensure that searches will lead applicants to your site, web optimization needs to be considered. The design of the site is vitally important. Keeping people engaged with interactive features is a good idea: 'the more they click, the more they stick'. This way people hang around the site for longer and their interests can be monitored by following the clicks, giving the web designer and the recruiter some insight into the profiles and interests of site visitors.

Figure 8.4 shows the total volunteer applications via the internet and paper received by the Manchester Commonwealth Games from the launch of its recruitment programme in May 2001 to the end of the programme in August 2002. Figure 8.5 includes a good example of a volunteer application form.

Preparing for the interview

Once a number of applications have been received, they need to be sorted to see which meet the selection criteria. Candidates who are rejected should be advised immediately; those who make it to the next selection phase are usually interviewed.

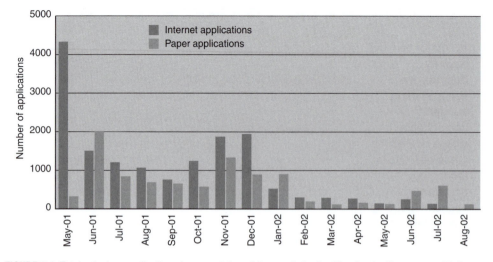

FIGURE 8.4 Total volunteer applications (paper v. internet) by month for the Manchester Commonwealth Games

Although there has been much debate about the validity of interviews for selection (De Cieri, 2003), they continue to be the mainstay of most human resource processes. One of the ways in which the validity of the interview can be improved is by asking all applicants the same carefully prepared questions. These questions should emerge from the job description and person specification. They should be 'behavioural' questions that reflect the person's past experience and not hypothetical questions about what they might do in the future. If we use the event sponsorship co-ordinator's position in Figure 8.3, the questions prepared for the interview could include:

Previous demonstrated experience in sponsorship development
Q: Describe the approach you took to securing sponsorship in your previous position.

Previous experience in negotiating and managing contractual relationships with key clients
Q: Explain some of the problems and pitfalls you have experienced in managing contractual relationships with key clients.

Project management skills, ability to meet tight deadlines
Q: Describe a project you have managed where the critical path has been impacted by something unforeseen.

Established relationships with key players in government and business
Q: How have your relationships with government impacted on your role?

Degree qualifications in Marketing, Business or Events Management
Q: Why do you think your qualification is helpful in meeting the challenges of this position?

Understanding of main legislative compliance issues for events
Q: Can you identify legislation that impacts on arrangements with sponsors?

Canmore Folk Music Festival
Volunteer Application Form

2005 Festival: July 30–August 1

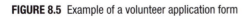

*= Required Field

1. *Last name [   ]   *First name [   ]

2. **Contact Information:**

    *Home phone: [   ]   Cell phone: [   ]

    Business phone: [   ]   Fax number: [   ]

3. **Email:** [   ]

4. ***Address:**

    Street [   ]

    City [   ]

    Province [   ]   Postal code [   ]

5. ***Have you volunteered for the festival before?** Yes: ○   No: ○

    If Yes, in which area? [   ]

    Who was your co-ordinator? [   ]

    What year(s)? [   ]

6. ***Would you like to be kept on file for next year if you don't get placed?** Yes: ○   No: ○

    (*Note*: You must be available from Saturday to Monday of the festival in order to be placed as a volunteer)

7. ***Do you have a valid driver's licence?** Yes: ○   No: ○

8. **In case of emergency the festival should contact:**

    *Name: [   ]

    *Relationship: [   ]

    *Contact number: [   ]

9. ***Do you have any medical/physical restrictions of which we should be aware?**

    No: ○   Yes: ○   If Yes, please specify

    [   ]

    [   ]

10. **Do you have a valid first aid certificate?** Yes: ○   No: ○

    If Yes, level [   ]

FIGURE 8.5 Example of a volunteer application form

Lynch and Smith (2009) question the effectiveness of volunteer interviews when job descriptions and specifications are not developed, this leading to informal one-one meetings. Dashper (2013) recommends further research into the 'embodied dispositions' required to succeed in the event industry, suggesting that there are implicit assumptions in online advertisements regarding physical attractiveness ('impeccable'), communication skills, gender, class and cultural background.

Conducting the interview

There are two main parts to the interview: explaining the job to the applicant and seeking information about how they meet the selection criteria. Most human resource professionals ask the questions first and explain the job later as this gives the person time to relax and absorb the information. By this time, the interviewer also has a fairly good idea of the person's likely success and can gauge how much time to spend in explanation. In some cases, of course, the interview turns into a sales pitch if the applicant is clearly outstanding and would be a potential asset to the organization.

Testing and evaluating candidates

There are many different types of tests that are used to test psychological attributes and general intelligence, as well as tests for specific skills such as word processing.

Psychological tests, despite their popularity, remain questionable in terms of validity and reliability, and there is much ongoing debate on this topic (Cook and Cripps, 2005; Downey et al., 2011). Where used, the tests should be carried out by professionals qualified to conduct assessment and interpret results. It is typically an employment agency that performs this role. The test needs to be reliable, delivering consistent results over time, and valid in that it measures what it sets out to measure (construct validity). Finally, the results should have validity by predicting how well the individual will perform on the job (predictive validity).

References are another part of the selection process. While many employers are not prepared to make evaluative remarks due to legal and ethical problems, there is every reason why an employer should check the accuracy of the information provided in the candidate's resume. According to the Society for Human Resource Management (2004):

- About 40 per cent of HR professionals report increasing the amount of time spent checking references for potential employees over the past three years.
- Of all organizations, 96 per cent conduct some kind of background or reference check on prospective hires.
- Almost 50 per cent of survey respondents reported that reference checks found inconsistencies in dates of previous employment, criminal records, former job titles and past salaries.

Guinn (2013) highlight the least effective and most effective methods for evaluating job candidates, suggesting that traditional selection criteria such as education, experience and job knowledge are not the most likely predictors of candidate success. Multiple meetings with candidates, behavioural interviewing and psychometric profiling are more successful methods of selection. This is particularly important for senior event management roles.

Maintaining records

It is essential to be aware that a selection decision may be challenged. For this reason, documentation should be maintained throughout the process of selection. This could include, for example, a rating scale when evaluating written applications and another when evaluating interview performance. Reference and background checks should also be fully documented. Employment on merit is the expectation and this can be justified long after the process if this has been done methodically. Comments made about applicants should not breach equal opportunity guidelines.

Everyone who has been through a selection process knows how stressful it is. Since this is potentially the first stage of the person's psychological contract with the organization, first impressions count. An upbeat, positive and informative approach is essential.

CASE STUDY 8.2
Edinburgh International Book Festival

Job description: press officer

Contract

Full-time temporary

Key dates

The Edinburgh International Festival runs 12–28 August. The launch is on 15 June. Ticket sales open on 16 June.

Background

The Edinburgh International Book Festival began in 1983 and is now a key event in the August Festival season, celebrated annually in Scotland's capital city. Biennial at first, the Book Festival became a yearly celebration in 1997.

Throughout its history, the Book Festival has grown rapidly in size and scope to become the largest and most dynamic festival of its kind in the world. In its first year the Book Festival played host to just 30 'Meet the Author' events. Today, the Festival programmes over 700 events, which are enjoyed by people of all ages.

In 2001 Catherine Lockerbie, the Book Festival's fifth director, took the Festival to a new level by developing a high-profile debates and discussions series that is now one of the festival's hallmarks. Each year writers from all over the world gather to become part of this unique forum in which audience and author meet to exchange thoughts and opinions on some of the world's most pressing issues.

Running alongside the general programme is the highly acclaimed Children's Programme, which has grown to become a leading showcase for children's writers and illustrators. Incorporating workshops, storytelling, panel discussions, author events and book signings, the Children's Programme is popular with both the public and schools alike and now ranks as the world's premier books and reading event for young people.

The Book Festival receives just 18 per cent of its income from public funds (Scottish Arts Council, City of Edinburgh Council). An unusually high proportion of over 80 per cent of income is self-generated, raised from ticket sales, book sales and sponsorship. The Festival runs a unique independent book-selling operation, now a trading subsidiary, which has become increasingly important in the generation of revenue.

The Edinburgh International Book Festival is a VAT registered company limited by guarantee and has charitable status.

Press team

The Edinburgh International Book Festival Press Office comprises a Press Manager, a Press Officer and a Press and Marketing Assistant. The press team is very busy, working long days and, during the festival itself, working a seven-day week. The press team will work at the Book Festival's offices in Charlotte Square in the lead-up to the festival, and on site in the Press Pod in Charlotte Square Gardens during the festival.

The Press Officer reports to the Press Manager and is responsible for:

1   being one of the main points of contact for all media enquiries in the lead-up to, and during, the Book Festival;
2   proactively selling the Book Festival to targeted media sectors (including online channels) and regions and responding to all media enquiries;
3   developing and nurturing strong two-way communication with these contacts to secure coverage/visits to the Book Festival in 2006 and future years;
4   identifying and pitching strong news lines and clear feature angles (either generic or author-based). This will require a good working knowledge of the 2006 programme and the authors attending;
5   maintaining an up-to-date database of journalists and publications;
6   managing the media accreditation system and ticketing procedure;
7   organizing the Book Festival press launch with the Press Manager and Marketing and PR Manager;
8   liaising effectively with authors and authors' publicists as necessary;
9   setting up, manning and helping to oversee the effective operation of the Press Pod – the service point for all media on site at the Book Festival;

10 organizing photocalls and interview schedules in conjunction with the Press Manager and effectively supervising freelance and contracted photographers on site;

11 overseeing television and broadcast crews on site;

12 monitoring and archiving all coverage and chasing any outstanding copies of broadcast/print coverage for files;

13 assisting the Joint Festivals Travel and Tourism Press Officer to maximize positive coverage in the travel media;

14 regularly and proactively feeding Book Festival news to the Joint Festivals Web Content Coordinator and writing news stories and updates for the Book Festival website;

15 along with all other staff, assisting with the clear-up of the Book Festival site and Press Pod – this will involve some moderate lifting and carrying;

16 assisting the Press Manager prepare a debrief report evaluating the press operation during 2006 and making recommendations for 2007.

Person specification

The successful candidate will possess the following:

- ideally, three years experience in an event-based PR role;
- excellent communication and organizational skills;
- an enthusiastic personality with a flexible can-do attitude;
- the ability to manage and report on projects and work under pressure to meet deadlines;
- the ability to work effectively as part of a small team.

We are committed to making the Book Festival as accessible as possible to customers, participants and staff. If you have any specific access requirements or concerns, please let us know and we will do our best to meet your needs.

Source: Reproduced with permission of Edinburgh International Book Festival; for further information see www. edbookfest.co.uk

Reflective practice 8.2

1 Discuss the best placement for this advertisement (e.g. newspapers, festival website, industry magazines). Which do you think would be most effective?

2 Develop a range of behavioural interview questions to match the position advertised. Which of these would you ask first?

3 Do you think educational qualifications would be relevant to this position?

Chapter summary and key points

This chapter has looked at two distinct processes, recruitment and selection. Recruitment attracts applicants to the organization, while selection is the process whereby the best of these are chosen and offered the jobs. Equal employment opportunity needs to be applied at every step to ensure that only job-relevant selection criteria are used.

Recruitment for an event organization is often a public relations exercise too, as it raises awareness and impacts on the profile of the event. For these reasons, the recruitment process needs to be managed particularly well to prevent the oversubscribing of paid and volunteer positions. Smaller events have the opposite problem and their approach has to be more targeted. By approaching clubs, associations, schools and colleges, many of these event planners find people they need who are well matched to the event type (sports, arts, community, etc.).

The validity of job interviews can be improved using behavioural interviewing techniques and asking the same questions of every candidate. Once the selection decision has been made and references checked, the person should be offered the position in writing.

Revision questions

1   Define recruitment.
2   Define selection.
3   Using a diagram, illustrate the staffing process.
4   List and describe the attributes of three primary sources of event employees.
5   List and describe the attributes of three primary sources of event volunteers.
6   Provide some simple guidelines for employment advertising.
7   Develop a job description and person specification for a volunteer working at an event information kiosk.
8   Using the above documents, prepare some questions for the volunteer interviews.

Industry voice by Kerrie Nash

Workforce is the biggest item of discretionary spend in any organizing committee, so clearly that's going to be a prime area of focus. Whenever we have to try and find money, which is all the time, HR never stops recalculating and re-versioning and rethinking the HR plan to make sure that across the business it's coming in within budget. We work very, very closely with finance to make that a reality and to get the right systems and processes and information in place to be able to do that. Recruitment needs to be handled very, very carefully.

I think the battle from an HR point of view is that the functional areas will all want to grow too fast. That creates budget pressure later on and one of the things that you have to do as an HR director is control recruitment very tightly. It's one of those things that once one person comes on they create work for someone else, so we have to hire someone else and that creates work. You can just see it snowballing and of course finances are limited. Every person that you hire early on obviously has a huge cost in terms of the lifetime of the organizing committee. Just generally with functional areas it is about trying to really keep a lid on their growth in the early days. It is very important to us because there will be a real tendency to recruit too early in many, many parts of the business.

Discussion questions

1 What are the financial and other risks associated with recruiting 'too many too early'?
2 Differentiate between the recruitment approach taken by the following event organizations:
   - mega-event run every four years in different bid countries (e.g. World Cup);
   - major annual event run in the same location;
   - one-off fundraising event in response to a natural disaster;
   - small annual community event;
   - association annual conference (e.g. Physiotherapy Association);
   - international conference run every four years, different bid countries (e.g. medical research).

References

Arcodia, C. and Axelson, M. (2005). 'A review of event management job advertisements in Australian newspapers', conference paper for *The Impact of Events: Event Management Research Conference* 13–14 July 2005, UTS: Australian Centre For Event Management, pp. 575–586. Available at: https://www.uts.edu.au/sites/default/files/conference_proceedings05%20-%20 3rd%20International%20.pdf; viewed 2 September 2014..

Bowdin, G., McPherson, G. and Flinn, J. (2006). *Identifying and Analysing Existing Research Undertaken in the Events Industry: A Literature Review for People 1st*. London: People 1st.

Cook, M. and Cripps, B. (2005). *Psychological Assessment in the Workplace: A Manager's Guide*. Hoboken: Wiley.

Dashper, K. L. (2013). 'The right person for the job: exploring the aesthetics of labor within the events industry', *Event Management*, 17(2), 135–144.

De Cieri, H. (2003). *Human Resource Management in Australia: Strategy, People, Performance*. Sydney: McGraw-Hill.

Downey, L. A., Lee, B. and Stough, C. (2011). 'Recruitment consultant revenue: relationships with IQ, personality, and emotional intelligence', *International Journal of Selection and Assessment*, 19(3), 280–286.

Guinn, S. (2013). 'Predicting successful people', *Strategic HR Review*, 12(1), 26–31.

Lynch, S. and Smith, K. (2009). 'The dilemma of judging unpaid workers', *Personnel Review*, 39(1), 80–95.

Manchester City Council (2003). *Manchester Commonwealth Games Post Games Report*. Available at: www.gameslegacy.com; viewed 17 May 2006.

People 1st. (2010). *Labour Market Review of the Events Industry*. January. Available at: http://www. people1st.co.uk/research/reports/other-reports/researchprojects; viewed 2 January 2014.

Sinha, V. and Thaly, P. (2013). 'A review on changing trend of recruitment practice to enhance the quality of hiring in global organisations', *Management*, 18(2), 141–156.

Society for Human Resource Management (2004). *Reference and Background Checking Survey Report*. Denver: Society for Human Resource Management.

Williamson, P. (2005). 'Event management students' reflections on their placement year: an examination of their critical experiences'. In J. Allen (ed.), *International Event Research Conference 2005*. Sydney: University of Technology.

9

Workforce training

Learning objectives

After reading through this chapter you will be able to:

- Differentiate between the different types of training typically offered at major and mega events.
- Discuss the budget implications of volunteer training.
- Explain how to go about conducting a training needs analysis.
- Explain how the responsibility for training is split between functional areas.
- Identify key steps in designing web-based training.
- Discuss whether leadership training is important in the event environment and how this might differ from the traditional business environment.

Introduction

Training an event workforce is quite a challenge. Work for the core management team starts months or even years before the event and so many different types of training may be necessary, the most common being project management, risk analysis and legislative awareness. The core planning team tends to be made up of a very diverse group, everyone coming from different backgrounds and industries. To make life even more complicated, there are rolling starts, with people coming on board right through to the event operational period. How much simpler it would be if the planning team were all to start at once!

The second large group of people requiring training are engaged just for the event itself, most starting work on day one just before the doors open. This group includes most volunteers, contract workers and a few casual paid staff. For a large event, this group would participate in one or more training sessions in the days or weeks before the event to give them a general overview of the event and information on the venue. Importantly, emergency and incident planning would usually be covered at this time.

Job-specific training can seldom be done before the venues have been hired and transformed in readiness for the event. For most events the build happens only the day before the event. Workers start several hours before the audience arrives and training usually occurs on the job, just before the gates or doors open. Problems are then ironed out along the way. This situation dictates a higher than usual focus on pre-planning tasks and control measures before the event commences, as from that time on controlled chaos usually reigns. However, most problems are generally solved through a combination of common sense, commitment and goodwill, particularly if these values have been instilled prior to the event.

The training needs analysis

A training needs analysis is the basis for the training plan. It covers the training needs of both managers and the general workforce. The questions asked should include the following:

- What is the context for training?
- What are the profiles of the candidates undertaking training?
- How many people need to be trained?
- When and where do these people need to be trained?
- How could technology support the training?
- Who will be responsible for the various types of training?
- What approach should be taken (e.g. lecture, seminar, simulation) to each of these?
- Should training be outsourced to a contractor?
- What is the role of the trainer?
- Is assessment necessary?
- How will training be documented?
- What will it cost?
- Which aspects of training present the highest risk?
- How will the training be evaluated?

The training needs analysis can take many forms, from an informal approach where all functional and venue areas are responsible for their own training to a more formal approach where training needs are analysed across the organization. In this latter case, core training can be identified and delivery integrated across the organization wherever possible.

Where a formal approach is taken, this can be done by document analysis, research into previous events and approaches to training, individual interviews, observation and focus groups. A pilot programme is recommended for feedback and fine-tuning wherever possible, particularly for customer service training.

Prior to the Sydney 2000 Olympic Games there were two dilemmas (among many others): how to record attendance at large-scale orientation and venue training sessions where numbers in the audience ranged from 200 to 2,000; and whether or not to provide refreshments. As trivial as these questions may seem, there were budget and logistical implications for both. A cup of tea and a biscuit for each volunteer attending training would cost in the region of $50,000, while attendance records would require manual registration and subsequent data entry or a more sophisticated barcode/identification card system. This seemed unnecessary as each person would receive an accreditation badge closer to the event, but this system was not yet operational.

The budget and time allocated to training varies widely, depending on the type and duration of the event. Long-term personnel need extensive, just-in-time programmes, while casual or hourly staff working for only three days would need the bare minimum training. In the area of business events, hotels and convention centres are generally relied upon to provide skilled staff, particularly in the area of food and beverage. However, the quality of service provided could be improved if the team was provided with a short, informal briefing about the event audience and programme. Rogers (2007) provides a chapter on conference and convention staffing and training. However, specific research on training relevant to business events is lacking. Ladkin and McCabe's (2010) research focuses on the stresses and poor quality of the working environment and the toll this takes on motivation.

In the current environment, recording attendance at training sessions (or participation in online training) ensures that there are records in relation to safety knowledge, this being a risk treatment option for health and safety of the event workforce and audience. Many venues now provide online safety training as a pre-requisite for the many and varied people that work at the venue. Glastonbury was one of the first events to start using the Event Safety Passport scheme to ensure everyone working on site had basic safe working knowledge. Playbill Venues Safety Induction is another such programme, this one being offered fully online.

The audience for training is an important consideration. Reeser et al. (2005) found that the highly qualified health professionals working at the 2002 Winter Games environment were dissatisfied with training, the study finding that physicians tended to have lower overall satisfaction scores with regard to the administrative aspects of the volunteer experience, such as pre-games training, despite being generally well satisfied with the overall experience.

Costa et al. (2006: 165) suggest that training can contribute to volunteer satisfaction, arguing that 'the training of event volunteers should be conceived and designed as an opportunity to build a sense of community among volunteers and staff so as to enhance volunteer commitment and satisfaction'.

Management training

The management team usually needs training in specific topic areas since it is common for the core team to come from a range of different backgrounds. Training can be formal or informal, and run internally or outsourced to expert facilitators. Given the expertise of the management group, training has to be well delivered by someone experienced in adult learning and the event context. Because of the pressures of time faced by people in this role, a training room can be emptied after the coffee break if the learning is not relevant and meaningful to the group!

The following topics are indicative of material covered during induction training and later on during the planning period as needs emerge:

- history and purpose of the event, strategic plan;
- project management principles and techniques, including software;
- risk management for all aspects of the operation, including safety;
- legislative awareness, compliance issues;
- roles of stakeholders such as police, traffic authority, sponsors, etc.
- cultural and disability awareness;
- recruitment and selection, including equal opportunity;
- supervision/leadership (more on this later in the chapter);
- operational planning, systems and procedures;
- contract negotiation, contractor management;
- delivering training at the venue or on the job for large and small audiences;
- customer service management.

This training can be delivered in a variety of formats, ranging from online tutorials (e.g. software use) to short sessions conducted by experts or visiting speakers during lunch periods. Conventional training would seldom take more than a day. Depending on the size of the event, some of the above topics could be merged into one or more sessions.

Professional development

There are an increasing number of universities and colleges offering diplomas, degrees and post-graduate qualifications in this field. In China and other parts of Asia the focus of these qualifications is the business events sector (MICE). There have been several initiatives to define the curriculum (Xu and Luo, 2007; Silvers et al., 2006) and there are several certifications available from industry associations such as Certified Meeting Professional (CMP) and the Certified Special Event Professional (CSEP). For updates in this area the AEME (Association for Events Management Education) website is recommended. The objectives of this association are to

- provide a discussion forum for issues affecting events education and industry;
- establish communication opportunities between events stakeholders;
- encourage the development and dissemination of the events management body of knowledge;
- support, undertake and disseminate events research;
- encourage international exchange of ideas and best practice in events.

Getz (2012) in his book, *Event Studies: Theory, Research and Policy for Planned Events*, links various interdisciplinary fields for study and research in the field and Silvers et al. (2006) have initiated the EMBOK (event management body of knowledge) as the basis for curriculum in this area. The authors Bowdin, Getz, Silvers and McCabe have produced an outstanding body of work to support the status of the event professional and the field of event studies as an important area for research.

CASE STUDY 9.1
The International Special Events Society (ISES)

The International Special Events Society provides members and stakeholders with:

- collaborative networking
- education and professional development
- inspiration
- outward awareness and credibility

to ensure a thriving global creative events profession.

ISES was founded in 1987 to foster enlightened performance through education while promoting ethical conduct. ISES works to join event and meeting professionals to focus on the 'event as a whole' rather than its individual parts. ISES has grown to involve over 5,500 members active in over 50 chapters throughout the world.

ISES offers comprehensive, year-round, local and international educational experiences for professionals in the creative events industry such as ISES Live. ISES Live is a continuing education conference for the creative events industry where attendees have the opportunity to improve their professional skills and knowledge.

Certification is offered and the CSEP (Certified Special Events Professional) designation is the hallmark of professional achievement in the special events industry. It is earned through education, performance, experience, and service to the industry, and reflects a commitment to professional conduct and ethics. The CSEP designation is awarded by the International Special Events Society (ISES) and its Certification Committee. ISES is the only international umbrella organization representing professionals in all disciplines of the special events industry. Education and a commitment to professionalism are cornerstones of ISES.

Source: http://www.ises.com/ises/home. Reprinted with permission from the International Special Events Society, Inc. (2014). All rights reserved.

Reflective practice 9.1

- Discuss the statement, 'Event managers have not achieved professional status'.
- Discuss the statement, 'Event studies is firmly established as a field of academic research'.
- Explain how associations, such as ISES can contribute to the reputation of professional event managers.

General workforce training

Most major events follow the same formula for workforce training delivery and some examples are listed below. For all of the following events there were three types of training for the general workforce – orientation (general) training, venue training and job-specific/ role training:

- Sydney 2000 Olympic Games
- Manchester 2002 Commonwealth Games
- Salt Lake City Winter Olympic Games 2002
- Asian Games Doha 2006
- Torino Winter Olympic Games 2006
- Melbourne Commonwealth Games 2006
- London Olympic Games 2012
- Manchester Commonwealth Games 2014.

In Sochi (2014) the programme consisted of three main parts: 'My Games', 'Job Specific Training' and 'Venue Specific Training', and a special English language course with an emphasis on event themes. While these can be merged for smaller events, it is nonetheless worthwhile to look at each separately.

Orientation training

This training is a general introduction to the event, its history, mission, purpose, planning and programme. For sporting events it covers all the different sports and the different venues at which they will take place. For music events, this session would explain the different bands and stages; for an agricultural show it would cover the competition and commercial zones. There is usually a general introduction to customer service, disability awareness and cultural awareness. More than this, however, most orientation training is highly motivational, and this is achieved through the use of celebrity speakers, national songs and dance, music and inspiring words from key members of the organizing committee.

The two main aims are that people leaving the session are informed and inspired. This is an interesting point, as the discussion later in the chapter on web-based training will illustrate, since much of this information could be delivered online. The question is whether this approach would meet the psychological needs of volunteers, in particular, to feel included, involved and inspired.

Following are examples of the topics that might be covered in orientation training:

- event overview
- event history
- event aims
- symbols
- organization
- sponsors
- event programme

- event venues
- performers or athletes
- previous shows/events
- workforce roles
- what to expect
- commitment and expectations
- customer service.

Venue training

As the title suggests, this type of training usually takes place at the venue to familiarize people with their working environment (a treasure hunt is a good way to do this) and their teams. Functional areas, teams and reporting relationships are discussed during this training and work groups get the opportunity to meet each other. The most significant part covers safety and emergency training, which is often venue specific. In some cases, orientation training and venue training can be combined as they were with the 1996 Atlanta Olympic Games.

Following are some of the topics that might be covered in venue training sessions:

- the event precinct (general area of operations);
- the event venue (performance location);
- locations within the venue (e.g. stairs, lifts, exits, communications control);
- functional areas represented at the venue (e.g. medical, accreditation, security);
- accreditation zones/areas (who can go where);
- safety of staff and visitors;
- emergency procedures;
- incident reporting;

PLATE 9.1 Event orientation training session

- crowd control;
- recycling and waste management;
- staff procedures, check-in, meals, etc.;
- communicating in the team;
- staff rules;
- common questions customers will ask;
- venue management team and their support.

Job-specific training

This is very specific training for the particular job that the person is going to do. For the majority of roles this takes only an hour or two. However, there are some positions that require many hours of training in the lead-up to the event. This can sometimes be short-circuited using video or web-based multimedia for core training (e.g. in the use of two-way radios). Job-specific training will be covered in detail in the next chapter.

The issue raised in many event evaluation reports (Sydney 2000 Paralympic Games Post Games Report, 2001; Strategic training issues for the 2006 Commonwealth Games, 2002; Manchester Commonwealth Games Post Games Report, 2003; Delhi Commonwealth Games Post Games Report, 2010) is the sequence in which this training is delivered. The

PLATE 9.2 Workflow planning and training are essential for catering teams who work at a frantic pace

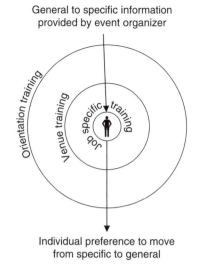

General to specific information
provided by event organizer

Individual preference to move
from specific to general

FIGURE 9.1 Different preferences for order of training

order suggested in Figure 9.1 is most logical from the event organizer's perspective as it follows the general project plan of moving from the general to the specific. The information required for orientation training is generally available some time out, while venue overlays are only finalized shortly before the event and specific planning for particular jobs is finalized very late in the process, with small details requiring input from other functional areas.

From the volunteer's perspective, on the other hand, what they most urgently want to know is where they will work, what they will do, what they will wear, when they will start and finish, whether meals will be hot or cold, whether particular dietary needs will be met, and so on. Details such as rosters, meal voucher systems and locker allocation are seldom available right from the start. Thus, as Figure 9.1 shows, the event organizer needs to be mindful of the workforce's priority for personally relevant information over event history!

For the smaller event, all of this can be collapsed into a pre-event tour of the site and a briefing. Checklists and careful supervision will then ensure that things go smoothly.

Web-based training

Many of the above problems could of course be avoided if most of the training were delivered online. People would not need cups of tea, they would not have to travel or park, they would not need invitations or books or videos. Brandon Hall (1997) has written a primer on planning web-based training for anyone working in training and development. This book provides outstanding advice for the design and development of this type of training but recommends specialist support for the finer details. He also suggests posing the following questions before setting off on this pathway and these are answered as follows:

Is this the best method of training?

While there are significant efficiencies associated with Web based training, the most important question is whether the motivational content can be delivered using this medium. The informational content can definitely be provided on the Web, and with good instructional design this can become quite interactive. By monitoring use of the website, and the pathways people follow in navigating it, the organizing committee has a very accurate idea of the level of interest. Furthermore, the website can be used for conducting assessment on key topics such as health and safety, thus demonstrating an adequate level of learning.

Should we do this in-house or outsource it?

Events with a website designed for ticket sales to the general public may be extended to provide training information to staff. This is often done using a user name and password so that employees can access the instructional parts of the site. Many human resource functions can be managed this way, including roster planning. One needs to consider the effort involved in development as well as maintenance of the site.

What are some of the problems that may be associated with online training (such as some individuals not having access or bandwidth)?

Although most people have access to computers, at the very least through public libraries and internet cafes, the issue of bandwidth is an important one. If the site includes sophisticated and memory hungry video, for example, this is going to prove difficult for many users. The alternative is burning the site to a USB format but this means that it cannot be maintained with the most up to date information available. One also needs to consider staff with a disability when preparing training materials, for instance, deciding whether materials need to be available in audio, large print, braille, etc.

Can the cost be justified?

A website with bells and whistles, one that has good instructional design, graphics etc. that can maintain the interest of a generation that has played computer games is likely to cost a small fortune, so the cost needs to be carefully considered.

Who will be needed on the development team?

The development team needs to include a project manager; an instructional designer who develops scripts and story boards; a programmer or author who can use the authoring tool; a graphic artist; writers or subject matter experts; and of course a webmaster for hosting the programme.

Are there issues with approving the content of web information and graphics?

Major events often have an approved style for all communications including website, ticketing and signage. This includes font types and sizes, font colours, background colours, graphics etc. In addition to this sponsors and other stakeholders need to approve all logos and content relevant to their roles. The approvals process is arduous, statements about safety need to be checked by the relevant functional area, statements about meals need to be checked by catering, the list is endless. However this is not unique to online training, it is just as big a task with print materials.

What level of interactivity will there be?

A website can be simply informative, with the user navigating their way through links to find the information they want to find. Alternatively, sophisticated design can guide learners through a process where interaction is indicative of learning. Asking how much multimedia is realistic is a related question, linked to design, outcomes and budget.

Is there any assessment planned?

This question is important for any type of training, whether online or not. Will there be any assessment of how much learning has taken place? This is increasingly the case in the area of workplace health and safety. Even the smallest event these days is likely to issue a multiple choice test on safety with a requirement that everyone must score over 80 per cent. One such test had all the answers as (d) just to make it easy for most people and to eliminate those who were not listening and not very bright!

Who will have access to the training material?

This is a most interesting question. For many mega and hallmark events there are many people clamouring for information including sponsors, universities and organizations 'outside the tent'. They are serving the interests of the event and want to train their people. In a pre-emptive move the Beijing Organizing Committee for the Olympic Games launched their pre-Games training guide on their website a full three years before the event (see Figure 9.2). This enabled all these parties to commence orientation type training a long way ahead.

The decision regarding web-based training is a difficult one if the event is a one-off occurrence. If, on the other hand, the event is held annually, then the investment made in training can be carried through to the following year (see Figure 9.3). Event organizations such as Cleanevent, mentioned in the last chapter, are well placed to develop web-based human resource systems for training and rostering as they are involved in so many events year after year.

Leadership training

Leadership training has become a common feature of training for event supervisors and managers. The training aims are to develop workforce motivation and increase retention. One of the first of these programmes was developed for the 2000 Sydney Olympic Games in response to problems experienced in Atlanta in 1996, which included staff poaching, wage blowouts and volunteer attrition (Webb, 2001). While industrial relations initiatives were largely credited with the success that ensued, it was also widely accepted that recruitment, selection and training strategies also worked towards developing a sophisticated and well-trained workforce – according to Juan Antonio Samaranch, 'the best volunteers ever'.

The training needs analysis for event leadership for the 2000 Olympic Games included a literature review, analysis of previous event training materials, individual interviews and focus group sessions. The last of these were exceptionally useful, bringing a large number of experienced event professionals from around the world into one room to discuss the

CONTENTS		
Beijing Olympic Games Organizing Committee President Liu Qi's Message		⊕
Chinese Olympic Committee President Yuan Weimin's Message		
Prologue		
A. Introduction		⊕
Map of China: Administrative Regions	Map of China: Major Scenic Areas	
Map of Beijing	Introduction to China	
Introduction to Chinese Olympic Committee	Beijing Olympic Games Overview	
Attention		
B. Training sites and facilities by sport	⊕ 1st	⊕ 2nd
1. Athletics	2. Rowing	
3. Badminton	4. Baseball	
5. Basketball	6. Boxing etc. (28 sports)	
C. Training sites and facilities by region		
Beijing Municipality ⊕	Tianjin Municipality	⊕
Hebei Province ⊕	Shanxi Province	⊕
Liaoning Province ⊕	Heilongjiang Province	⊕
Qinghai Province ⊕	Etc. (25 regions)	
D. Others		⊕
Application Form	Key Contacts	
Acknowledgment		

FIGURE 9.2 Website training guide for the Beijing Olympic Games 2008 released three years prior to the Games

programme. The model illustrated in Figure 9.4 emerged directly from comments made by these experienced leaders. This in turn led to development of a video and a game to match the model. While subsequent models have been developed (e.g. Van Der Wagen, 2010), the first model is discussed and illustrated here as a direct outcome of the training needs analysis for Sydney 2000:

> As a result of our research the model that we developed is called the 'Special Events Leadership Model'. One of the features of this model is the contrasting nature of leadership roles. In some situations, a leader has to be directive and autocratic, such as in a crisis, and in others a leader needs to be collaborative and appreciative. This paradoxical and flexible approach seemed well suited to the dynamic event context.

Proposal development – overview, audience and learning objectives

⇩

Media design – consistent appearance, inclusion of style standards

⇩

Flowchart of training – linking learning strategies

⇩

Scripts and storyboards for programming

⇩

Prototype development and testing

⇩

Release within the organization

⇩

Release to the event workforce

FIGURE 9.3 Stages of development for web-based training

Leadership roles	Event leadership competencies
Planning	• visioning, planning and goal setting • designing and organizing work • workforce contingency planning
Co-ordinating/controlling	• training • delegating work • monitoring and tracking performance
Directing	• maintaining focus and priority • communicating effectively • using leadership styles effectively
Decision-making	• understanding policy and procedure • making and implementing decisions, escalating • negotiating agreement and commitment
Informing	• providing timely, updated information • listening, harnessing feedback • presenting and reinforcing messages
Appreciating	• matching rewards and recognition to individual needs • recognizing and appreciating individual performance • recognizing and appreciating team performance
Managing time/stress	• managing time • managing self/stress • managing conflict
Energizing	• initiating and energizing the team • acting as a role model • building 'fun factors'

FIGURE 9.4 Event leadership model

Another feature of the model is an illustration of roles as part of a circle without sequential order. In most organizations in which business is conducted over a longer time span, the processes of leadership are largely sequential, moving from planning through to organizing and controlling. In contrast, event leadership requires a higher level of flexibility. Three roles were specifically identified as being important, and these are appreciating, managing time and stress, and energizing. These are not roles that are generally made explicit in traditional leadership texts.

The quote that follows is an explanation of the concept of energizing and the role it has to play in maintaining an upbeat atmosphere, which was one of the volunteers' main expectations (see also Figure 9.5). They would work hard, but they wanted to have fun too.

Energizing

One of the biggest challenges for most events is the creation of a celebratory atmosphere. Look at it like hosting a party – you are the host and have to look like you are enjoying yourself while you are working like crazy for everyone's enjoyment. Both customers and team members look to you to take the initiative to build and maintain the atmosphere and create the ambience. Many event staff say that one of their motivators is the opportunity to join in and enjoy the atmosphere. The positive buzz that this can create can be quickly destroyed through poor leadership. Energizing is the most intangible leadership role but it is arguably the most important. Careful use of gestures, tone of voice and the building of the 'fun factors' is required to meet the expectations of all staff. For many of those involved fun is an essential motivator, and spontaneity, humour and high levels of energy are required. This is very different from traditional leadership roles within most business environments. Many energizing strategies, as with appreciation strategies, can be planned in advance. Using icebreakers, games and jokes can help to create the right atmosphere.

FIGURE 9.5 Energizing – an important aspect of event leadership

Managing and co-ordinating the training programme

While for some events there is a specific functional area responsible for training, in many cases responsibility for training devolves to the supervisors. A marathon, for example, is unlikely to have more than one person assigned to the training role. A community children's festival might not have anyone in the role but expect training to simply evolve as the need arises. Learning would be largely an outcome of many planning meetings, and training would occur in the form of briefings before commencement. Where it is a multi-venue, multi-session event, training requires much more attention. Typically, Human Resources or Training and Development (if there are such functional areas) would take overall responsibility for co-ordinating planning for the three workforce training sessions described earlier in this chapter, but would prepare and present only core components of the programme, including orientation. The event management team would be responsible for venue training, and supervisors for job-specific training. And sometimes training is outsourced, as it was for the volunteers in Case Study 9.2.

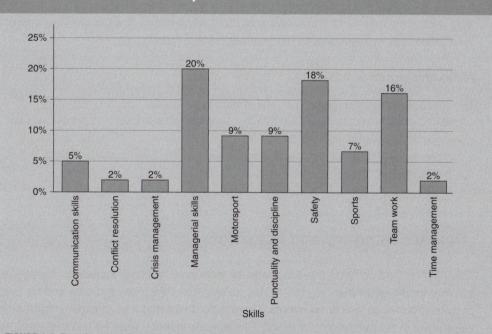

CASE STUDY 9.2
Transferable skills for sports volunteers

FIGURE 9.6 Transferable skills attained by volunteers, Abu Dhabi F1 Grand Prix
Source: www.fia.com/sites/default/files/basicpage/file/ATCUnitedArabEmiratesVolunteers-0.pdf

Transferable skill acquisition is again very much linked to levels of training. Based on this premise, the team investigated if the skills taken from their volunteering experiences were deemed to be of any benefit outside of their duties. From those volunteers who answered this question, an alarming 49 per cent felt that they were not, with the remaining 51 per cent in more positive agreement. It is important to note that a sizeable number of volunteers did not answer this question; this was taken to mean that they disagreed with the statement suggested to them. Approximately 20 per cent of this subset agreed that their managerial skills were improved as a result of the training they had received. Improvements in safety awareness were reported by 18 per cent of the group. Team working skills were noted by some 16 per cent and 9 per cent acknowledged increases in motor sport and punctuality skills. Other notable advances were recorded in sport skills (7 per cent), communication (5 per cent), conflict resolution, crisis management and time management (2 per cent). The prospect of learning new skills and using these skills to advance career prospects is an important belief which motivates a large number of volunteers. ATCUAE is committed to these ideals, providing opportunities for volunteers to develop skills required beyond the realm of motor sport. Therefore it is pleasing to see that a number of the volunteers realised some transferable skills advancement in important competencies such as management and team work. This outcome is to be welcomed and improves the chances of retaining volunteers for future events in the Formula 1 calendar.

However, it is important to highlight that 49 per cent felt that the training they had received offered no improvements to their transferable skills set. In acknowledging this fact, it is timely to remember that significant numbers did not attend many training sessions. Furthermore a lot of the volunteers questioned were highly experienced. It is possible that a lot of these individuals, in their own view, had nothing more to learn.

Reflective practice 9.2

1 Which areas showed the highest level of skills attainment?
2 Many survey participants did not see any improvements in their transferable skill set. Discuss the potential reasons for this.
3 How can training design and work practice increase the transferability of skills to new environments?

Chapter summary and key points

This chapter has covered the full scope of workforce training, including management training, for the event planning team. This training can take many formats, and be formal or quite informal, as with small events. There is no doubt that a lot of experiential learning takes place in the planning of an event. This is aided in many ways by training, mentoring and learning through trial and error.

In order to prepare the workforce for the operational period there are typically three levels of training: orientation training, venue training and job-specific training. The larger the event, the greater the time between the first training session and the start date of the event. For a mega event, the majority of training would occur approximately three months

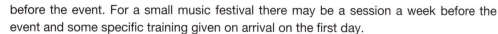

before the event. For a small music festival there may be a session a week before the event and some specific training given on arrival on the first day.

Event leadership training is an essential component for all supervisors, particularly those who have volunteers as their responsibility. The energy and commitment developed by event leaders translates into outstanding customer service.

Revision questions

1   List and expand on four training topics for managers involved in the event organization during the planning phase. For a specific event, identify which of these would be the highest priority.
2   Explain the three levels of training: orientation (general) training, venue training, and job-specific (job role) training.
3   What are three of the logistical considerations associated with developing the overall training plan for the event organization?
4   Discuss why it is difficult to make a decision regarding online training for the event workforce.
5   What is the aim of event leadership training? Give an example of an event for which you think this type of training would be imperative.

Industry voice by Kerrie Nash

I often talk about the fact that in a Games environment there are different attributes of the three different workforces. First of all, there is the paid staff who of course are known to us and work with us every day. The volunteers, once they have gone through the recruitment process, are known to us but don't work with us every day, so they're sitting out in the community waiting for their day. That's an interesting concept from an HR point of view. You have this workforce that you've recruited, but you've got them on standby for something like 12 months before they start working.

Finally, of course, the contractor's workforces are completely unknown to us. We might know which contracting organizations we are working with 6–12 months or so out, give or take. You bring those organizations on board and you can start talking to the organizations, but the individuals are completely unknown to you until such time as they go through accreditation, and they turn up at the venue.

To me the tools that you have to build those three groups together is your communications and engagement programmes and your training programmes, which are certainly very much geared towards trying to build that one team culture.

Things to think about in workforce training are the fact that the volunteer and contractor workforces are often working between 10 to 20 shifts. So the time spent in training has to be commensurate – you can't ask a volunteer to give up a week of their time in training to work 10 shifts. Training has to be extremely focused, relevant and outcome-oriented.

Discussion questions

1   Explain the three different workforces and their different training needs.
2   What are the core components of focused training?
3   Do you think training for volunteers could be fully online in future?

References

Automobile and Touring Club of the United Arab Emirates (2012). *Economic Impact Report for Volunteers Of The 2012 Abu Dhabi F1 Grand Prix*. Available at: http://www.fia.com/sites/default/files/basicpage/file/ATC%20United%20Arab%20Emirates%20Volunteers_0.pdf; viewed 18 February 2014.

Beijing Organising Committee for the Olympic Games (2005). *The Pre-Games Training Guide: The 29th Olympic Games China 2004–2008*. Available at: http:/len.beijing-2008.org/71/76/column211637671.shtml, viewed 12 July 2005.

Costa, C. A., Chalip, L., Christine Green, B. and Simes, C. (2006). 'Reconsidering the role of training in event volunteers' satisfaction', *Sport Management Review*, 9(2), 165–182.

Getz, D. (2012). *Event Studies: Theory, Research and Policy for Planned Events*. London: Routledge.

Hall, B. (1997). *Web-based Training Cookbook*. New York: John Wiley.

Ladkin, A. and McCabe, V. (2010). Human Resource Issues and Trends in the UK Conventions and Exhibitions Industry. Available at: http://eprints.bournemouth.ac.uk/18969/3/cautladka%28Revised%29.pdf; viewed 8 June 2014.

Manchester City Council (2003). Manchester Commonwealth Games Post Games Report. Viewed 2 July 2013, http://www.thecgf.com/media/games/2002/volume1.pdf.

Organising Committee Commonwealth Games Delhi 2010 (2010). *Commonwealth Games Post Games Report*. Available at: http://www.thecgf.com/games/2010/D2010-Post-Games-Report.pdf; viewed 3 June 2014.

Reeser, J. C., Berg, R. L., Rhea, D. and Willick, S. (2005). 'Motivation and satisfaction among polyclinic volunteers at the 2002 Winter Olympic and Paralympic Games', *British Journal of Sports Medicine*, 39(4), e20–e20.

Rogers, T. (2007). *Conferences and Conventions*. London: Routledge.

Silvers, J. R., Bowdin, G. A., O'Toole, W. J. and Nelson, K. B. (2006). 'Towards an international event management body of knowledge (EMBOK)', *Event Management*, 9(4), 185–198.

Sydney Paralympic Organising Committee (2001). *Sydney 2000 Paralympic Games Post Games Report 2001*. Olympic Co-ordination Authority. Available at: http://fulltext.ausport.gov.au/fulltext/2002/nsw/fin_cont_report.pdf; viewed 20 December 2013.

Tourism Training Victoria (2002). Strategic Training Issues for the 2006 Commonwealth Games, Melbourne. Available at: www.gamesinfo.com.au/postgames/pa/pg001301.htm; viewed 20 February 2002.

Van Der Wagen, L. (2010). *Event Management*, 4th edn. Sydney: Pearson Education.

Webb, T. (2001). *The Collaborative Games: The Story Behind the Spectacle*. Sydney: Pluto Press.

Xu, Hong-gang and Luo, Qui-ju (2007). 'International event management educational models and implications', *Journal of Guilin Institute of Tourism* (2), 83–84.

Job-specific training

Learning objectives

After reading through this chapter you will be able to:

- Plan job-specific training.
- Link training to job requirements.
- Deliver small group training.
- Describe a range of training methods.
- Evaluate training.

Introduction

Job-specific (role specific) training is required for every event regardless of size. Each person on site needs to know what to do. In this chapter we will use the simple formula of plan, deliver, assess and evaluate training (see Figure 10.1). These four steps are the basic elements of small group and individual training for specific skills and knowledge.

Food safety training will be used as an example to illustrate job-specific training as it is a rare event that does not provide food as part of the event experience, whether provided by the event organization's caterers or a contractor. In each case, food safety planning and food safety training still must be carried out. The starting point for developing job-specific training is the job description and, if available, the pertinent parts of the project plan. These enable the trainer to take the first step, preparing for one-to-one or group instruction.

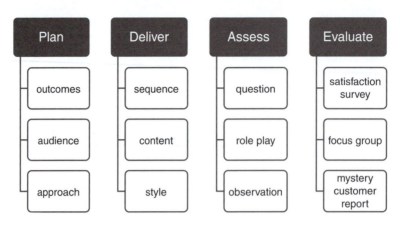

FIGURE 10.1 Planning training for specific jobs

Planning training

Planning is one of the most crucial parts of training. It involves breaking down the task into elements, deciding how best to explain and demonstrate these elements and then obtaining feedback from the learner about their progress. While this sounds easy, Burns points out 'the act of training does not lend itself well to techniques, formulas, dogma or event logic; it is a dynamic process of interaction between humans that unfolds over time and is dependent on the elegant execution of complex skills' (Burns, 2000: 31). While this seems a contradiction of the opening remarks in this chapter, even the most spontaneous of trainers would agree that their dynamic approach to meeting audience needs is based on a plan. This plan provides the bedrock for training: identifying learning outcomes. Thus, while the trainer might deviate, expand or become side-tracked, it is ultimately necessary to work back to the learning outcomes in the training plan and make sure that these, as a minimum, are achieved.

Placing ourselves in the position of event catering co-ordinator, we can see from the extract that follows that there is a role to play in training staff in food safety (State Government of Victoria, Australia, 2006). This is replicated across nearly every functional area. However, in this case there are regulations that have to be met, making this training vitally important.

When your organization holds an event where there will be food sold – for instance, a fete, sausage sizzle or cake stall – you will need to appoint an event co-ordinator. It is the role of the event co-ordinator to ensure that all food handlers at the event, whether they are volunteers or paid workers, understand the relevant food safety and safe food handling practices for the tasks which they are to be carrying out. To communicate such information to all food handlers, the event co-ordinator will have to conduct training or group discussions about food safety before the event.

The event co-ordinator must be familiar with the following:

- the food safety programme for the event;
- safe food-handling practices;
- personal hygiene – for instance, correct washing and drying of hands;
- efficient cleaning procedures;
- safe food preparation;
- correct storage and transportation of food;
- how to conduct temperature checks;
- safe food display.

Having seen a specific example of a clearly identified training need, let us look at the training needs analysis for other roles and tasks before returning to this example of food safety training.

The training needs analysis for job-specific training generally needs to be facilitated by the event co-ordinator. This is done by discussing training with the relevant functional area supervisor.

The following questions are a guide for a training needs analysis:

1   What is the job title?
2   Who is responsible for conducting this training?

PLATE 10.1 Job specific training on site (the beach)

3 How many people are going to do this job (individual or group)?
4 What are the skills required?
5 What is the knowledge required?
6 What are the training objectives or learning outcomes?
7 How much does this person/group already know?
8 Are there any special requirements such as accredited training?
9 Having reviewed the common training modules (e.g. orientation training, customer service, health and safety awareness), what are the remaining training objectives for this specific job?
10 What training method will be used (small group training, one-to-one training, self-directed training)?
11 When and where will training take place?
12 How long will it take?
13 Is equipment required?
14 What training materials are needed, including print materials?
15 Will there be any form of assessment?
16 How difficult is this likely to be for the participants?
17 How critical is this training to the success of the event?

The most important of these questions is number six: what are the training objectives or learning outcomes? A training objective (or learning outcome) states what the person can do or should know on completion of training, generally beginning with a verb. For example: 'On completion of training the catering assistant will be able to prevent food poisoning by practising good personal hygiene'. Another example would be: 'On completion of training the customer services officer will be able to explain the layout of the event site and provide directions to services and facilities'.

Once the overall job training plan has been developed, instruction needs to be planned in detail, including the particular steps that the trainer would follow. For the training objective, 'practising good personal hygiene', the State Government of Victoria, Australia, Department of Human Services (2006) recommends that the following skills and knowledge are required:

Objective: Prevent food poisoning by practising good personal hygiene

Demonstrable skills (these would be covered by demonstration and practice):

• Wear clean protective clothing, like an apron.
• Thoroughly wash and dry your hands before handling food.
• Dry your hands with clean towels, disposable paper towels or under an air dryer.
• Use disposable gloves.

Knowledge (these would be covered by explanation, example and questioning):

• Never smoke, chew gum, spit, change a baby's nappy or eat in a food handling or food storage area.
• Never cough or sneeze over food or where food is prepared or stored.
• Keep your spare clothes and other personal items away from where food is stored and prepared.

- If you have long hair, tie it back or cover it.
- Keep your nails short so they are easy to clean; don't wear nail polish which can chip into the food.
- Avoid wearing jewellery, only plain banded rings and sleeper earrings.
- If you have cuts or wounds, make sure they are completely covered by a waterproof wound strip or bandage. Use brightly coloured wound strips, so they can be easily seen if they fall off.
- Wear disposable gloves over the top of the wound strip if you have wounds on your hands.
- Change disposable gloves regularly.
- Don't handle food if you feel unwell, advise your supervisor.
- Follow the event Food Safety Programme.
- Follow the advice given by the Food Safety Supervisor.
- Be trained in safe food handling (this to follow in detail).

As Figure 10.2 illustrates, once the training objectives or learning outcomes have been developed, planning can commence. However, it is necessary to be mindful of the participants' prior skills and knowledge to ensure that they are not being taught something they already know. Performance deficiencies, such as not wearing gloves while preparing food, may be a result of laziness and poor supervision, not a lack of knowledge.

Training delivery

A training session for food safety is most effectively delivered using demonstration and practice, explanations, questions and answers. Following is an example of a demonstration of how hands should be washed prior to handling food. While it may be self-evident that people should wash their hands, do they do it properly? A test of this is to put zinc cream (the sort cricketers wear on their noses) on participants' hands and ask them to wash them. It is surprising how long it takes and how thorough one has to be to do it properly. This results in an indelible lesson, and hopefully no indelible zinc on the hands! Imaginative presentation is always appreciated.

Using the zinc (which comes in many vibrant colours), the trainer can also demonstrate how the 'germs' are transferred to utensils, plates, pot handles, etc.

Role plays are another way to make a point. At one venue training session, for example, the event manager and the event assistant manager played out a charade about the 'good volunteer' and the 'bad volunteer', which was hugely appreciated by the audience. The bad guy got waylaid on the way home from his first shift, went drinking in his volunteer uniform, forgot his accreditation pass in the morning and missed the train. The message was clear and everyone appreciated the participation of senior staff acting out their roles. Of course the 'good volunteer' laid out her clothes for the next morning (not forgetting her accreditation pass), was polite to people on the train, arrived on time as bright as a button and so on.

The following approaches to training delivery are a few of the many available to experienced trainers.

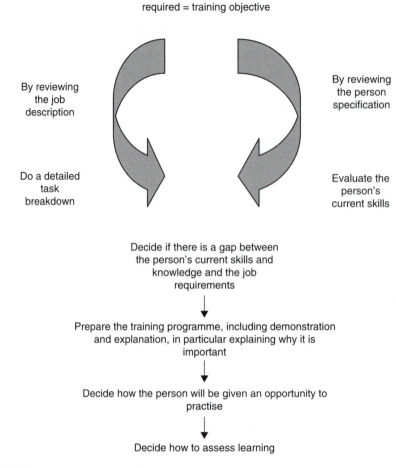

Describe the performance
required = training objective

By reviewing
the job
description

By reviewing
the person
specification

Do a detailed
task
breakdown

Evaluate the
person's
current skills

Decide if there is a gap between
the person's current skills and
knowledge and the job
requirements

Prepare the training programme, including demonstration
and explanation, in particular explaining why it is
important

Decide how the person will be given an opportunity to
practise

Decide how to assess learning

FIGURE 10.2 Planning and delivering training

Demonstration

'Show and tell' is sometimes used as a demonstration approach to training. But any elderly person who has been 'taught' anything on a computer by a teenager would know that watching someone else's fingers fly across the keyboard with screens changing faster than you can blink, would tell you that there is more to learning than simply watching. The information needs to be chunked into logical bits that the person can cope with and, even more importantly, the learner needs time to practise and consolidate at regular intervals. Otherwise the session just falls apart and the learner becomes completely overloaded. By shaping behaviour using modules of demonstration, practice and revision, the learner is more likely to grow in confidence. Thus the sequence for demonstration-style learning should be tell, show, do, review. As Figure 10.3 illustrates, the training session is broken down into a series of small tasks that are demonstrated and practised, in this case the training session is on how to use a two-way radio for the first time.

Turning on and off
• To Turn ON press and hold the Power button. A special 'beep' sound will be heard and the LCD Screen will display the current channel. • To switch OFF press and hold the Power button. A special 'beep' sound will be heard and the LCD Screen will turn blank. • To adjust the speaker volume, press the UP button to increase, or press the DOWN button to decrease.
Receiving a call
• Press the Menu button once, the Channel icon '8' will start blinking on the LCD. • Screen 2. While the Channel icon is blinking, press the UP or DOWN button to select the desired channel. The channel changes from 1 to 8, or from 8 to 1. 3. Press the TALK button again to confirm your selected channel. • The unit is continuously in Receive mode when the unit is turned ON and not transmitting. When a signal is received on the current channel, the receive signal icon 'RX' will be displayed on the LCD Screen.
Transmitting (sending)
• Press and hold the TALK (Push to Talk) button to transmit your voice. The transmit signal icon 'TX' will display on the LCD Screen and the RED LED indicator will light. • Hold the unit in a vertical position with the mic (Microphone) 5–10 cm away from the mouth. While holding the TALK button, speak into the mic (microphone) in a normal tone of voice. Release the TALK button when you have finished transmitting.

FIGURE 10.3 Explaining, practising and consolidating training using a task breakdown

Additionally, throughout the training the rationale, or logic of the action, should be explained. With the earlier example of hand washing, it would be appropriate to talk about the various types of food poisoning, their causes and symptoms. It would also be appropriate to discuss the repercussions for the event organization if a large number of people suffered from food poisoning. It is a very serious issue: for example, 200 Russian train travellers were hospitalized and another 450 treated after they had visited a festival (Mosnews, 2005).

Lecture

This training approach is best suited to a large audience. Most commonly it is used to explain emergency and evacuation procedures using demonstrations of the fire alarms, the preparatory alarm, 'please evacuate as directed by the fire wardens', and finally the rising tone 'woop woop' instructing all to evacuate. This training is usually delivered by the fire department or someone appropriately qualified.

Mentoring

Mentoring is used at management level to build expertise. An individual is assigned a mentor who monitors their learning, providing suggestions and provocation to stimulate learning. At lower skill levels, the buddy system is a sound approach to skills training, providing that the buddy is doing their job correctly and can explain why it is important. In the high-pressure event environment it is important to monitor this role as the training may deteriorate as it is passed on from one person to another. Checklists or diagrams can be helpful in preventing this occurrence.

Brainstorming

The creative field of event concept development and the unique features of event planning lend themselves well to brainstorming as an approach to learning. As plans become more and more specific, it is important to ensure that people are not locked in, but instead are stimulated to think of new and better ways to do things. According to Beckett and Hager (2002), organic learning needs to grow explicitly. They suggest three questions to bear in mind during hot action:

- What are we doing?
- Why are we doing it?
- What comes next?

These three questions can be immensely valuable as a focus for learning, for evolving plans, and for visionary and creative responses to complex problems.

Debate

While debating appears to be a very formal training method, when used in an energetic and humorous way it can emphasize two positions, highlighting sensitivity to differences in fact or opinion. For example, the topic of waste management and recycling as it is typically covered at event briefings can be quite a dry topic. An energetic debate on the merits of maintaining waste streams (and the associated costs) and against (why bother?) could be highly entertaining and get the message across.

Presentation

Presentations by visiting speakers such as police and first aid supervisors, sometimes as a segment of a programme, can contribute enormously to effective training. Likewise, an experienced volunteer with inspirational stories can raise the level of enthusiasm dramatically. If the presentation is followed by questions, they can also be used as an assessment approach to consolidate learning, enabling participants to explore and defend their learning.

Role play

This acting technique can be used to good effect in customer relations, disability and cultural awareness training. For example, it is clearly a most appropriate way to train staff working on the information booth at an event.

Group discussion

Group discussions can promote inclusiveness providing that they are run democratically, giving everyone a chance to participate. They also need to have a clear goal. Occupational health and safety committees can be run along these lines, although principles of effective meetings need to be applied, including minutes and agreements on emerging actions.

Guided discussion – conversational learning

This much more sophisticated idea is pitched at higher management levels: 'The role of the HR/HRD professional in conversational learning focuses on creating space for conversation, inviting different voices into the conversation, and cultivating a safe space for deliberation about difficult but meaningful issues' (Baker et al., 2002: 204). As these authors point out, this type of conversation can occur in a face-to-face interaction or online. Risk management planning or discussion about emerging threats to the organization or running of the event would be appropriate topics for conversational learning. Here the outcomes would be less clear-cut and the issues more nebulous.

Case studies

Problem-based case studies have been widely used in medicine and more recently in the business environment (Gallagher, 2011; Hmelo-Silver, 2012; Beetham and Sharpe, 2013). Case studies are an effective way for participants to become involved in realistic and problematic situations, away from the pressure of the real situation. This type of experiential learning is likely to foster learning on a higher order level, such as critical thinking. In the event environment, problem-based case studies for customer service are particularly useful.

Simulations – experiential learning

In the mega event business it is typical to run a series of 'test events', which are a training ground for event staff, most particularly those responsible for managing the competition. For example, the Nordic Skiing World Cup held in January 2005 was a test event for the Winter Olympic Games in Torino in 2006. This is as close a simulation as you can get!

Many trainers use a combination of techniques. For example, following a test event, a brainstorming session could be held to iron out procedures and finalize job descriptions for specific roles. Specific incidents that occurred could be part of a group discussion. A visiting speaker (such as a competition manager) could make a presentation or a volunteer could talk about their experience. A trainer needs to be attentive to the needs of the audience and remain highly responsive to their feedback. This usually comes in the form of enthusiastic participation, ranging from doodling through to text messaging.

There are a number of ways in which a trainer can obtain feedback during delivery to make sure that the session is on track and meeting audience needs:

- Ask the group how many would like to step through the information again.
- Provide a self-check quiz and find out what people scored (1–5, 6–10,11–15, etc.).
- Reinforce information by providing a framework (such as a flow chart) for learners to complete during the presentation.
- Ask learners to check their skills by practising with a procedure checklist and then without one.
- Leave out a key step on a list of steps and see how many can remember what to do.
- Ask learners to rate their skill level against your learning outcomes.
- Find out which parts are not clear.
- Find out which parts are perceived by learners to be most important.
- Ask specific questions.
- Use both closed and open questions.
- Ask if there are any questions.
- Use a matching exercise to check understanding.
- Ask learners to check one another when trying out a skill.
- Provide self-check procedures, diagrams and lists to take home so that learners can check themselves.
- Develop a rating scale, or barometer, to check confidence at the start and finish of training.

Training assessment

The term 'assessment' is generally used in the context of assessing the learner, while evaluation focuses on the overall success (or otherwise) of the training programme, which will be discussed in the next section. Some of the suggestions for obtaining feedback listed in the last section are also assessment methods – ways in which the trainer can test understanding and skills. Observation and questioning are the two main methods of assessing a learner's progress.

Few events have the luxury of allowing novices to practise in real-time situations; most can only observe and correct staff and volunteers on the job. There are, however, some reasons why assessment may be required. The most significant of these is for risk management and insurance purposes. It may therefore be useful to be able to demonstrate that each person on site (including contractors) has undergone training and assessment in health and safety on site and is familiar with evacuation plans.

At all stages of training, it is important to carefully manage expectations. As Case Study 10.1 illustrates this can be done by pointing out the highs and lows of the role. Case Study 10.1 indicates the importance of managing volunteers' expectations.

Training evaluation

Where briefings and training sessions are planned and prepared prior to an event, it is a good idea to run a pilot session to evaluate the effectiveness of the programme to

CASE STUDY 10.1
Highs and lows

The highs ...

You will be performing a vital role, making sure venues operate safely. You will also get to meet and help people from all around the world, adding to their experience of the event.

... and possible lows

You will be working long days, often standing outside for extended periods. You won't get to see the field of play. The days will be intensive from start to finish and an exceptionally high level of service will be expected throughout.

Reflective practice 10.1

Reinforcing expectations by putting this wording in the training material is one way to deal with this issue. What are other ways in which you could ensure that the volunteer has a realistic understanding of job demands?

see that it is fit for the purpose. A focus group can be invited to the session to critique it and make suggestions for improvement. However, in the mega event environment of the Olympic Games, for example, this can sometimes lead to deficiencies in the final programme as a result of endless cycles of change and review by multiple stakeholders (Van Der Wagen, 2005).

Figure 10.4 provides a format for evaluation of a training session.

There are a number of other ways in which training can be evaluated, and this information should be included in the final event report. However, it is necessary to be aware that there are many variables at play and clear-cut research into the merits, benefits and outcomes of training is not easily achieved. Despite this, those responsible for training prior to a successful event like to claim that the success was a direct result of their efforts (Van Der Wagen, 2005), as do many other functional areas and stakeholders! Despite the difficulty associated with conducting scientific research in this complex area of social interaction, a post-event evaluation report is immensely valuable for events that follow. Qualitative data, in the form of quotes and case studies, are a useful legacy.

Training participant feedback sheets

These feedback sheets are given to participants immediately after the training session requesting feedback very similar to that illustrated in Figure 10.4. In the human resource development (HRD) world, these are known as 'happy sheets' as they indicate how happy

Presentation Please rate the following on a scale of 1–5 (with 1 the least successful and 5 the most successful)	Learning
Planning – room set-up and materials [ ] [ ] [ ] [ ] [ ]	Posed questions and used other ways to check learning [ ] [ ] [ ] [ ] [ ]
Purpose/objectives – clearly explained, people welcomed [ ] [ ] [ ] [ ] [ ]	Practice/application – given with guidance for learners [ ] [ ] [ ] [ ] [ ]
Process (session outline) – clearly explained [ ] [ ] [ ] [ ] [ ]	Practice/application – occurred independently for learners [ ] [ ] [ ] [ ] [ ]
Presentation – in small steps, logical, just enough information [ ] [ ] [ ] [ ] [ ]	Provided learners with support such as diagrams and checklists [ ] [ ] [ ] [ ] [ ]
Presentation – easy to hear, interesting and well paced [ ] [ ] [ ] [ ] [ ]	Problems solved if needed [ ] [ ] [ ] [ ] [ ]
Presentation – supported with visuals [ ] [ ] [ ] [ ] [ ]	Purpose/objectives – reviewed and closed with learners confident [ ] [ ] [ ] [ ] [ ]

FIGURE 10.4 Evaluation of pilot training programme by focus group

participants felt about the session. Note of course that they do not accurately indicate how much everyone learned.

Pre- and post-event interviews

A longitudinal study can be done, interviewing staff and volunteers pre- and post-event. This qualitative approach can also be matched with a quantitative skills rating sheet. To achieve research results that are valid and reliable would need careful planning, including selection of an appropriate sample group.

Mystery people studies

Evaluation of the effectiveness of training can also be conducted by using mystery customers, staff members and volunteers armed with key observation points and questions. These 'mystery shoppers' are much more aware of what they are looking for and may, for example, ask specific questions to evaluate responses on the job. The mystery customer may be primed to simulate heat exhaustion, for example, to evaluate the actions/responses of staff or volunteers. A mystery volunteer would likewise be well attuned to contextual factors and to the needs, expectations and experiences of their volunteer associates, including their satisfaction with the information provided during training, the skills needed and utilized, and unanticipated issues arising on the job.

On-the-job surveys and observation

Researchers armed with questionnaires can visit members of the event workforce and interview them on the job. They can also use observation techniques to evaluate skills in customer service, crowd management and information provision.

Critical incident analysis

This research methodology is used in many different circumstances. It is very valuable in that it uses one critical incident to highlight deficiencies in planning or execution. Likewise, it emphasizes successes, which are just as important a legacy of an event. Essentially, the questions are 'what worked' and 'what didn't work', with a specific example and an explanation for the reasons.

Case Study 10.2 illustrates the approach taken in a critical incident focus group.

Post-event management evaluation focus groups

There is another type of focus group that can be used for event evaluation, which is much more open ended, with general feedback about human resource strategies, including training. A number of focus groups could be arranged, including the following people:

- event management/organizing committee
- human resources and human resource development (trainers)
- functional and zone area managers
- supervisors
- paid staff
- volunteers.

For a smaller event, a focus group with each of the above representatives would be adequate.

Post-event analysis of risk planning and incident reports

Finally, it is essential that risk management plans for human resource management and training are revisited after the event to evaluate their accuracy. The risk ratings may or may

CASE STUDY 10.2
What worked? What didn't work?

The aim is to describe two incidents that illustrate positive and negative outcomes of the project with a view to developing recommendations for improvements in training for the next event or for future similar projects.

Please answer the following questions:

1   Please describe a negative incident (relevant to training effectiveness).
2   Why do you think this occurred?
3   What can we learn from this (to improve training effectiveness)?
4   Please describe a positive incident (relevant to training effectiveness).
5   Why do you think this occurred?
6   What can we learn from this (to improve training effectiveness)?
7   Do you have any other recommendations on training provided to the workforce for future events?
8   Do you have any other recommendations for future related projects?

Reflective practice 10.2

1   What is critical incident analysis?
2   Why is this approach useful for training evaluation?
3   Describe an alternative approach to training evaluation in detail.

not have been accurate, and there may be issues that emerged that were not anticipated at all.

Incident reports are another rich source of information about training effectiveness, particularly in the area of safety and customer service.

The training evaluation report

The training evaluation report is a valuable source of information for future event organizers. It can cover a wide scope including effectiveness of the following:

- contractual arrangements for delivery of training including venues and presenters;
- online training judged on many criteria, including user friendliness, accessibility, learner outcomes;
- training administration and record keeping;
- stakeholder involvement, including sponsors;
- media response to training initiatives;
- copyright clearance and other project timeline issues.

Surveys of participants are only one aspect of training evaluation.

Kraiger et al. (2004) take a strategic approach to training evaluation, suggesting that the first step is to develop a theory of impact. In doing so, business results that matter are linked to the knowledge and skills to do the job. Second, they suggest that the focus of the evaluation should be on evidence – evidence to show that training has been a success. Third, to claim success, the effects of training must be isolated, which is very difficult to do. Finally, as suggested throughout this and the previous chapter, it must be clear who is accountable for training. As these authors point out:

> research on training effectiveness suggests that training has its greatest impact when all parties in the organization share responsibility for identifying training needs, ensuring that trainees have the time and opportunity to focus on training, and have the opportunity and support to apply and practise trained skills on the job.
>
> (Kraiger et al., 2004: 347)

Giangreco et al. (2010) call for training evaluation tools that align better with modern organizational reality. In the event industry approaches need to be pragmatic and cost-effective if they are to be done at all.

Completion of the task at the end of Case Study 10.3 will test understanding of the material contained in this chapter.

CASE STUDY 10.3
Training for an exhibition project

This is a plan for installing an exhibition stand:

1   Plan exhibition
    1.1 Obtain requirements from marketing.
    1.2 Agree on build materials.
2   Assemble equipment
    2.1 Identify current stock of build materials.
    2.2 Reserve required stock.
    2.3 Generate list of equipment to be procured.
    2.4 Identify suppliers.
    2.5 Negotiate price and delivery.
    2.6 Raise and approve purchase orders.
    2.7 Place orders with suppliers.
    2.8 Deliver materials.
    2.9 Check materials and store materials.
3   Build exhibition stand
    3.1 Ship exhibition materials.
    3.2 Unpack materials.

3.3 Build stands.

3.4 Fit electrics.

3.5 Fit audio visual.

3.6 Check stand.

3.7 Install sales and marketing brochures, posters, etc.

4 Dismantle exhibition stand

4.1 Remove audiovisual equipment.

4.2 Dismantle electrics.

4.3 Pack up materials.

4.4 Ship to base.

Reflective practice 10.3

For Stage 2 of this project, 'assemble equipment', you need to develop a training plan, which should include the following information:

1 learning outcomes/training objectives;

2 training method/s;

3 equipment required;

4 demonstrable skills, including break down into steps;

5 knowledge (hint – don't forget health and safety);

6 Assessment – key points for observation and questions to ask.

Chapter summary and key points

Job-specific training is arguably the most important part of preparing an event workforce. This is where people learn how to use two-way radios, how to set up athletic equipment, who to admit at the VIP entrance, and how to provide customers with the information they need. For this to work successfully, jobs need to be broken down into tasks and basic knowledge, which form the basis for the training plan. A number of training methods can be used, such as demonstrations, case studies and brainstorming, and at the end of the training it must be evident that the trainees are competent to undertake their specific event roles. Evaluating the success of the training project is helpful and informative for subsequent events. Workforce morale is closely linked to the level of confidence employees and volunteers have in their ability to put on a good show.

Revision questions

1 What are the four steps in small group and individual training for specific skills? Explain the steps.

2   Using two specific events, can you identify at least three areas in which skills training will be required?
3   What are four different approaches to training delivery? Summarize these approaches.
4   Discuss the following statement: 'There is no point in evaluating training post event as the event is over and will never be replicated'.

Industry voice by Kerrie Nash

One of the things I think HR managers in the event world should focus on in the future, is event-specific training for the paid workforce. I mean there are obviously university courses, but one of the things that I like to do is look at the unique aspects of the event and tailor training to meet this need – for example: training on how to write operational policies and procedures. Or let's run a training session on how to read a CAD diagram or how to develop your Games-time staffing plan. I mean these short, event-specific courses just don't exist. If you do need to 'grow your own' event staff, which I think will happen in the future, we're going to have more of a challenge to do that. We need to have good training programmes that can take good skilled generalists and turn them into specialists in the event world.

With volunteer job-specific training, every event develops modules for the many hundreds of different jobs that are done at Games-time. There are great opportunities for knowledge transfer in this area, as the training requirement is pretty much the same from event to event – at least for the international multi-sport events such as Olympic and Paralympic Games, Commonwealth Games.

Discussion questions

1   In addition to training in how to write operational policies and procedures, what other short training sessions would be useful for the core planning team?
2   What does Kerrie mean when she talks about turning 'skilled generalists' into 'event specialists'?
3   What is knowledge transfer and how is it relevant to training?

References

Baker, A. C., Kolb, D. A. and Jensen, P. J. (2002). *Conversational Learning: An Experiential Approach to Knowledge Creation*. Westport, CT: Quorum Books.

Beckett, D. and Hager, P. J. (2002). 'Life, work and learning: practice in postmodernity', *Routledge International Studies in the Philosophy of Education*, 14. London: Routledge.

Beetham, H. and Sharpe, R. (eds). (2013). *Rethinking Pedagogy for a Digital Age: Designing for 21st Century Learning*. London: Routledge.

Burns, S. (2000). *Artistry in Training*. Melbourne: Woodslane Press.

Gallagher, J. (2011). 'Trigger questions: their role in problem based learning; do they add to the quality of interactive business case study solutions?', *Journal of Business Case Studies (JBCS)*, 3(4), 9–22.

Giangreco, A., Carugati, A. and Sebastiano, A. (2010). 'Are we doing the right thing? Food for thought on training evaluation and its context', *Personnel Review*, 39(2), 162–177.

Hmelo-Silver, C. E. (2012). 'International perspectives on problem-based learning: contexts, cultures, challenges, and adaptations', *Interdisciplinary Journal of Problem-based Learning*, 6(1), 3.

Kraiger, K., McLinden, D. and Casper, W. (2004). 'Collaborative planning for training impact', *Human Resource Management*, 43(4), 337–351.

Mosnews (2005). '200 festival visitors hospitalized with food poisoning in Southern Russia', *Mosnews.com*, 6 November. Available at: http:/lmosnews.com/news/2005lll/06l passengerspoisoned shtrnl; viewed 8 May 2006.

State Government of Victoria, Australia, Department of Human Services (2006). *Food Safety*. Available at: www.health.vic.gov.au/foodsafety/; viewed 8 May 2006.

Van Der Wagen, L. (2005). 'Olympic Games event leadership course design'. In: *The Impacts of Events*. Sydney: University of Technology.

Workforce policies and procedures

Learning objectives

After reading through this chapter you will be able to:

- List a number of areas of human resource management in which policies are required.
- Provide examples of procedures that support these policies.
- Discuss ethical and unethical human resource practices.
- Describe logistical challenges for workforce planning.

Introduction

The logistics associated with having the right people doing the right thing at the right time are challenging as events generally run for a very short time. Staff and volunteers need their rosters, they need uniforms, they need food and they need somewhere to sit during their breaks. Among the most common complaints from volunteers are those concerning the most elementary of needs, for example, being left on a gate collecting tickets for too long without being 'relieved' or given a drink.

Getting people into place and assigning work is the first hurdle. The next is to make sure that they are appropriately cared for in terms of their physical and emotional needs, such as having a supervisor stop by from time to time to talk to those working in isolated positions. The third hurdle is to make sure that the conduct of staff and volunteers is beyond reproach. This requires careful supervision, and in rare cases it may require asking the person to leave.

Developing policies and procedures to deal with such eventualities will mean that every event you participate in is more likely to run smoothly.

Policy planning

A policy is an intended course of action for an organization. A procedure is more specific, detailing the steps involved in seeing through the intent of the policy. For example, there may be a policy that every contractor should attend a safety induction session prior to working on site. To implement this policy, a record of attendance at these briefings would be necessary and a procedure would also be needed for contractors assigned at the very last minute. An example might be to have them go to staff check-in and be issued with a short booklet or watch a three-minute video presentation, much as they do in many fast food outlets with high staff turnovers.

UK Sports (2005) has an outstanding guide to ethics in their planning guidelines for major sporting events in which there are a number of points to be taken into consideration in the development of policy guidelines for human resource management, as follows.

Data protection and privacy

Good standards should be in place for protection of personal data, which should be used only for a specific purpose and be accurate and secure. Many websites have statements to this effect. The following extract illustrates the importance of careful record keeping:

> One area which event organisers need to take note of and act on is the Data Protection Act. The Act applies to all individuals. It sets out rules for processing personal information – i.e. data about identifiable living individuals – and applies to manual records such as paper files, as well as those held on computers.
>
> In planning for your event, you will need to consider the compliance requirements of the Act. Before collecting data for any purpose it is important to understand the principles of the Act, and to comply with the relevant conditions of processing personal data.
>
> The Act protects individuals from the inappropriate or inaccurate use of their personal data, and provides many people and organisations with a systematic framework for the proper handling of information.
>
> (UK Sports, 2005)

Human rights

Respect for others is demonstrated in a number of ways, an example being a breach of confidentiality regarding a high-profile sports person or celebrity. Most codes of conduct include a requirement that staff and volunteers do not behave in inappropriate ways such as taking photographs, asking for autographs or generally being a nuisance. Members of the event audience also expect exemplary conduct. Problems can occur when conversations between staff members are overheard (sometimes with bad language) or a volunteer may make a joke embarrassing someone in front of a crowd. In the most serious cases, athletes and celebrities may be the target for stealing souvenirs and this is particularly serious if the item is needed for the performance.

Diversity

Linked to human rights is the topic of diversity. Event organizations should champion and encourage diversity in the working environment. Valuing diversity is an organizational ideal that can be achieved only if embedded in policy and procedures and supported in the organizational practices. Internal communications is a means to achieve this end and this is the topic of the final chapter.

Equity/equal opportunity

In the staffing area the focus for this is the planning and organization of the event, resulting in the equitable treatment of everyone on site. Suitable arrangements may need to be made including, for example, access to the venue by wheelchairs and arrangements for people with hearing or sight impairment. Rotation and redeployment are ways in which one can ensure that team members are provided with a range of opportunities. In particular, those far from the field of play can be alternated with those closer to the field of play. Inequity in this regard is a major source of dissatisfaction for volunteers.

UK Sports (2005) recommends that

> Those hosting major events have a responsibility to provide suitable access not only to athletes, but also to spectators and employees, service providers and volunteers. Access can refer to physical aspects of the event – such as wheelchair access or Braille signage – but it can also be less tangible. Creating a culture surrounding the event so that people feel safe and free from harm makes the event truly accessible. Key questions to ask yourself are:
>
> • Are you aware of the different needs of diverse groups of people?
> • Do you have a policy statement and procedures in place for equity?
> • Have staff, service providers and volunteers been trained to deal with equity issues – do they understand the implications of inequitable behaviour?

Working with children

Staff training, working practices and codes of conduct need to be put in place to minimize situations where abuse of children may occur. In some countries, such as the United Kingdom and Australia, screening processes are in place to assess an applicant's suitability for working with children. In particular, procedures are needed for employees or volunteers dealing with missing children and general guidance is needed on appropriate behaviour of adults around children.

Drugs and alcohol

For safety reasons, nobody on site should be working under the influence of drugs or alcohol (see Case Study 11.1). For some music events, this is somewhat problematic, Woodstock being a good example:

> The first of many things to go wrong with the Woodstock Festival was the location. No matter how the young men and their lawyers spun it, the citizens of Wallkill did not want a bunch of drugged-out hippies descending on their town. After much wrangling, the town of Wallkill passed a law on July 2, 1969 that effectively banned the concert from their vicinity. Everyone involved with the Woodstock Festival panicked. Stores refused to sell any more tickets and the negotiations with the musicians got shaky. Only a month-and-a half before the Woodstock Festival was to begin, a new location had to be found.
>
> (Rosenberg, 2014)

   To this day, the use of drugs and alcohol by team members on an event site remains one of the highest safety risks, affecting judgement in case of emergency.

Dealing with the public

Members of the workforce team should understand that they are not spokespeople for the event organization. However, as representatives of the organization, their dealings with the public should be positive and pro-active. Many event organizers go to great pains to ensure that their staff do not admit liability in case of an accident or incident.

Grievance procedures

A grievance policy and related procedures should be developed and explained to all members of the workforce. This topic will be covered in more detail at the end of the chapter.

Sexual harassment and bullying

Harassment should not be tolerated and should be reported in accordance with carefully constructed guidelines. The policy should define harassment, state that it is not tolerated, define the role of managers in preventing and dealing with harassment and set out specific procedures.

Health and safety

Everyone should be aware of their responsibility to report health and safety hazards. Furthermore, they should also report behaviour of others that is risky or dangerous.

Code of conduct

Any of the following including the aiding and abetting of others constitutes a breach of the HOTBOX Terms and Conditions of employment and/or voluntary position.

- Failure to comply with the HOTBOX Terms and Conditions; Code of Conduct; Code of Practice; Instructions; Policies and Procedures and instructions of HOTBOX clients.
- Neglecting to complete a required task promptly and diligently, without sufficient cause.
- Leaving a position without permission or without sufficient cause.
- Making or signing any false statements, of any description.
- Destroying, altering or erasing documents, records or electronic data without permission or through negligence.
- Divulging matters confidential to HOTBOX and/or its clients, either past or present, without permission.
- Soliciting or receipt of gratuities or other consideration from any person, or failure to account for keys, money or property received in connection with the business of HOTBOX or HOTBOX clients.
- Incivility to persons encountered in the course of duties or misuse of authority in connection with the business of HOTBOX or HOTBOX clients.
- Conduct in a manner likely to bring discredit to HOTBOX, a fellow employee, HOTBOX clients, or HOTBOX client's customers.
- Use of uniform, equipment or identification without permission.
- Reporting for duty under the influence of alcohol or restricted drugs, or use of these whilst on duty.
- Failure to notify HOTBOX immediately of any:
    - Conviction for a criminal and/or motoring offence;
    - Indictment for any offence that may affect your work with HOTBOX;
    - Police caution or legal summons that may affect your work with HOTBOX.
- Permitting unauthorised access to premises; event site; place of work.
- Carrying of equipment not issued as essential to an individual's role or duties, or use of a HOTBOX client's and/or HOTBOX client's customer's equipment or facilities without permission.
- Not maintaining agreed standards of appearance; identification; and deportment whilst at work.

Source: http://www.hotboxevents.com/about/code-of-conduct/

Reflective practice 11.1

1   What is the purpose of developing a code of conduct for volunteers?
2   Give an example of unsatisfactory behaviour covered by one of these policies that would be reason for dismissal.

Most built centres have excellent procedures in this regard, however outdoor exhibitions (such as boat shows) and music events carry the highest risks for health and safety. One of the issues is that health and safety responsibility is often shared and specific areas can be overlooked by the various parties involved. This could be the venue owner, security contractor, set builder, caterer, etc.

Personal advantage

Members of the event workforce should not use their position for personal advantage, including receiving gifts and personal use of equipment.

Confidentiality

All event-related information is confidential. Staff should refer the media to the media centre or event control room. Many large events profiling celebrities require staff to sign confidentiality statements.

Lost and found

Any lost and found items should be reported and submitted for storage.

Use of the internet

Some organizations develop a policy to explicitly monitor private use of the internet. All employees and volunteers should be given a copy of the policy and procedure guidelines and should sign that they understand that violations may lead to dismissal.

While many organizations express their policies in a fairly negative 'will not' way, the well-known Burning Man Festival (2014) expresses their ten guiding principles in a more positive, pro-active way:

1 Radical inclusion ('welcome and respect the stranger')
2 Gifting ('unconditional')
3 Decommodification
4 Radical self-reliance
5 Radical self-expression
6 Communal effort
7 Civic responsibility
8 Leaving no trace
9 Participation ('transformative change')
10 Immediacy.

At this values-based event, the workforce are expected to uphold and demonstrate these principles.

Staffing logistics and procedures

Each of the following logistics issues needs to be considered. These are common consequences of not planning these in detail:

- not having enough staff rostered;
- not having enough small volunteer t-shirts;
- running out of hot meals;
- losing track of where people are (may be watching rather than working!);
- finding staff in the wrong areas;
- losing valuable equipment to theft;
- receiving reports of staff/volunteers misbehaving (in the bar perhaps).

Rosters

Fortunately, not many events have the numbers of staff illustrated in Table 11.1. However, this table illustrates the level of attention needed for roster planning. The benefits of a contingency group of multiskilled roving workers are also evident from this illustration. For larger events, timetabling online has been a progressive step, enabling staff to access and change their roster themselves, sometimes so that they can work with friends, which is a major benefit.

When planning the staffing schedule, decisions are not just about which days people should work. Micro-level planning is needed to identify the peaks and ebbs of staffing. For example, a large number of staff might be needed in the hour before a performance and again during an interval. This is quite predictable. If, however, the timetable is being done for a multi-venue, multi-session series of events, crowd flow planning forms a key part of planning. Many anxious punters arrive very early, even for ticketed events, and the level of readiness is important. The alternative is that some staff and volunteers are still checking in while the venue fills and this is where things can start to slide. Those key hours before the gates open are critical.

Uniforms

Uniforms are a major expense for a winter event, so care must be taken in the design and sizing. The design of uniforms or t-shirts is often determined with the audience in mind. However, it is also necessary to consider staff's response to uniforms, the size and colour of t-shirts being the most elementary consideration. Many events supply too few very small t-shirts. If a men's small is the smallest size, it will be more like a dress than a t-shirt on a tiny woman. Differentiation of status between paid, volunteer and contractor staff may be highlighted in the design of uniforms and this can cause some dissatisfaction if not handled well. At many events these three groups are not easily distinguished as they form one workforce in one uniform. This is an important decision, with implications for motivation.

Venue	15-Jul-02	16-Jul-02	17-Jul-02	18-Jul-02	19-Jul-02	20-Jul-02	21-Jul-02	22-Jul-02	23-Jul-02	24-Jul-02
TABLE 11.1 Peak shift numbers by venue and day, 2002 Manchester Commonwealth Games										
Sportcity	109	104	97	129	169	95	101	114	477	95
Commonwealth Games Village	34	31	32	34	33	31	31	35	33	32
Bessmer Street (MAUC)	30	27	28	30	29	27	27	33	32	30
Rivington Mountain Biking Crowd Management	–	–	–	–	–	–	–	–	–	48
Salford Quays	–	–	–	–	–	–	–	–	–	–
MEN-Arena	–	–	–	–	–	–	–	–	–	–
International Broadcast Centre	69	43	43	63	52	55	61	51	53	45
National Cycling Centre	9	9	9	9	9	9	9	9	9	9
Bolton Arena	14	11	10	12	10	10	10	9	9	8
G-Mex	12	7	14	15	15	18	24	17	15	22
Flying Squad (attrition – covering all venues)	–	–	–	–	–	–	–	–	–	–
Heaton Park	–	–	–	–	–	–	–	–	–	–
Hough End Fleet Car Park	16	16	16	16	16	16	16	16	16	16
Aquatics Centre	15	15	15	15	15	15	15	15	15	15
Belle Vue	12	12	12	12	12	12	12	12	12	12
Heron House	8	8	7	7	7	6	7	7	7	9
International Convention Centre	–	–	–	–	–	1	1	1	1	1
Forum Centre, Wythenshawe	–	–	–	–	–	–	–	–	–	–
Fleet Commissioning Depot Redvers Street	7	7	7	7	7	7	7	7	7	7
Technical Officials' Village	2	2	2	2	2	2	2	4	5	4
Bus Operations Depot Sheffield Street	4	4	4	4	4	4	4	4	4	4
Commonwealth House	4	4	4	4	4	4	4	4	4	4
Fleet Operations Depot Bessemer Street	4	4	4	4	4	4	4	4	4	4
Main Press Centre	1	1	1	1	1	2	2	1	2	2
Mobile Drivers	–	–	–	2	2	2	2	2	2	2
Broadcast & Rate Card Car Parks	–	1	1	1	1	1	1	1	1	1

Source: Manchester City Council (2003)

25-Jul-02	26-Jul-02	27-Jul-02	28-Jul-02	29-Jul-02	30-Jul-02	31-Jul-02	1-Aug-02	2-Aug-02	3-Aug-02	4-Aug-02	Peak
504	611	650	553	540	657	488	306	603	539	862	862
58	173	200	192	183	202	220	218	205	217	219	220
57	172	198	191	182	199	219	28	30	31	25	219
–	–	125	–	–	–	–	–	–	51	–	125
–	–	2	2	–	21	–	14	14	13	88	88
–	62	84	70	75	69	74	87	66	60	–	87
50	44	48	60	44	43	60	45	47	53	46	69
11	9	9	11	11	31	45	36	43	10	10	45
11	37	32	35	24	25	26	36	37	27	26	37
22	34	34	34	35	32	36	35	33	33	33	36
23	17	21	20	22	22	20	–	–	–	–	23
–	15	14	20	21	22	20	19	16	18	22	22
16	16	16	16	16	16	16	16	16	16	16	16
15	15	15	15	15	15	15	15	15	15	15	15
12	12	12	12	12	12	12	12	12	12	12	12
8	10	6	7	8	10	9	9	8	10	9	10
1	1	1	1	1	8	8	9	10	5	1	10
1	1	1	1	1	1	1	9	7	7	9	9
–	–	–	–	–	–	–	–	–	–	–	7
5	5	4	5	5	5	5	5	5	5	5	5
4	4	4	4	4	4	4	4	4	4	4	4
4	4	4	4	4	4	4	4	4	4	4	4
4	4	4	4	4	4	4	4	4	4	4	4
2	2	2	2	2	2	2	2	2	2	1	2
2	2	2	2	2	2	2	2	2	2	2	2
1	1	1	1	1	1	1	1	1	1	1	1

Accreditation

Workforce members need to be identifiable by security, by one another and by the event audience. A name badge is the simplest method, although for sophisticated events an accreditation badge would be produced, with precinct and access codes, a photograph and provision for electronic access to specific areas.

Sign-on and sign-off

A sign-on and sign-off system is important, both for staff and volunteers. For legal and ethical reasons, the event organizers should be able to account for everyone on duty.

Meal vouchers

The earlier example of staff numbers at different venues in Table 11.1 raises the issue of meal planning. Members of the workforce all need to be fed at least one hot meal per day. Forecasting is thus vitally important to avoid waste or, worse still, run out of food. There are two things that make catering planning a nightmare. First, many of the staff, such as security, have wide-ranging access and might eat at a different venue on each shift depending on where they are at the time. Generally, the news of which menu is best travels on two-way radio pretty quickly. Second, contract staff need to be catered for, requiring some sort of voucher system to allow the event organizer to redeem the cost of contractor meals post-event.

As Figure 11.1 illustrates, detailed planning is needed to estimate and account for the number of meals served at each meal period. Using the system illustrated, each contractor group (e.g. police, transport, security, cleaning) would need to be issued with a different coloured voucher.

Camping

At many music festivals, facilities for camping are provided for people working on site. In some cases they bring their families, friends and pets too. The need for a policy, procedures and control measures for this aspect of the event is immediately evident. At the Falcon Ridge Folk Festival, Hillsdale, New York, volunteers can expect three meals a day as well as camping facilities. The expense of running a three-meals-a-day canteen for staff (and possibly family and friends) is enough to give the event organizer the jitters – catering for the event audience would be a difficult enough task.

Lockers

If lockers are not provided for staff, they need to be aware of this and the fact that they are responsible for their own valuables.

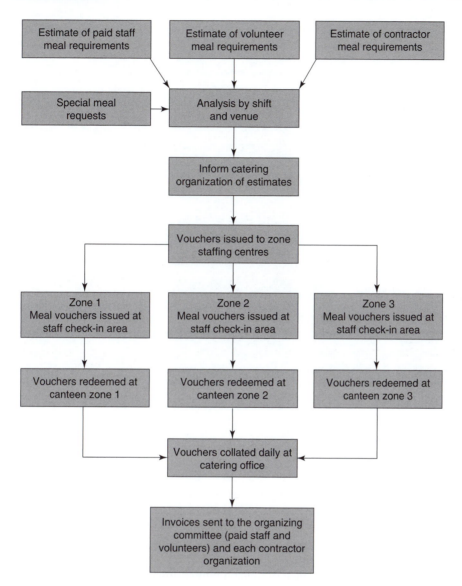

FIGURE 11.1 Estimating meal requirements and accounting for meals served

Communications equipment (two-way radios)

Management and supervisory staff require communication equipment, usually in the form of two-way radios. These may be issued on arrival at the staff desk or from the adjacent communications command centre.

PLATE 11.1 Food safety training and systems are essential for commercial kitchens

Briefing and debriefing

It is traditional for staff arriving at an event to be given a briefing, regardless of whether they have already attended a training session. The briefing allows management to communicate important recent changes in operational planning. Likewise, the debriefing enables staff to air their thoughts about operational problems that may be able to be ironed out overnight. For the smaller event, the pre-event briefing could be all the training that is required.

Authority

When arriving for work people need to be told what to do and a checklist is exceptionally useful for this purpose. A common reason for frustration on the part of volunteers is that they are underemployed and therefore don't feel that their support is valuable. Furthermore, all staff, supervisors and volunteers should understand the limits of their authority.

It is not uncommon for the more senior volunteers to attempt to take control and the younger volunteers then find themselves in a situation in which they are given contradictory instructions by several people bossing them around.

PLATE 11.2 Customer demands go from zero to 100 per cent within minutes

Incident report forms

Employees and volunteers should report all criminal or suspicious behaviour, so on arrival they should be shown where the incident report forms can be found and where to put them when completed. At this time they can also be reminded about potentially more serious accidents and emergencies and how to respond to them. Strategically placed posters in staff areas are useful for informing personnel of these important aspects of events.

Dealing with no-shows

It is inevitable that some people will not turn up, and estimates need to be made for how many extra people will be needed to take their place. These estimates are hard to come by due to the varied nature of events, such as duration. Weather has the biggest impact on attendance as rain is likely to detract some volunteers.

Surveillance

Some events have cameras placed in many of the working areas. In Australia, for example, it is necessary to advise staff of their existence as covert surveillance of work areas is not permitted.

Access

Employees and volunteers should not enter areas where they do not have authorized access. A policy is often required on after-hours access to events which, for some, is an anticipated benefit of working at them. At other events, people are asked to leave the precinct on completion of their shift. The author remembers a volunteer, accompanied by two small children, fraternizing with sponsors at the bar. When she became very intoxicated, she and the children were sent home by taxi by a sponsorship manager. Unfortunately this was not reported until the next day.

Performance management

While most long-life organizations have formal performance appraisal systems, this is seldom the case in the project environment of the event business where performance management takes a different format. This is not to say, however, that the absence of a formal programme of annual interviews and appraisal precludes performance management. A simplified system of using the job description as the basis of an interview form was recommended in Chapter 7. Elements of performance management thus appear in the processes of job analysis, selection, induction and training.

Any organization, whether it has a formal or informal system, needs to do the following:

- Set standards of performance.
- Set deadlines and outcomes.

- Monitor and facilitate performance.
- Provide feedback.
- Develop and implement remedial action plans if necessary.

Kramer et al. (2002) suggest that there are five criteria for evaluation of performance management systems: strategic congruence, validity, reliability, acceptability and specificity. The first of these, strategic congruence, 'refers to the extent to which performance appraisals encourage job performance that supports the organisation's strategy, goals and culture' (p. 307). Thus, in the event organization, any performance management system, whether project based or formal performance appraisal in the traditional sense, needs to serve the needs of the event. These authors recommend linking strategic objectives to a set of financial and operational measures. This would sit very comfortably with most event organizations.

Grievance procedures and dismissal

The first question it is necessary to ask is whether a grievance procedure is necessary. For small temporary teams operating for short periods of time such a procedure may be unnecessary as most problems will be readily solved. However, for large-scale events, this type of procedure is an invaluable way to deal with grievances, including those put forward by volunteers. The aims of an effective grievance procedure are immediate and confidential attention to conflict issues, consistency and a fair outcome. A grievance procedure should have the following features:

- It should be agreed between all stakeholders.
- It should be explained in plain English to everyone involved.
- The steps to be taken in making a complaint should be clear.
- People should be dealt with consistently and objectively.
- Confidentiality of all concerned should be maintained.
- There should be a means of escalating the issue through several levels of the organization.
- The process should be fully documented.

Essentially, this procedure ensures that people are dealt with fairly and objectively, particularly when there is a performance deficiency. Furthermore, allegations of unfairness can be investigated. There are two significant benefits of such a system: first, conflicts can be resolved and work resumed in a harmonious environment; and second, litigation can be avoided for most cases of alleged discrimination and unfair dismissal once the matter has been given this level of attention.

Dismissal procedures should include counselling and a series of warning letters. At each stage the full facts must be evident, the performance gap clearly identified and the individual given the opportunity to remedy the situation.

Disciplinary procedures

These are the issues that need to be considered in disciplinary procedures to ensure that procedural fairness occurs.

Specific issue

- What specifically was the offence, the action or inaction, or misconduct?
- Was this clearly a breach of the written code of conduct?
- Was this a minor or major disciplinary issue?
- How does this disciplinary issue relate to the person's job performance?

Awareness and evidence

- Did the person know that they were doing something wrong?
- Was the person warned?
- What are the facts and sources of information?
- Are there witnesses or evidence?

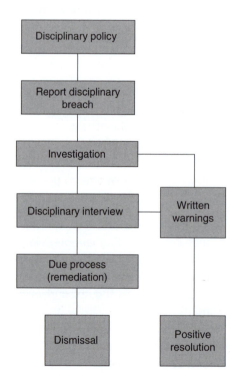

FIGURE 11.2 Disciplinary process

Circumstances

- Were there extenuating circumstances?
- Have these been taken into account?
- Have other people been committing the same offence?

Safety and crisis management

- Does the breach impact on workplace safety?
- What are the risks associated with the misconduct?
- Is this a potential media issue?

In a case of gross misconduct, the employee is asked to leave immediately without following the full process of warnings. This is known as summary dismissal and can apply also to volunteers.

Grounds for summary dismissal include:

- gross dishonesty
- wilful damage to property
- endangering the safety of self and others
- assault and fighting
- gross insubordination or insolence
- intoxication on duty.

Procedural fairness in respect of a disciplinary action (South African Labour Guide, 2014) in South Africa is described below.

The following requirements for procedural fairness (misconduct) should be met:

- An employer must inform the employee of allegations in a manner the employee can understand.
- The employee should be allowed reasonable time to prepare a response to the allegations.
- The employee must be given an opportunity to state his/her case during the proceedings.
- An employee has the right to be assisted by a shop steward or other employee during the proceedings.
- The employer must inform the employee of a decision regarding a disciplinary sanction, preferably in writing – in a manner that the employee can understand.
- The employer must give clear reasons for dismissing the employee.
- The employer must keep records of disciplinary actions taken against each employee, stating the nature of misconduct, disciplinary action taken and the reasons for the disciplinary action.

CASE STUDY 11.2
General terms and conditions, Better Festival Group

General

- If you have any queries regarding these Terms and Conditions please contact us by email before applying.
- Submitting an application indicates that you are agreeing to these Terms and Conditions and Code of Conduct.
- Submitting an application indicates that you agree for The Better Festival Group to store your application details in our database. Your information will never be passed onto another organisation with the exception of point 1 below.
- Submitting an application indicates that you agree that if you fail to arrive and work at a festival you have been confirmed for without giving 4 weeks' notice or your performance whilst on site is less than acceptable you will get blacklisted. You will be unable to apply to work with The Better Festival Group in the future and some of your details maybe shared with other staffing providers and/or events to inform them that you are blacklisted with The Better Festival Group.
- Submitting an application indicates that you agree that any photographs or videos of you or by you may be used by us for promotional purposes. Obviously if we use a photograph you really don't want us to use, you can email us to discuss it.
- All volunteers MUST camp within the allocated Crew Camping Area.
- All staff will be issued with a wristband/pass giving them access to the areas of the event which they need to perform their duties. These wristbands will remain the property of the event at all times. Anyone found abusing access their pass has given them will have their pass taken, be removed from site and will subsequently become blacklisted.
- The misuse of any issued radio communications will result in a verbal warning, only 1 verbal warning will be issued and further issues will result in further action being taken. This includes but is not limited to disclosing any sensitive information heard over the radio, using bad language and too much chit chat.
- Your confirmation of acceptance can be revoked at any time due to cancellation of an event or contracts not being gained at named events. If it is deemed necessary to revoke your confirmation of acceptance for any other reason you will be advised of the reasons via email.
- If you are dissatisfied with any disciplinary decision or wish to discuss anything regarding your volunteering experience please contact us by email.
- You will need to bring proof of your Entitlement to Work in the UK to the first event you volunteer at with us, we will copy it, keep it safe and return it at the end of the event. You will not have to bring it again. More information can be found HERE please read before applying.
- We are introducing a deposit scheme this year. Please ensure you have read the Deposit Terms and Conditions HERE before applying.

Employment rights

(Statement of the Terms and Conditions of employment under the employment rights act 1996)

1   You are required to carry out your roles and responsibilities as detailed in the job description/position specification/On Site Briefing.
2   Your place of work will be the address of the event and is where you are required to work.
3   Staff are responsible for their own travel, subsistence (unless otherwise stated in Confirmation of Acceptance) and accommodation expenses (in the unlikely event that camping is not available on site).
4   Provision of meals or allowances are not negotiable and are, where available, provided by the event and distributed by The Better Festival Group.
5   All of our vacancies are VOLUNTARY unless otherwise stated in your Confirmation of Acceptance.

Hours and breaks

- Hours of work will be no more than 8 hours per shift, majority of our vacancies are 6 hours per shift.
- Adults (18+) – If you work over 6 hours you will be required to take a 20 minute break during your shift. Shift supervisors will arrange this on site.
- 16 & 17 – If you work over 4.5 hours you will be required to take a 30 minute break during your shift. Shift supervisors will arrange this on site.
- Adults (18+) – You will have at least an 11 hour break between shifts.
- 16 & 17 – You will have at least a 12 hour break between shifts – if your shift pattern does not adhere to this please let your shift supervisor know immediately and they will look into it.

Code of conduct

Any of the following, including the aiding and abetting of others is a breach of our Terms and Conditions and will result in some or all of your deposit being retained.

1   Failure to comply with our Terms and Conditions or On-Site Instructions.
2   Failure to complete a required task promptly and conscientiously, without a valid and confirmed reason.
3   Leaving a position during your shift without permission.
4   Making any false declarations.
5   Revealing or discussing any confidential information relating to The Better Festival Group or its clients without permission.
6   Inappropriate or unacceptable behaviour towards persons encountered during your time on site.
7   Conducting yourself in a manner that is liable to damage the credibility or reputation of The Better Festival Group, its clients or its other volunteers.

8   Failure to wear a Hi Visibility vest when on shift, this includes having it tucked in your trousers, slung over your shoulder, tied round your waist etc.

9   Reporting for duty under the influence of alcohol or restricted drugs, or use of these whilst on duty.

10   Permitting unauthorised access to premises, event site or place of work.

SUBMITTING AN APPLICATION INDICATES THAT YOU AGREE TO ALL THE INFORMATION IN THIS DOCUMENT AND THOSE LINKED FROM IT.

Source: http://www.thebetterfestivalgroup.co.uk/get-involved/gentandc

Reflective practice 11.2

1   Why is it necessary for an event of this size to develop such a comprehensive code?

2   This list of rules is quite extensive. Assume that you are running a much smaller event and consolidate them to develop your own guidelines in plain English.

Revision questions

1   What is the difference between a policy and a procedure?

2   List and describe some of the logistics challenges of the workforce co-ordinator.

3   Write a short code of conduct for volunteers at a small community festival.

4   How would you go about communicating the above code to staff and volunteers?

Industry voice by Kerrie Nash

Policies and procedures in an event organization need to be adapted to work firstly for the 'corporate' office-based environment, where the workforce is all paid staff. These policies and procedures need to be adapted, rewritten for event-time, where a blended workforce population of paid, volunteer and contractor workforces are located in multiple venues, at multiple locations.

Discussion

Discuss the issue of discipline (specifically misconduct) and the policies that would vary from the 'office environment' of the planning period to the event implementation period. List the challenges and make recommendations for developing such a policy and procedure in consultation with other workforce stakeholders.

References

Burning Man Festival (2014). *10 Principles*. Available at: http://www.burningman.com/whatisburningman/about_burningman/principles.html#.UsuCzvv87cw; viewed 8 January 2014.

Kramer, R., O'Connor, M. and Davis, E. (2002). 'Appraising and managing performance'. In *Australian Master Human Resources Guide*. CCH, pp. 301–322.

Manchester City Council (2003). *Manchester Commonwealth Games Post Games Report*. Available at: www.gameslegacy.com; viewed 17 May 2006.

Rosenberg, J. (2014). *The Woodstock Festival of 1969*. Available at: http://history1900s.about.com/od/1960s/p/woodstock.htm; viewed 8 January 2014.

The South African Labour Guide (2014). *Procedural Fairness*. Available at: http://www.labourguide.co.za/procedural-fairness; viewed 5 January 2014.

UK Sports (2005). Major Sports Events – The Guide. Available at: www.uksport.gov.uk/generic_template.asp?id=12237; viewed 5 January 2014.

Event service culture

Learning objectives

After reading through this chapter you will be able to:

*   Define the term organizational culture and describe an event organizational culture.
*   List and describe ways in which organizational culture is established.
*   Discuss service culture in terms of the event product and its features.
*   Describe stakeholders and how they impact on event organizational culture.

Introduction

The culture of an organization is reflected in the way things are done within the organization. For example, the level of formality with which senior management are addressed is one feature of an organization's culture. Wimbledon would have a fairly formal culture, with highly developed policies and procedures based on the event's long history. In contrast, relationships between staff planning the Woodstock 1969 Music and Art Festival would undoubtedly have been quite frenetic, given that 50,000 people were expected and 500,000 turned up! In fact, it would have been quite different from any similar event held today, given the values held by those who staged the event and the fact that it was the climax of the hippie era.

   Organizations mould a common set of attitudes and values, whether intentionally or not. In most cases it is done intentionally, the culture developing through selection and socialization of members. The language used in the organization is another feature of its unique culture; indeed, the field of event management has a language of its own, summarized in the glossary. Staff at mega events often use more acronyms than words, with the result that outsiders find it hard to understand what they are saying!

Shone and Parry (2013: 194) sum up, in general terms, the culture of events: 'events are significant social activities; they are often communal and good natured, and this is reflected in their culture'. This chapter looks at the culture of event organizations, specifically at those aspects of the culture that impact on service provision. Much has been said in this text about the workforce and its unique characteristics compared to a traditional organization in which a service culture is built more easily. The hotel industry has developed fairly clear cut perceptions in the minds of customers and it is hoped that in the long run this aspect of event management is given the same attention.

What is organizational culture?

Culture is a system of learned patterns of behaviour, ideas and products characteristic of a group or society. Organizational culture can be described in terms of patterns of cross-individual behavioural consistency within an organization. For example, when people say that culture is 'the way we do things around here', they are defining the consistent way in which people perform tasks, solve problems, resolve conflicts, and treat customers and employees. Culture is also defined by the informal values, norms and beliefs that guide how individuals and groups in an organization interact with each other and with people outside the organization. A strong organizational culture gives people a sense of identity, encourages commitment to the organization's values and mission, and promotes stability. Parent (2010) describes the event environment as having 'high velocity' and it is this environment of rapid change that makes it difficult to create an appropriate service culture unless it is done as part of the strategic vision.

A culture is conveyed internally through the following means.

Organizational structure

This may be stable or unstable. It is unstable, for example, when there is constant reorganization or when there is a high turnover of staff. It can be tall, with many levels to the hierarchy, or low, where there are few levels to the hierarchy.

Mission and objectives

Many organizations and events have very clear mission statements that encapsulate their culture, as those of the Indigenous Heritage Festival and the Southeastern Surgical Congress indicate:

The Indigenous Heritage Festival provides crucial opportunities for indigenous peoples of the world to share self expression and wisdom with communities and initiate inter-tribal relationships that promote cultural exchange and build economic co-operation. Our ultimate vision is to witness the establishment of a united network of flourishing indigenous nations and our global society enriched and strengthened by cultural diversity.

(Indigenous Festival, 2006)

The Southeastern Surgical Congress was founded to provide opportunities for surgeons and surgeons in training to come together for educational, scientific and social purposes to promote and advance the study and practice of surgery.

(Southeastern Surgical Congress, 2006)

Devolution of decision making

Where there are few levels to the hierarchy, individuals at the lower levels are more likely to be empowered to make decisions without sending them up the line. Thus they have higher levels of responsibility.

Policies and procedures

Approvals for equipment acquisition, petty cash systems, grievance procedures, and reward and recognition programmes are all examples of policies with associated procedures, and their content is indicative of the organization's culture.

Language specific to the workplace

Unfortunately, the specific language of the workplace becomes second nature to those immersed in the culture, making them oblivious to the fact that some of their communication is incomprehensible to others. For example:

Our contingency plan must be linked to the risk assessment which is weighted according to probability and consequence. The VCC (venue command centre) will be the base for implementing the VERP (venue emergency response plan).

(Van Der Wagen, 2011)

Distribution of rewards

Remuneration at different levels of the organization is another feature of the culture, with large differences in some organizations and smaller differences in others. This has a major impact on how people work together.

Communication flows

Both vertical and horizontal communication varies from organization to organization. There is also the 'grapevine', the informal communication network, where supposition and rumour prevail, which at times can be damaging. The final chapter will cover the topic of internal communications, the media and messages that can be used to develop an organizational and service culture.

Resource allocation

The amount of financial and other resources allocated to different departments distinguishes their position in the pecking order. In the event business, if the functional area of waste management is given a very small budget and only one staff member, this is indicative of the value placed on environmental impact by the organization.

How does event organizational culture differ?

Primarily events are service enterprises, not manufacturing enterprises, so it is necessary to look at the event product and service features in order to better grasp the concept of event organizational culture.

Service orientation of events

Here we are looking at the organization's culture as it is expressed in its external relationships. Customers have contact with the event at the following four points and at each point the organization's service culture is communicated (Van Der Wagen, 2011):

1   Pre-purchase
    (a) interactive website
    (b) email
    (c) telephone enquiry.
2   Purchase/pre-event
    (a) ticket sale
    (b) transportation
    (c) parking
    (d) queuing
    (e) entry
    (f) security check.
3   Event
    (a) seat allocation/usher
    (b) food and beverage
    (c) information
    (d) entertainment
    (e) performance/participation (e.g. in concert/fun run)
    (f) first aid
    (g) merchandise sales
    (h) lost and found.
4   Post-event
    (a) exit
    (b) queue

(c) transport
(d) online results
(e) photographs/memorabilia.

Furthermore, the event product is characterized by the following well-known services marketing characteristics (Parasuraman et al., 2004; Jemmasi et al., 2011) which have implications for human resource management.

Intangibility

Services cannot be seen, touched or taken home, and for this reason the customer has difficulty assessing quality and value until after the service experience. A ticket to an event, such as a concert, is often the only tangible reminder of an experience that is judged worthwhile, but it is difficult for the customer to describe, particularly the fleeting points of service contact described earlier. All form part of a cumulative experience which is intangible.

The implication for human resource management is the necessity for a strong culture built on induction and training. Consistent and positive responses by staff and volunteers that reflect the organization's values need to be developed for every service interaction. Some workforce members refer to orientation as 'indoctrination' as this form of training aims to have everyone understand the event's mission and in some cases (particularly fundraising events) to be inspired and motivated by it. This mission and culture could be peace and harmony; novelty and extremism; political posturing; appreciation of a unique artform; or a love of books. For many events, there is an upbeat mood of community celebration.

Perishability

An event organization cannot keep an event experience such as a seat in a stadium for a cricket match and sell it the next day because by then the match is over – the commodity is perishable. In contrast, a hardware store can sell a hammer any time for months and years after it is put on the shelf. The perishability of the event product means that it must sell at the time it is offered and marketing efforts are generally directed at developing demand for tickets. This often means that large crowds attend and there are queues for tickets, entry, cloakrooms and exits. This puts pressure on service personnel to deal with sudden peaks and high-level consumer demands. If there is any prospect of missing the show, tempers flare. Training to deal with these possibilities is essential. The event organization has to capitalize on the moment, and needs staff to help it do so at an optimal level of efficiency.

Inseparability

Services quality and consistency are subject to great variability because they are delivered by people, and human behaviour is difficult to control. The service is inseparable from the service provider. The mood or facial expression of the service provider characterizes the service for that encounter. Judgements are made by both service provider and customer affecting subsequent communication. By paying careful attention to recruitment of staff and volunteers and selecting for sound customer relations skills, it is possible to achieve higher levels of service quality. Training, specifically in service provision, is also recommended. For a service-based enterprise, the investment is in preparing the workforce and not in developing systems of quality control checks as would be done for a production line.

Variability

Following the concept of inseparability, every interaction with the customer is a unique communication. It is thus subject to considerable variation, and in most cases so it should be. The provider customizes their response to meet the customer's needs. However, for this to work successfully, the provider must be empowered to make decisions and solve customer problems. Working closely with management during briefings and debriefings can lead to resolution of many problems, which in turn leads to greater consistency in customer service interactions between staff and clients. Better decision making on the part of frontline personnel is essential for quality service.

Dynamic quality of events

It is difficult to describe the culture of an event organization unless it is an ongoing concern such as a music promoter, exhibition hire company or convention centre with a core team of permanent staff. Even this type of organization would be quite a turbulent environment in which to work. Each new performance, road show or exhibition would provide different challenges. Often the culture of the pre-event period is quite different from the culture of the operational and post-event periods. One thing that is common to all events is that they tend to operate in an environment of relative uncertainty:

> The more complex and the more unique an event is, the more likely it is to be more labour-intensive, both in terms of organization and operation. The organizational issue relates to the need for relatively complicated planning to enable the service delivery to be efficient, or put more simply, for the event to be a good one (this is why some events may be outsourced to event management companies, caterers or other types of suppliers). The uniqueness of this type of service implies a high level of communication between the organizer and the event manager. Such a high level of communication and planning will take time and effort, even where the event may be repeating a well-known formula, or operating within a common framework such as a conference. The operational element may also require high levels of staffing in order to deliver the event properly.
>
> (Shone and Parry, 2013: 17)

Much has been made of the idea that the event organization is dynamic and responsive to many situational changes in the life of each event project, and thus theorists are now looking more carefully at the role of human resource managers in non-static organizations.

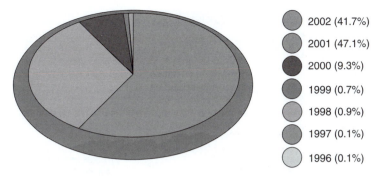

2002 (41.7%)

2001 (47.1%)

2000 (9.3%)

1999 (0.7%)

1998 (0.9%)

1997 (0.1%)

1996 (0.1%)

FIGURE 12.1 Yearly recruitment of full-time employees for the 2002 Manchester Commonwealth Games

Tyson (1999, 2013) suggests that greater weighting needs to be given to process and diagnostic skills on the part of the human resource practitioner than to detailed technical knowledge of human resource management. This is a valuable perspective. From the growth of the event workforce over time, as shown for paid staff alone for the Manchester Commonwealth Games in Figure 12.1, it is easy to see that a process and diagnostic focus would better serve the evolutionary character of events.

Relationships with external stakeholders

It would be impossible to discuss event service culture without covering the important relationships developed with external organizations. Multiple stakeholders are part of the event communication structure and these external bodies have a profound impact on operational planning and execution. Police and traffic authorities are an example of stakeholders; sponsorship providers are another, having considerable input into ensuring that the event meets their sponsorship and branding expectations.

Eunson (2012) uses the term 'boundary spanner' to describe people working at the interface between the organization and the environment of stakeholders. Boundary spanners have a job role that places them in contact with clients and others, sometimes spending more time with people outside the organization than within it. This role is also played out within the event organization, for example, where the marketing manager has considerable ongoing communication with the naming rights sponsor. Figure 12.2 illustrates the most common stakeholders with which the event organization has relationships, and these are described in more detail below.

Government

Legislative compliance and approval processes are often quite taxing, involving long periods of negotiation by the event organizer with local and regional government bodies, tourism bodies, and authorities such as police, traffic management and environmental protection.

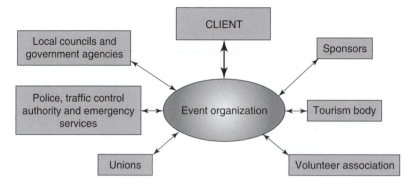

FIGURE 12.2 Common stakeholder relationships with the event organization

Sponsors

The level of interaction with sponsors varies in accordance with their financial commitment to the event. In some cases sponsors are happy to leave the running of the event to the organizers; in others, sponsors have a great deal at stake and play a significant role in staging the event to suit their aims. This requires endless communication and negotiation, and approval at every step along the way. Sponsors might wish to play a part in designing

PLATE 12.1 Working with media stakeholders

the event programme, providing goods and services at the event, and managing marketing and publicity, and many sponsors like to run corporate hospitality programmes for their business contacts and staff.

Unions

The role of unions in events was discussed in Chapter 6. For organizations operating in South Africa, United Kingdom and Australia, for example, these relationships are an important consideration for organizational communication. Keeping the unions in the loop can be a proactive measure with significant and positive outcomes, including simplified planning and improved staff retention (Webb, 2001). Also important are the relationships between contractors and unions, which have been highlighted in Chapter 5. While, theoretically, these contractor organizations operate at arms length from the event organization, the relationship between contractor and union/s is crucial to meeting deadlines. The alternative could be a dispute which could disrupt planning and execution of the event.

In the United Kingdom interest is growing in the role trade unions play in supporting those people employed in freelance or contingent work. Research conducted by Heery et al. (2004) has focused on case studies of the media and entertainment unions as well as those representing freelance guides, interpreters and translators. These members of the event workforce have mobile careers and are increasingly concerned with the security, tenure and development potential of their appointments:

> The focus of our research was on trade unions but also yielded information on the reactions of employers. What emerged most strongly from this evidence was the ambiguity with which employers regard the regulation of freelance labour markets, an ambiguity that arguably characterizes the employer view of institutionalized job regulation per se. They cavil at constraint, and avoidance of union-authored rules is common in the industries in which freelance unions operate. The primary purpose of avoiding regulation is to reduce costs and ensure maximum flexibility in the use of labour although, in some cases, such as major film companies, avoidance takes the form of offering high rates of pay that allow the recruitment and retention of the most skilled labour. Where regulation is institutionalized, however, employers frequently accept it and acknowledge its efficiencies.
>
> (Heery et al., 2004: 32)

Volunteer associations

Associations that support volunteering can provide outstanding support when planning the volunteer programme. For example, Volunteering England provides advice on managing volunteers, including such topics as occupational health and safety.

Case Study 12.1 reinforces previous comments regarding the status of volunteers.

Some event organizations have an outstanding relationship with their highly motivated volunteers, so much so that these volunteers meet for years after the event

CASE STUDY 12.1
Oxford City of Culture

A world-class cultural city

The City Council and its partners believe that culture – whether it takes the form of the architecture that surrounds us, the museums that reflect our past and present, or the literature and performing and visual arts through which we celebrate our experiences – plays a profound role in shaping people's experiences and attitudes.

We believe that access to high quality cultural experiences is the right of all our citizens. Our ambition – developed with our partners, including business, community organisations, the health and education sectors, and the County Council – is to make Oxford a world-class city for everyone.

Our shared vision for culture

To work in partnership with Oxford's key stakeholders and cultural partners to develop and promote cultural activities and events that enhance and leave a legacy in the lives of individuals and communities, offer affordable, excellent experiences, encourage attainment amongst young people and promote cultural ambition. Our three key priorities for culture:

- Lead a partnership-based approach to sustaining, developing and improving the cultural life of the city.
- Improve opportunities for young people to access and actively participate in high quality cultural activities.
- Improve opportunities for the diverse range of communities in the city to actively participate in high quality cultural activities that reflect their own identities and can be shared with the whole community.

Source: *Oxford Culture Strategy 2012–2015*. Available at: http://www.oxford.gov.uk/culture; viewed 6 January 2014

Reflective practice 12.1

The website for Oxford City outlines the vision for cultural activities. With this information in mind describe how you would go about developing a team of long-term volunteers to support their vision and events.

and even continue to wear their colourful uniforms! However, in other cases, this level of camaraderie is not achieved and volunteers leave feeling that they have been exploited or underutilized. Developing relationships with volunteer organizations to support the volunteer programme can lead to more effective management of such programmes.

Clients

Of course, the most significant stakeholder for most events is the client. This could be the person booking the meeting, organizing the company conference, planning the incentive trip or booking the wedding or party. Communication with the client needs to be frequent and clear, so that every expectation is realized. Of course, in some cases, it is impossible to meet every need for the price quoted! Communication with the client needs to be supported by written documentation such as the booking contract. However, from that time on there are likely to be many meetings and conversations that likewise need to be recorded (however briefly), with any changes to service provision and contract price agreed in writing, for which emails will generally suffice.

Reliance on customer satisfaction

In their study, Getz et al. (2001) constructed a service map for an event in which they identified the processes – listed earlier in the chapter – through which visitors experienced the event, judged the effectiveness of encounters with staff, viewed tangible evidence of services provided, conducted observations of crowd behaviour, and applied knowledge of management systems and operations. The study was undertaken using trained observers to supplement visitor surveys. The resulting narratives produced by observers led to numerous recommendations for service improvement, including providing more visible and welcoming staff/volunteers.

While it is impossible to cover all aspects of this study and their implications for evaluation, service mapping was one of the main recommendations. This study also provides a baseline for comparative research.

The authors concluded:

> Events are different from other service encounters, as demonstrated by this research. The event product is unique each time it is offered, and there are no routine service encounters. No matter what management systems are in place, interactions between setting, management and visitors result in unpredictable elements. Indeed, customers help shape the experience through expectations, emotional states and their social interaction.
>
> (Getz et al., 2001: 389)

Social impacts of events

Studies of the key impacts currently being used for event evaluation focus on the concept of triple bottom line (TBL) evaluation which covers economic, environmental and social impacts (Jago 2005). While it is impossible to do justice to the topic of event evaluation here, suffice it to say that human resource management contributes, at least in part, to the social impact of an event. For example, an estimate of the workforce for the FIFA World Cup 2010 in South Africa is the equivalent of 159,000 annual jobs (Swart and

PLATE 12.2 Team spirit is evident here

Urmilla, 2005). Large-scale events can contribute to direct short-term employment at the event and, in some cases, to long-term employment if there is significant tourism impact. Depending on the scale and scope of the event, training initiatives can be quite significant in attaining such an outcome, particularly if they cover the full scope of training, from management development through to specific skill acquisition.

There are also more intangible benefits such as increase in community pride, leading to greater self-confidence and a 'can do' attitude on the part of individuals and the community. The culture of the event can thus transmit to the general community, bringing long-term benefits. In the IOC report, Case Study 12.2, on the Beijing Olympic Games, excellence and relevance are differentiated, as 'doing things right' and 'doing the right things'. This chapter is all about doing the right things, looking at the intangible aspects of event management rather than the technical.

While it is tempting to consider only the positive outcomes of events, we must be mindful that some events are not successful. In his analysis of why some festivals fail, Getz (2002) points to the following reasons.

Human resources:

- incompetent event managers or staff;
- volunteer burnout;
- corruption or theft from within;
- high turnover among volunteers.

Organizational culture:

- lack of strong leadership;
- internal divisions over goals, programme, strategy, etc;
- the event founders had not permitted needed changes;
- the structure of the organization prevented necessary changes.

   Further, he goes on to point out that an event might fail, not because it has reached the end of the product life cycle or because of market forces, but due to an absence of strategic planning and a sound organizational culture.

CASE STUDY 12.2
Excellence and relevance – doing the right things

The power of the Games to inspire young people and a broader global audience requires both Excellence and Relevance. Excellence in the quality of the product – 'doing things right' (preparation, staging, service levels, responsiveness, etc.); and Relevance in how the Olympic experience is positioned – 'doing the right things' – for example, closely considering the context when choosing the ingredients and developing the elements that eventually make an Olympic experience truly unique (sports presentation, look elements, city atmosphere, messaging, etc).

Innovation is therefore essential at all stages of the Games' development: it allows for preparation and delivery of projects that are less complex to manage and cheaper to develop, while providing the different stakeholders and the fans with a more stunning Games experience.

Source: *Final Report of the IOC Coordination Commission Games of the XXIX Olympiad, Beijing* (2008: 21)

Reflective practice 12.2

1   Describe a host city's expectations of a mega event.
2   If 200 nations and international organizations participate in an event, explain how a 'best fit' between national cultures can be achieved.
3   If you were responsible for training the workforce for this event, what would you list as five priorities?

Chapter summary and key points

This chapter has looked at organizational and service culture and has highlighted some of the dimensions of a culture, such as policies, practices, communication flows and resource allocation. Looking specifically at the event industry's organizational culture, we saw that the emphasis was on characteristics of the service culture as they apply in this context, that is, intangibility, perishability, inseparability and variability. Providing quality service in this complex environment (with a temporary workforce) is exceptionally challenging and, from a human resource perspective, the importance of careful labour force planning, selection and training cannot be underestimated. Other defining features of the event organizational culture were seen to include the dynamic nature of events, the network of relationships with external stakeholders and the heavy reliance on customer satisfaction for the event's success. This requires a shift in thinking from the technical to the human side of service provision.

Revision questions

1   Select an event on the internet that you can investigate or visit one in person. Describe the culture of the event organization through your observations and by using the dimensions suggested in this chapter.
2   Elaborate on the statement, 'Events provide services that are intangible and inseparable, therefore staff communication and customer service training is vitally important'.
3   For a specific local event, describe three of the stakeholders and their communication relationships with the event organizers.
4   Events have social impacts. Compare two events in terms of their human resources impact.

Industry voice by Kerrie Nash

Doha was very interesting because it was culturally so different. In the Middle East it's a very hierarchical, risk adverse culture, very patriarchal. I had to learn to really prepare whatever I wanted to do, to sell it up the line to get people confident in that, whereas, I am much more used to having the blank sheet of paper. You're moving at a huge pace. Normally you might just decide on something and implement it. I couldn't do that in that environment. I had to be much more cognizant of the need to involve my manager and his manager and the need to explain why we were doing it this way and how that was actually going to help to de-risk.

The learning is, to listen, to take your cues, to focus on the output you want to achieve and adapt. Adapt, but also challenge. However, I do think that you do have to challenge the cultural stereotypes that can be associated with people. I keep coming back to this idea of the learning organization. I think that an event environment is a brilliant example of what should be a learning organization. Everybody in the organization, whether they have previous event experience or local knowledge (or both), should understand that they're on a journey and that they're learning from one another. It truly is a voyage of discovery where no two days are ever the same. Every day is advancing towards an immovable deadline.

We all bring something to the table. I think if you can try and embed that as a sort of a cultural norm in the event organization it can be hugely powerful.

Discussion questions

1 Why does Kerrie describe the event planning process as a voyage of discovery?
2 How is 'learning from one another' able to contribute to development of an event organizational culture and service standard?

References

Eunson, B. (2012). *Communication in the Workplace*. Milton, Queensland: Wiley.

Getz, D. (2002). 'Why festivals fail', *Event Management*, 7(4), 209–219.

Getz, D., O'Neill, M. and Carlsen, J. (2001). 'Service quality evaluation at events through service mapping', *Journal of Travel Research*, 39, 380–390.

Heery, E., Conley, J., Delbridge, R. and Stewart, P. (2004). 'Beyond the enterprise: trade union representation of freelancers in the UK', *Human Resources Management Journal*, 14(2), 20–34.

Indigenous Festival (2006). *Mission Statement*. Available at: www.indigenousfestival.org/MissionStatement.asp; viewed 21 March 2007.

Jago, L. (2005). 'The impacts of events: triple bottom line event evaluation'. In *The Impacts of Events*. Sydney: University of Technology Sydney.

Jemmasi, M., Strong, K. C. and Taylor, S. A. (2011). 'Measuring service quality for strategic planning and analysis in service firms', *Journal of Applied Business Research (JABR)*, 10(4), 24–34.

Manchester City Council (2003). *Manchester Commonwealth Games Post Games Report*. Available at: www.gameslegacy.com; viewed 17 May 2006.

Parasuraman, A., Zeithaml, V. A. and Berry, L. L. (2004). 'Refinement and reassessment of the SERVQUAL scale', *Journal of Retailing*, 67(4), 114.

Parent, M. M. (2010). 'Decision making in major sport events over time: parameters, drivers, and strategies', *Journal of Sport Management*, 24(3), 291–318.

Shone, A. and Parry, B. (2013). *Successful Event Management*, 4th edn. Andover, UK: Cengage Learning.

Southeastern Surgical Congress (2006). *Mission Statement*. Available at: www.sesc.org/member/information/MissionStatement.htm; viewed 22 June 2008.

Swart, K. and Urmilla, B. (2005). 'Leveraging anticipated benefits associated with hosting the 2010 Soccer World Cup in South Africa'. In *The Impacts of Events*. Sydney: University of Technology Sydney.

Tyson, S. (1999). 'How HR knowledge contributes to organizational performance', *Human Resource Management Journal*, 9(3), 42–53.

Tyson, S. (2013). 'The handbook of research on comparative human resource management', *Personnel Review*, 42(3), 366–368.

Van Der Wagen, L. (2011). *Event Management*, 4th edn. Sydney: Pearson Education.

Webb, T. (2001). *The Collaborative Games: The Story Behind the Spectacle*. Sydney: Pluto Press.

13

Collaboration and integration

Learning objectives

After reading through this chapter you will be able to:

- Describe the challenges of the event environment in terms of integration and collaboration.
- Describe the factors that can lead to conflict.
- Evaluate ways in which collaborative work practices can be improved.
- Describe the difference between national and organizational cultures.
- Briefly discuss research into cross-cultural communication.
- Discuss the issue of knowledge management: transmission of knowledge within and beyond the event.

Introduction

This chapter looks at communication processes, at the collaboration required to run a successful event. The event environment, due to its turbulent and temporary nature, can provide real challenges for effective communication. Sharing knowledge within and across events can be unreliable, although new technologies are assisting in storing and disseminating a wide range of information. The importance of data collection, research and evaluation cannot be stressed enough. For the industry to become more professional, the process of event operational planning needs to be improved and consolidated, particularly where there are serious threats to safety. Event evaluation provides a lasting legacy for future events.

Goldblatt (2005) points out that event management is a profession where success or failure depends on communication. He also stresses that there are often barriers to communication, such as noise and visual distractions in the event environment. Regardless of the communication channel chosen, and the barriers to communication, it is essential that messages are clear, action oriented and, in most cases, recorded for future reference. This is particularly the case if a contract variation is involved, where customers ask for more, and more, and more! While a good customer service orientation is essential, it is also essential to recognize when additional services have cost implications.

In the event environment there are two stages where good communication is essential: developing plans and communication on site. For the first of these, project management software can be a useful tool, facilitating the development of project plans on the network and updating by anyone on the team. Generally an email is automatically generated to advise team members of changes made. If this is not the case, another procedure needs to be developed to guard against timelines being modified without anyone noticing. As enticing as project management software sounds, it is not user friendly, and many people prefer to have ownership of part of the project rather than have teams contributing to a common plan or budget. If enough Gantt charts are developed to wallpaper a building it is taking it too far!

For communication on site two-way radio is the preferred option, although smaller events usually get by using mobile phones. Two-way radio allows multiple people to work together on the same channel. However, this runs the risk of there being too much communication and staff members are often advised to use the radio channel sparingly so that priorities can be managed effectively. And if the radio is used for chitchat others will be excluded, although there are, of course, overrides or alternative channels for emergency reporting.

Transmission models of communication emphasize that a 'message' be transmitted from one person to another. This message is converted into a signal, which is transmitted via a channel. If, for example, the channel is the telephone, there are various ways in which the transmission can be disrupted. First, there is mechanical noise, making it hard for the receiver to hear the message. Or there could be poor reception on a mobile phone (another form of mechanical noise), interfering with the transmission of the message. The second type of disruption is semantic noise. If your communication is unclear and the message confusing, through the use of words the receiver does not understand, this too can contribute to poor message transmission. Use of jargon or complex words contributes to semantic noise. Finally, psychological noise causes the receiver to block or object to the message, perhaps due to the tone or language used. If, for example, a supervisor used a swear word on a two-way radio this could interfere with the message content. The receiver might get offended and ignore the instruction. Ultimately, the aim is to ensure that the meaning of the sender is interpreted correctly by the receiver.

Conflict management

What better time to raise the subject of conflict management? Due to the dynamic nature of the event planning environment and the many pressures faced by the organizers, conflict is endemic. It can be resolved positively, leading to creative and innovative event designs and concepts, but equally it can lead to teams becoming dysfunctional. As Eunson (2005) points out, conflict can have positive payoffs, leading to better decision making. Equally, it can block communication.

According to Eunson, any of the following four factors may lead to conflict and they are elaborated from an event viewpoint:

1   Resource scarcity. This may include lack of time, money, people and tangible resources such as radios.
2   Workflow interdependence. Gantt charts, frequently used for event planning, illuminate the dependence of one task on another, thus impacting on the critical path.
3   Power and/or value asymmetry. People with high-low power relationships or significantly different values may find it extremely hard to work together. For example, the 'bean counters' are often derided by the creative team for harnessing their ideas.
4   Goal incompatibility. Goals of different departments, functional areas and teams can clash. For example, the demands made by the waste management team to ban the use of polystyrene and foil may seem unrealistic to the catering team.

Many studies have been done into the nature of conflict in building projects, which is similar to that occurring during event projects and different from the conflict which occurs in business enterprises. Clarke (2010: 82) describes the 'adverserial relationships between contractors and design teams' and this may relate to contractual obligations which are unclear. There may be disagreements about priorities, tasks, timing and resource allocation. This is due in part to goal interdependence.

Absolute goal congruence is difficult to achieve. By way of example, the environmental sustainability (green) team might demand that caterers do not bring various types of packaging on site, such as polystyrene. Their demands across the catering spectrum (including managing food waste) might lead to unanticipated time and cost. In the first chapter we looked at the three primary event impacts, economic, social and environmental. In this case the environmental objectives are at odds with the economic objective of profit for the caterer. Likewise social impact objectives such as recruitment of unemployed or jobless people will add to training costs. This is not to say that this is not a laudable objective, however it cannot emerge late in the planning process. This reinforces the importance of defining the event purpose and objectives as this in turn will reduce the level of conflict as a result of the 'moving goal posts' so familiar to event managers.

Working collaboratively

For an event to be successful issues need to be resolved by working collaboratively and productively. Issues may evolve around inequity in distribution of resources; problems with decision making and lines of communication; different values and interpersonal styles; inadequate project planning; or lack of leadership and direction.

So what do we know about collaboration? Here are some assumptions:

•   Management involvement in collaborative work planning is essential.
•   Teams benefit from regular, professional and neutral facilitation.
•   Conflict is inevitable.

Conflict can be reduced by:

- developing clear roles and responsibilities;
- setting ground rules;
- developing boundaries for acceptable behaviour;
- developing clear goals and targets;
- empowering individuals to negotiate and make binding decisions;
- focusing on super-ordinate goals (the event programme and deadline);
- establishing conflict resolution processes;
- establishing procedures for conflict escalation;
- meeting regularly and monitoring progress towards agreed goals.

On an individual level, conflict negotiation techniques include:

- asking questions;
- listening and providing feedback;
- refraining from taking absolute positions;
- repeating key phrases and statements of fact;
- restating the question as a point of focus;
- developing targets and action points;
- focusing on tasks and behaviours;
- avoiding emotional terms and personal blame;
- searching for alternatives;
- reaching agreement on the steps forward.

Chiocchio et al. (2011: 78) suggest that the configuration of work into functional and disciplinary areas negatively impacts the collaborative process and that many problems often fail to be resolved either quickly or to anyone's satisfaction:

> Teamwork during integrated design projects is complex. We address this by investigating how trust, collaboration, and conflict evolve over time to affect performance. Our results stem from data gathered using validated self-report questionnaires with 38 participants in 5 multidisciplinary teams at three points in time during a 6-week integrated design competition. Results show that without collaboration, trust and conflict have no bearing on performance. In addition to an unambiguous practical outcome – fostering collaboration helps build trust and manage conflict – our study points to theoretical developments: as trust- and conflict-performance relations grow over time, so does collaboration's mediating effect.

In summary, these authors suggest that building collaboration should be the main focus as this in turn leads to trust and reduces conflict. In practice then, 'collaboration boots the positive effect of trust and dampens the negative effect of conflict, offering the opportunity to substantially improve performance' (p. 87). Thus any attempt to mediate conflict between teams and individuals in the event workplace should have a collaboration as its focus using team building activities to this end.

One of the most interesting features of the event business that has not been widely documented is the 'magic moment' when everyone realizes that only collaboration from this point onwards will enable the event to meet its deadlines. This is the point at which everyone knows that the moment of doors opening to visitors is imminent, and that only positive teamwork will ensure that this will happen. This intense but positive period of co-operation occurs at different times, depending on the size and scope of the event. Complaining, sabotage, arguments and blaming cease and compromise is reached on almost every issue. Super-ordinate goals are those that sit above the nitty-gritty conflicts of every day. In the event business the super-ordinate goal is generally the successful production of the event programme on the date and time specified. Since this deadline is invariably inflexible this becomes the super-ordinate goal for negotiation. One of the tactics of the event manager could be to bring this moment in time forward in the perceptions of stakeholders and the wider workforce. An extra day or even an extra week of total commitment and collaboration by all involved is a bonus. This can be done by creating a 'fudge factor' in last minute timelines. Another suggestion would be holding the 'after party' before the event to give the team a sense of completion and celebration of their achievements.

Cross-cultural communication

Multinational teams are a feature of events. In addition, many event organizations work in different cities and countries. For example, specialists working in the fields of pyrotechnic displays and opening ceremonies typically work around the world. Cross-cultural communication is thus a significant issue for such individuals and organizations.

A company called Pyrovision in the United Kingdom produced the special effects for the Queen's Jubliee and the Shanghai Music Festival. In addition to numerous shows done in their home country, employees have worked in Monaco, China, Germany, France, USA and Russia, to name just a few places. To work in a global environment cross-cultural communication skills are essential for negotiation and operational implementation.

In this text we have described many of the common features of the event organizational culture, the most dominant being the project management orientation and the dynamic nature of the working environment (Allen et al., 2010; Bowdin et al., 2012; Hanlon and Cuskelly, 2002; Yeoman et al., 2012). When discussing national culture, and the impact this has on organizations, we are looking instead at international business relationships and the impact that national culture has on communication. Communication effectiveness is affected by the 'fit' between one national culture and another. Hofstede (1991) is one of the best-known theorists in this field and he describes national cultural dimensions in terms of:

- Power distance – focuses on the degree of equality, or inequality, between people in the country's society.
- Individualism – focuses on the degree to which the society reinforces individual or collective achievement and interpersonal relationships.

- Masculinity – focuses on the degree to which the society reinforces, or does not reinforce, the traditional masculine work role model of male achievement, control and power.
- Uncertainty avoidance – focuses on the level of tolerance for uncertainty and ambiguity within the society.
- Long-term orientation – focuses on the degree to which the society embraces, or does not embrace, long-term devotion to traditional, forward-thinking values.

This last dimension was added after Hofstede completed a study of Chinese managers. As an example, Brazil's highest Hofstede dimension is uncertainty avoidance, suggesting that, as a result, the society does not readily accept change and is very risk adverse (Geert Hofstede™ Cultural Dimensions, 2006). This would have implications for event planners. Koester and Lustig (2012) provide several other taxonomies of intercultural competence and practical guidelines on improving intercultural knowledge and communication competence.

While Hofstede's research has prompted much debate and discussion (largely over the sample chosen for the research), most writers agree that intercultural communication requires a global outlook. A model for communication effectiveness developed by Griffith and Harvey (2001) includes three communication competencies. Cognitive competence is the ability of the individual to ascertain meaning from verbal and nonverbal language; affective competence relates to an individual's emotional tendencies (e.g. willingness to accept culturally diverse communications); and behavioural competence. The last of these is indicated by flexibility and adaptability – the ability to respond appropriately in different cultural contexts.

Griffith goes further to suggest the following steps as an action plan to monitor and improve communication effectiveness in international organizations:

- assess communication competence of internal managers;
- match internal and external manager competencies;
- assess the effectiveness of the communication environment;
- develop an appropriate communication strategy;
- audit performance effectiveness of communication.

Event planning involves extensive negotiation with stakeholders, so event organizations operating offshore need to develop their knowledge of local conditions (including rules, regulations, laws and practices) and fine-tune their negotiation skills. An ability to work and communicate effectively in a global environment is a priority for those organizations and individuals working under these circumstances.

Knowledge management

Broadly, knowledge management is the process of systematically managing the stores of knowledge in an organization and transforming these information and intellectual

CASE STUDY 13.1
Different perceptions of crowd control

True picture on the parade 'problems'

I am writing to express my disgust at the one-sided piece of reporting on page three of the journal last week, headlined: 'Animal magic ends in upset'.

Maybe you should make yourself aware of all the facts before publishing such rubbish. Why did you publish only one person's point of view?

I was travelling with my daughter in Black Thunder, we were supposed to be part of the parade through Barnstaple with Father Christmas. Lantern FM were kind enough to take children from the Children's Hospice in their cars to see Father Christmas.

The problems started as we left the service ramp at Green Lanes, the crowd surged forward behind Father Christmas thus making it impossible for the Lantern cars to follow.

There were many children dressed up, I believe they were also supposed to be a part of the parade, but were swamped by the crowd.

As we reached the top of Joy Street a gentleman from the Rotary Club stood in front of the Lantern vehicles and refused to let us pass. Did he not understand that children from the hospice would want to be part of the parade, or did he not appreciate the support and generosity of the Lantern team? At this stage the police stepped in and diverted us down Joy Street as all three cars quickly became surrounded by people, demonstrating a frightening lack of crowd safety or control.

We sat in the cars at the bottom of Joy Street for about half an hour or so, until Father Christmas came past and we could rejoin the parade to the entrance at Green Lanes, where the children were supposed to follow Father Christmas to the Grotto.

We were advised by the police not to leave the cars as there were too many people, it would not be safe or possible for the children to follow. We sat in the cars until the crowds cleared and the reindeer moved off. We went straight back to the hospice.

The situation could have been a disaster, not only from our point of view in that the children could have become distressed or scared.

It was all thanks to PJ and the Lantern team that the situation was turned into a fun experience. From the crowd point of view, it shows credit to the people of North Devon (most of whom seemed to be in Barnstaple that night!) in that it was their goodwill and humour that kept the atmosphere happy.

Maybe the Rotary Club should think long and hard before marshalling an event of this size, or that has the potential to be this size, as it seems they were ill-equipped to deal with this situation.

But all credit and thanks should go to the police who were brilliant throughout, and to PJ and the Lantern FM team, not only for their support for the children from the Children's Hospice, but for also creating a fun atmosphere to salvage a potentially disastrous evening.

MRS CINDY STONE Barnstaple

Reproduced with permission of *North Devon Journal*, 2 December 2004

ROTARIANS ROLE WAS NOT CROWD CONTROL
In response to the letter by Mrs Cindy Stone headed 'True picture on the parade problems' in last week's journal may I take the liberty of correcting one of her misconceptions, namely the role played by the Rotary Clubs of Barnstaple.

The Christmas parade was organized by the Town Centre Management who in turn asked for volunteers from the Rotary Clubs, fourteen of us duly gave up our evening at home and turned up.

On arrival at the Green Lanes ramp we were given specific instructions. Two members were sent to Joy Street and told that under no circumstances were they to let any vehicle pass while the remainder were instructed to surround Santa's sled to prevent (for health and safety reasons one assumes) children touching the reindeer.

The assumption by Mrs Stone that we were in some way responsible for crowd control is ludicrous, such tasks are best left to the professionals, the police.

Volunteering for unenviable jobs is what we Rotarians do. We also raise vast sums of money for local, national and international charities one of which is the Children's Hospice to which it would appear Mrs Stone also lends a helping hand.

She is to be congratulated, as is the Town Centre Management, for putting on the parade, and the people of Barnstaple for responding so wholeheartedly.

EDWARD O'NEILL
President, The Rotary Club of Barnstaple Link Copley Drive, Barnstaple

Reproduced with permission of *North Devon Journal*, 9 December 2004

Reflective practice 13.1

1   Explain how these problems occurred.
2   How could clear communication have prevented these problems occurring?
3   Write a letter to the Rotarians, thanking them for their help and clarifying the situation.

assets into enduring value for the organization. Within the event operation, the focus of knowledge management is on the development and dissemination of information to the workforce and the management of post-event evaluation.

One of the characteristic features of the event environment is the speed at which decisions are made. When talking about the Wave Aid concert put on in quick response to the 2004 tsunami, Matthew Lazarus-Hall said that decisions were made in record time. On one occasion, he left a meeting to find that the decisions made there had changed before he reached the parking lot.

Responsiveness to operational contingencies often requires quick dissemination of information to staff and volunteers who are dealing with the public. Systems need to be in place to ensure that this happens. As seen above, two-way radio is used for this purpose, although today many event staff rely more on their mobile phones and other devices for communication.

Knowledge management in relation to event evaluation is increasingly viewed as a priority. The Olympic Games Knowledge Management repository is an example of an initiative developed in 1998 so that future events could build upon the planning of past events by accessing and transferring historical information. A similar system was developed by the Manchester Commonwealth Games and built on by the Melbourne Commonwealth Games. All events – whether one-off productions or annual events – can create a useful legacy for those that follow by assembling, storing and evaluating data related to the event.

Unlike the hotel industry in which standard accounting procedures and reporting statistics have been developed, the event industry has had a limited focus on knowledge management and analysis. Communicating knowledge gained from one event context to another occurs mostly informally through transmission of information by individuals who are experienced in the field. For knowledge to be used as the asset that it is, it has to be systematically collected and categorized. While it may appear that technological solutions are the answer, the question of human intent is critical as well. The right organizational climate is needed for people to willingly share information and to learn collaboratively in the interests of the industry.

There are a number of ways in which human resources can contribute to knowledge management:

- Developing a culture of trust and open communication.
- Developing systems for capturing tacit knowledge.
- Using training and mentoring as a means of disseminating expert knowledge.
- Providing rewards for projects which capture expert knowledge.
- Writing reports, such as training evaluation reports, to contribute to knowledge management in the area of human resources.
- Co-ordinating briefing and debriefing meetings.
- Developing and presenting training sessions on project management and evaluation, including post-event reporting for the event as a whole.

Emergency and crisis management communication

Communicating hazards and reporting incidents is a key responsibility for everyone on site. This topic is generally the core aspect of onsite training for events, particularly those held outdoors. Communication protocols should be in place for any occurrence

PLATE 13.1 Crowd management team sets off for duty

linked to health and safety and all staff should be fully aware of their roles should a serious incident occur.

The incident or emergency command structure (ICS) or emergency control organization (ECO) is likely to be quite different to the operational organization structure of an event as rescue services personnel overrule normal management personnel in these circumstances. There may be an event co-ordination centre to manage radio communications and keep a radio log of key communications. Roles and responsibilities of various parties need to be clarified in any emergency response plan including those of:

- police, fire, first aid, ambulance and other emergency response agencies;
- venue/facility management;
- event producer/manager;
- security;
- entertainers;
- ushers and other key personnel involved in evacuation.

The emergency communications plan should outline:

- how to contact emergency services;
- communication protocols during an emergency (such as how, and to whom, incidents are reported and logged);
- coded messages for incidents, such as:
  - Red – fire or smoke
  - Orange – evacuation

- Yellow – internal emergency
- Blue – medical
- Brown – external emergency
- Purple – bomb or substance threat
- Black – personal threat.

In times of crisis effective communication can save lives. While the emergency response plan (ERP) and crisis communication plan might never be used they are essential components of training. It is in preparing for such training that policies and procedures are clarified and resolved for the event organization. In this sense the HR team is often 'across' all aspects of event planning, often driving development to meeting training deadlines.

Chapter summary and key points

Having a clear purpose regarding communication can go a long way towards improving its effectiveness. Different people can make different meanings of the same message because of their different perceptions, but if communication is purposive and clear, fewer misunderstandings will occur. In this chapter we have also covered cross-cultural communication, explaining briefly how differences in cultural background can impact upon communication. It is dangerous, however, to stereotype cross-cultural communication. Instead, an emphasis on understanding differences in perception (by individuals and groups) and a focus on developing effective listening and clear communication is a more constructive approach.

Inevitably, conflict will arise at times in the pressured event environment, so conflict management skills and conflict negotiation techniques have been outlined in this chapter to help event personnel deal with such situations.

Finally, the field of knowledge management has been introduced briefly and its role in professionalizing event management emphasized. Assembling, storing and evaluating data on events provides a useful legacy for future event planning and implementation.

Revision questions

1 Select one communication channel and describe how it is commonly used in the event environment.
2 Give three reasons why conflict might emerge during the planning of an international convention.
3 Using an example, explain how collaborative processes can assist in developing win-win solutions.
4 Discuss the statement: 'Studies of cultural differences are counterproductive as they lead people to stereotype others'.
5 Explain the importance of training for emergency communication and response.

Industry voice by Kerrie Nash

It requires a huge level of integration and project management and I actually enjoy that piece of trying to bring all the strands together. Not just within the HR team, but broader in the organization because everything is so intertwined. I enjoy stitching the whole thing together and ensuring that what HR does is completely integrated with what the rest of the organization does. I do enjoy the challenge of trying to develop the unified culture when you have so many different individuals and different experiences within the organization.

Discussion questions

1   Integrating the functions across an event organization is essential. The HR staffing and training functions contribute to integration as they require 'buy in' from all functional areas. In the process of recruitment and training, many issues can be ironed out. This is particularly the case when job descriptions are developed as part of the staffing masterplan. Discuss the concept of Workforce Planning acting as the 'glue' in a mega or major event.

2   Smaller events do not have dedicated HR personnel. Explain how the event producer can facilitate team collaboration/communication across the project team including staff, contractors, clients and stakeholders. To do this create a table with two columns, one for the planning period and one for the operational period. In each column make at least 10 specific recommendations.

References

Allen, L., O'Toole, W., Harris, R. and McDonnell, I. (2010). *Festival and Special Event Management*, 5th edn. Milton, Queensland: John Wiley & Sons.

Bowdin, G., Allen, J., Harris, R., McDonnell, I. and O'Toole, W. (2012). *Events Management*. Oxford: Elsevier.

Chiocchio, F., Forgues, D., Paradis, D. and Iordanova, I. (2011). 'Teamwork in integrated design projects: understanding the effects of trust, conflict, and collaboration on performance', *Project Management Journal*, 42(6), 78–91.

Clarke, N. (2010). 'Emotional intelligence and its relationship to transformational leadership and key project manager competences', *Project Management Journal*, 41(2), 5–20.

Eunson, B. (2005). *Communicating in the 21st Century*. Milton, Queensland: John Wiley and Sons.

Geert Hofstede™ (2006). *Cultural Dimensions ITIM International*. Available at: www.geert-hofstede.com/hofstede_brazil.shtml; viewed 12 February 2006.

Goldblatt, J. J. (2005). *Special Events: Event Leadership for a New World*, 4th edn. Hoboken, NJ: Wiley.

Griffith, D. A. and Harvey, M. G. (2001). 'An intercultural communication model for use in global interorganizational networks', *Journal of International Marketing*, 9(3), 87–103.

Hanlon, C. and Cuskelly, G. (2002). 'Pulsating major sport event organizations: a framework for inducting managerial personnel', *Event Management*, 7, 231–243.

Hofstede, G. (1991). *Cultures and Organizations: Software of the Mind*. London: McGraw-Hill.

Koester, J. and Lustig, M. (2012). *Intercultural Competence: Interpersonal Communication Across Cultures*. Upper Saddle River, NY: Pearson Prentice Hall.

Yeoman, I., Robertson, M., Ali-Knight, J., Drummond, S. and McMahon-Beattie, U. (eds). (2012). *Festival and Events Management*. London: Routledge.

14

Leadership

Learning objectives

After reading through this chapter you will be able to:

- Differentiate between management and leadership.
- Describe stages of project management.
- Discuss the appropriateness of project management approaches for providing leadership in the event environment.
- Describe context factors for event leaders.
- Describe theories of leadership and their relevance to the event industry.
- Prepare leadership training.

Introduction

In this chapter we will look at the topic of leadership. In some respects this is quite problematic as so much has been written on the subject, but with the traditional business in mind. In the normal business environment, everything is pretty stable: policies and procedures are in place and there are ready-made systems for dealing with market force changes. Even if staff turnover is high, many organizational characteristics remain unchanged. Systems and procedures in hospitals, banks, supermarkets and fast food outlets come to mind. In these organizations, there is generally a legacy on which to build and move forward, and the organizational culture is well established.

For many events, however, it is a ground-up development, sometimes at an alarming pace. This involves new venues, policies, operational procedures and, most importantly, new temporary people. While some events, such as small meetings held in hotels and exhibitions staged at convention centres, have ready-made formulas, the majority of events, including diverse events in arts and entertainment, are unique in concept and execution, thus requiring flexible leadership.

Management or leadership?

Most people would agree that not every manager is a leader (although he or she should be) and that every leader is not a manager (some workers appoint themselves to this role). Informal leaders often emerge in the event environment: for example, an experienced business person might step in to lead a group of volunteers where there appears to be a leadership vacuum. The problematic informal leader is one who takes the lead, but is essentially clueless!

Management is generally characterized as tactical, i.e. following the processes of planning, organizing, leading and controlling. Planning involves setting the direction and operationalizing organizational strategies; organizing means creating structures and assigning tasks; leading means inspiring effort; and controlling ensures that tasks are completed (see Figure 14.1). From this can be seen that leading is part of a manager's role. Some are better at it than others!

Project management was discussed in Chapter 3 because of its similarity to event management, but here we will outline the five phases of project management to see that for a one-off event they are more linear.

Initiating. During this phase the vision for the project is developed and the goals are established. Stakeholders are engaged. The core planning team is in place and the planning process begins.

Planning. Work breakdown is analysed, resources are allocated and schedules are developed. During this phase tasks and activities that lead to project goals are defined more clearly. Throughout this phase there is an emphasis on determining the scope of work.

Executing. Here the work is completed according to the project plan. The focus is on task completion, meeting milestones and managing critical paths. Communication is vitally important during this phase.

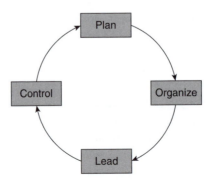

FIGURE 14.1 Management cycle

Controlling. Monitoring the outcomes achieved, rescheduling and reallocating resources occurs during the controlling phase, helping to keep the project on track. Where project goals are varied, approval is required from stakeholders. Note that in the event environment a project timeline overrun is seldom possible; the media and the audience are waiting for the performance to begin. Viewers around the world are ready for kickoff and conference delegates are waiting for the live broadcast from the CEO.

Closing. Before the team is disbanded, the project needs to be reviewed, bills paid and people acknowledged. An evaluation of the project is essential, the final report being the legacy of achievement and results.

Readers will notice that throughout these phases, the issue of leadership does not emerge clearly and the process appears quite clinical. Perhaps this is because projects in information technology or engineering are not as creative, complex, problematic, dynamic or stakeholder reliant as special events. However, this is doubtful, because vision and leadership are required in all workplaces, particularly when working on ground-breaking projects.

Thomsett (2002), in his discussion on the project management revolution, talks about the increasing technical complexity of projects making it impossible for project managers to undertake technical reviews. He differentiates between content and context. Content includes the project tasks, the technical deliverables, while context involves the business, social and political environment of the project. He argues that the role of the project manager is shifting to ensuring that the project achieves its business goals: 'Build a relationship with your stakeholders and you will be doing your job. It is all about relationships' (p. 26). In fact, he goes further to suggest that the less the project manager knows about the technical details the better! Thus the project manager's role is all about power and influence, about making things happen. Thomsett concludes by pointing out that leadership is about change whereas management is about order and consistency.

Other authors highlight the association between leadership and vision. Christenson and Walker (2008) found that vision that was effectively communicated made a strong and positive impact upon project success. Silvers (2012) also provides a convincing argument for convergence of artististic and technical abilities driven by creative vision. In this chapter we will look in more detail at leadership in the event context, sources of power, and old and new theories of leadership, including contemporary ideas about transformational leadership. Case Study 14.1 illustrates contemporary views on visionary leadership.

Definitions of leadership

Leadership is generally defined as the ability to inspire confidence and support among the people who are needed to achieve organizational goals and it is about the capacity of an individual to inspire and motivate. As stated earlier, leadership can be exhibited by non-managerial personnel such as union leaders. In recent years researchers have looked at leadership in terms of 'near' and 'far' leadership (Alimo-Metcalfe and Alban-Metcalf, 2005).

They have done this because most previous analysis has been of very senior executives and they believe that the focus for leadership study should be 'near leadership', that is at lower levels of the organizational structure where leaders define organizational reality rather than exert wide-ranging influence over goal achievement.

The concept of 'followership' has also been introduced in more recent times, possibly in response to the diverse nature of the workforce. Leadership and 'followership' are distributed through every level of organizations.

Recent studies are more inclusive of gender and culture. The women's perspective claims that finding collaborative, interdependent relationships between leader and followers is more common in gender inclusive research. It also suggests that linear models of group development, particularly those that view power struggles as one of these phases, are unsuited to the modern work environment. In general terms leaders are known for:

- exerting influence;
- having followers;
- lifting people to a new level;
- persuading others to act towards achieving a common goal;
- leading by example so that others follow.

The theme of influence is found in most definitions.

Organizational contexts for leadership

Before looking at leadership theory, past and present, let us revisit the topic of the event context discussed in Chapter 1. Here we will contrast various contexts for leadership: long-life organizations, short-life organizations and organizations manned primarily by contractors or volunteers.

Shone and Parry (2004) use the description 'short-life' to describe the special event context. This is a helpful basis on which to review leadership literature since the short-life organization is quite different from the long-life organization, which has been the basis for most leadership research. Tyssen et al. reiterate that 'projects and other temporary forms of organising are different from standard organisational processes' (2013: 52).

Long-life organizations

Strategic planning for a long-life, stable organization requires a vision of the future in which the organization operates: the internal and external forces that might impact on the organization as time progresses; competitive forces; and responses that the organization may need to make to remain ahead of the game. This is generally the role of executives in large corporations, such as media, finance and telecommunications. However, this is also the general direction for many event suppliers, such as hire companies, who plan to run their organizations over a long period and remain profitable in a changing climate. It is also essential for events that have long-term sustainability as a goal, such as the

Schützenausmarsch or Marksmen's Parade in Hanover which is claimed to be the longest parade in the world. Around 5,000 marksmen and 5,000 musicians from more than 100 marching bands made their way through the streets of the northern German city in a parade that lasted three hours. The annual festival, which dates back to the fifteenth century, was originally a celebration of archery skills and evolved into a display of target shooting prowess. Carnival festivities in Brazil date back to 1723 and continue to evolve, these days providing valuable tourism income for Rio de Janeiro.

Short-life organizations (project based)

In contrast to long-life organizations, most events and event organizations do not operate on the scale of major corporations. Often, their vision is more creative than strategic. As we have seen, many events have project characteristics, such as defined timelines and resources. In this context, leadership is about harnessing energy and commitment to achieve the creative vision of the director (Shone and Parry, 2004).

Project-based organizations

Hanisch and Wald (2011: 5) point out that projects are different from standard organizational processes,

> due to their temporary and unique nature, projects are characterized by discontinuous personal constellations and work contents. This goes hand in hand with a lack of organizational routines, a short-term orientation, and the necessary transdisciplinary integration of internal and external experts.

Volunteer-based organizations

When people are not paid they are not easily coerced into doing things. In fact, to keep attrition of the workforce to a minimum, programmes need to be designed to reward and retain volunteers for the period of the event. Leadership is vitally important in the volunteer-based organization in conveying the event's purpose, as volunteers frequently cite their commitment to an ideal as their primary motivation for event volunteering.

Contractor-based organizations

For many events nearly every element is outsourced. In some cases, contractors employ sub-contractors and the hierarchy devolves further still. In many cases the employees on the ground are not appointed by their agencies until the week or day before the event. In these circumstances it is very difficult to develop a culture in the organization or provide seamless customer service at the event. In these circumstances project management planning has to rise to the level of planning often unnecessary when the workforce is flexible, willing, co-operative and committed.

Leadership is tested in an environment in which many of the event components are outsourced to contractors and subcontractors. As with volunteers, contractors are not paid staff of the organization and therefore highly effective communication, negotiation and conflict management skills are needed to manage them. The earlier definition of leadership is useful in that it referred to 'the people who are needed to achieve organizational goals' and is thus inclusive of contractor employees.

Leadership is also tested when an event organization shifts into emergency mode, for example, in the case of a fire, bomb threat or crowd control issue. When there are sudden and dramatic threats such as these, leadership is sometimes handed over to other authorities such as emergency services, as a military-style command and control mode is generally more useful in response to this type of situation.

Sources of power

A leader has various sources of power. The most common in most organizations is the legitimate power of employer over employee. This power is of course limited in the case of volunteers and contractor representatives.

In the event environment, as in most organizations, influence can be exerted in a number of ways depending on the power source (Mintzberg, 1983):

- Legitimate power comes from the person's place in the managerial hierarchy and is vested in the position. People working as police officers, fire fighters, etc. also carry legitimate power vested in them through legislation.
- Reward power is the realm of leaders who are in a position to provide rewards, both tangible (salary increase, prize, bonus) and intangible (praise, recommendation).
- Coercive power is the ability to use negative means to control behaviour. These can include criticism, demotion, written warnings and ultimately dismissal.
- Expert power is gained by a leader through the admiration by subordinates of his or her expertise and knowledge.
- Information power is achieved through the access to and control of information – those 'in the know' have more data on which to base decisions and to exert their power.
- Referent power comes from loyalty and admiration. This leader is admired and people identify with him or her.

In most situations subordinates will resist coercion (and volunteers will simply walk off the job), while referent and expert power are most likely to lead to commitment.

Theoretical models of leadership

The following theories of leadership are summarized more or less in historical sequence. The evolution of leadership theory has resulted from changes in society, including changes to work practices and increased diversity in the workforce.

Leadership traits

Early theorists were keen to identify the traits of highly effective leaders, as they assumed that people with these traits would become equally effective leaders. Some of the traits identified were confidence, decisiveness and charisma. Edwin Locke (2000) identified the following personality traits among successful leaders: drive, self-confidence, creativity and cognitive ability, among others. More recent work in the United Kingdom has led to the development of leadership scales in which personal qualities include being honest and consistent, acting with integrity, being decisive, inspiring others and resolving complex problems (Alimo-Metcalfe and Alban-Metcalf, 2005).

Emotional intelligence is a construct that has great popular appeal – managing one's emotions and having empathy for others are believed to improve interpersonal effectiveness. Goleman (1995) suggests that there are four dimensions to emotional intelligence: self-awareness, self-management, social awareness and relationship management.

Goldblatt (2005) lists the most important leadership qualities as integrity, confidence, persistence, collaboration, problem solving, communication skills and vision. As he suggests, 'it is important to note that event leadership is neither charisma or control, the ability to command nor the talent to inspire. Rather, it is that rare commodity, like good taste, that one recognizes when one sees it' (p. 153).

Leadership style

Leadership-style theorists looked at the two dimensions of leadership, concern for production (task orientation) and concern for people. The best known of these is the Leadership Grid of Blake and Mouton (1985). Their argument was that the best leader would exhibit concern for both people and production, with a resultant team management style.

Contingency theories

Recognizing that different contexts required different leadership approaches led to the development of contingency theories. Broadly speaking, contingency theories suggest that leaders need to be responsive to a range of situational variables. Many such variables exist. Fiedler (1967) matched style (task orientation and relationship orientation) to situational variables of leader-member relations, task structure and position power. The Hersey-Blanchard (1993) model, on the other hand, looked at the maturity of followers. Here it was suggested that new (low job maturity) employees needed a telling style of leadership, graduating to selling and participative styles. However, once an employee had high job maturity, little guidance was required and a delegating style was appropriate. Looking at the relevance of this approach to the events business, it is clear that most personnel, who see the event infrastructure only just before the event and are briefed only minutes before the gates open, would need a telling style of clear instructions.

In this book there has been much discussion about the event context. There are many situational factors that could be considered in relation to leadership style: primarily the amount of time available to issue instructions and make decisions; and the level of risk associated with, for example, delegating a decision about crowd management.

Transformational leadership

Burns et al. (2004) and Avolio and Bass (1994) have worked on the concepts of transactional and transformational leadership as illustrated in Table 14.1. Transactional leadership is characterized by rewards contingent upon goal achievement, while transformational leadership requires that the leader convince followers of the task importance and value, that everyone is committed to the vision. In most cases this is leadership by inspiration. This can work positively when positive goals and values are espoused by the leader and genuine concern for others' well-being is exhibited. In rare cases, however, there is the visionary-charismatic leader whose power is used for antisocial purposes, leading to corruption or corporate scandal, so it is necessary to remain mindful of the dark side of charisma.

In the event business there is occasionally a scandal or two: such as when event tickets are allocated to the rich and famous leaving scarce pickings for the general public or celebrity patrons fail to turn up to their fundraising events. One person's creative vision can lead to unexpected reactions despite positive intentions, such as the London mascot described as 'creepy' and 'childish' and several other unprintable descriptions.

Avolio and Bass (1994) define transformational leadership in terms of how the leader affects followers, who are intended to trust, admire and respect the transformational leader. They identified three ways in which leaders transform followers:

- increasing their awareness of task importance and value
- getting them to focus on team or organizational goals
- activating their higher order needs and enabling self-actualization.

Avolio and Bass suggest that authentic transformational leadership is grounded in moral foundations, and that transformational leaders are value-driven change agents.

Parent (2010) has a descriptor of a high change business context as a 'high velocity' environment. This would undoubtedly describe the short period immediately before a major concert, festival, exhibition or conference. In his research, he suggests that the notion of a singular change agent in an organization is inappropriate and should be replaced with a

TABLE 14.1 Characteristics of transactional and transformational leadership

Transactional	Transformational
Works within the organizational culture, generally maintains status quo	Works to change the organizational culture by implementing new ideas
Employees achieve objectives through extrinsic rewards and punishments	Employees achieve objectives through higher ideals and moral values
Motivates followers by appealing to their self-interest	Motivates followers by encouraging them to put group interests first

much more diverse range of people, all of whom are change agents in their own right. This he suggests is not commonly considered at the recruitment stage, but recommends that it should be. He describes it as a capability to withstand challenges and stresses, and an ability to manage in ways suited to the contingencies of the environment. He suggests, for example, involving those who are already acknowledged change agents in conducting the screening process.

This argument is useful in that it prioritizes change management attributes as selection criteria for event people in senior roles. While the absence of these attributes might be discovered during a performance appraisal process, this could already be too late for remedial action. In the event business, there are few opportunities to learn and grow and mistakes can have serious repercussions, including delays to the project timeline. If, for example, a poor decision about ticket releases created a storm in the media, the whole organization could be scuttled for a time as plans were changed in response to this pressure. It would also be embarrassing for the organization and could damage morale. This highlights the importance of recognizing the pace of change in the event planning environment and selecting people who can manage well in this context.

Müller and Turner (2010) in their study of 400 successful project leaders found high expressions of one intelligence sub-dimension (i.e. critical thinking) and three emotional intelligence sub-dimensions (i.e. influence, motivation and conscientiousness) in successful managers in all types of projects. They suggest that

> Implications derived are the need for practitioners to be trained in the soft factors of leadership, particular for their types of projects. Theoretical implications include the need for more transactional styles in relatively simple projects and more transformational leadership styles in complex projects.
>
> (Müller and Turner, 2010: 447)

This has implications for recruitment and human resources development (training) of event project managers in working in different event contexts ranging from simple to complex.

Leadership and decision making

Leadership is exhibited in decision making. Each time a manager makes a decision there are a number of factors that come to bear. First, the leader brings his or her attributes, knowledge and experience, and the attributes of followers to the decision. These could be their personal traits, cultural background or their status in the organization (employee, volunteer, contractor). The given task needs careful consideration, perhaps the most important being the level of risk involved. Finally, every decision is situated in the wider context of the event environment or the socio-political environment in which the leader finds him or herself. Given that each time a leader acts, these factors are likely to vary, so each decision is unique. This is shown in Figure 14.2 in which the leadership behaviour/

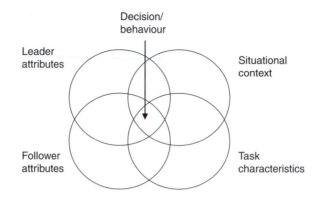

FIGURE 14.2 Decision-making model

decision is illustrated at the intersection of the four factors. Note that this is not a leadership style, but a fleeting, instantaneous decision or action.

Leadership and diversity

Theories of leadership have neglected diversity issues. Maylor et al. (2006) refer to the increasing projectification of the business world and allude to the diversity of the project team. On the other hand, the HR literature refers mainly to demographic characteristics, such as age, ethnicity, gender, physical abilities/qualities, race, sexual orientation, educational background, geographic location, income, marital status, parental status and work experience in the context of equal opportunity and workforce diversity. In the event environment the project team is diverse across these criteria and several more:

- area of expertise (production, staging, lighting, logistics, waste management, cleaning);
- role status (core team, contractor, sponsor, government agency, volunteer);
- employment status (full-time, hourly, contractor, sub-contractor);
- competence (technical, artistic);
- value to team (dispensable, not dispensable to implementation);
- experience (type and size of event, if any).

   This level of diversity takes project management leadership to a new level of complexity, which is part of the context of leadership discussed in detail later in the chapter.
   According to Chin (2010: 150), attention to diversity is not simply about representation of leaders from diverse groups in the ranks of leadership,

   diversity means paradigm shifts in our theories of leadership so as to make them inclusive; it means incorporating explanations of how dimensions of diversity shape our understanding of leadership. It means paying attention to the perceptions and expectations of diverse leaders by diverse followers and to how bias influences the exercise of leadership.

Leadership training

Event leadership training is conducted for most major events, the main purpose being to enable participants to better understand the event environment and the people they will need to supervise. The training must therefore cover the factors in Figure 14.3.

A leadership model specifically for the mega-event context was introduced in Chapter 9, including soft skills of informing, appreciating, managing stress and energizing. This type

Topic	Content
Entry music	Upbeat entry music
Welcome	Event leadership • What we will cover • The event environment • The event workforce • Event team leadership skills How we will do it • Discussion • Video • Activity and skill building What else you need to know • Who people are • Facilities • Session outline • Finish time Training objectives – list
Introduction	The biggest event you have been to and your role, e.g. wedding, office party, awards ceremony, sports match
Context for leadership	Introduce and show the welcome video (CEO)
The event environment	What are the unique features of the event environment? (flipchart)
Video	Show Part 1 of video 'The big challenges'
Your leadership skills in an event environment	Participants fill out questionnaire
Stakeholders	Who are the stakeholders (refer to notes) and fill in blanks
Expectations	As a staff member what do I expect from my leader? (flipchart) As an event leader, what do I expect from my workforce? (flipchart) What does event management expect from a leader at the event? (flipchart) As a customer what do I expect from the workforce? (flipchart)
Workforce	Paid, volunteer and contractor – motivations for each (flipchart)
Motivation	Why people volunteer (flipchart) – then show video or introduce volunteer speaker Worst case scenario: you lose your workforce (paid/volunteer/contract) How can we as leaders retain our workforce? COVERED WHAT WE NEED TO LEARN AND WHY NOW LET'S LOOK AT THE HOW

FIGURE 14.3 Event leadership training session plan

PLATE 14.1 First aid volunteers, also a source of general event information, need briefing

of training has its focus as the short event implementation period and not the planning period for the long lead up to the event.

Situational context

Most event training starts with a description of the aims of the event, whether they are to meet a business client's brief, celebrate culture or make a profit. This section answers the broader questions of 'Why are we here?' and 'What are we trying to achieve?' This part of training may involve a presentation by the CEO of the sponsor organization, the event creative director or the fundraising manager.

Task context

The specifics of the tasks to be supervised may or may not be covered in detail depending on the diverse roles of the leaders attending training. Job-specific information is generally covered in other training sessions. However, human resource planning for rosters, uniforms, pay, meals, discipline policy, etc. is important.

Follower attributes

A volunteer speaker often features at training if leadership of volunteers is a key part of the supervisor's role. Understanding workforce composition and expectations is a training objective.

Leader attributes

A degree of self-analysis is useful, many trainers using personality profile tests and games to introduce this session. However, since leader attributes are not easily changed, the focus for this part of training is more likely to be self-acknowledged deficiencies such as inexperience in the event environment and lack of knowledge of event conditions. Developing event leaders' knowledge of the new environment is often done using problem-based scenario exercises.

Leader decision making/behaviours

Tools and tips for leadership can be provided by experienced personnel who may be called upon in this part of the training. Specific ideas for motivating staff, planning rosters, dealing with staff problems and tackling unexpected staffing crises may be provided for discussion. In the ideal situation, leaders in training are provided with a range of problems and issues that require solutions. These can be table-based exercises, games or role plays. The illustrated plan for event leadership training in Figure 14.3 incorporates these elements in various ways.

In research undertaken during the 2010 Winter Olympic Games in Vancouver, Parent and McIntosh (2013) conducted a longitudinal case study to examine organizational cultural evolution in a dynamic event environment in which there was 'almost continual integration of new members at the function and venue levels' (p. 225):

> Closing in on the opening ceremonies, there was a change in time/velocity where members now felt rushed (additional pressures), and leadership, power, decision making, and protecting sponsors dominated members' attention. Members moved from being focused internally on their function and developing their capacity/

CASE STUDY 14.1
Leadership vision

This major international event could provide the platform for a millennium of multi-racial and multicultural harmony. Our policy of encouraging the maintenance of cultural diversity in an harmonious society that was nevertheless united in its patriotism could be a blueprint for the way the whole world should conduct itself in the next millennium.

Reflective practice 14.1

1   From reading the above quote, how do you think this vision could be realized in the context of event planning?
2   Many organizations are looking at supply chains to ensure that ethical employment and work practices are in place. How could this apply to the event context?

processes to being venue-focused and looking externally to servicing the various clients/stakeholders. By Games-time, members had to navigate different subcultures in order to perform their jobs.

(Parent and McIntosh, 2013: 232)

According to the authors, this resulted in communication and co-ordination issues, decision-making inconsistencies and power relation issues. Their study includes quotes from staff which illustrate these points well. In conclusion they offer the following applied implications:

> Managers within temporary organizations should focus on the importance of top management leaders in developing the 'corporate' culture and on the middle-level managers as they not only create the function and venue subcultures but are also key in the socialization process of newcomers. Choosing individuals with expertise or previous experience is critical given the time-limited nature of such organizations. As well, a broader view of HR management practices within temporary organizations may be needed given that subculture creation and new members' socialization processes run parallel to each other and then combine for the ultimate outcome/performance phase of the organization. While this may be different depending on the lifecycle of temporary organizations, it nonetheless seems to be critical to the deployment of strategy related to the achievement of larger organizational objectives. Finally, having different subcultures is necessary as each function and venue team must ultimately perform unique duties and serve specific clients. Games management should foster the creation of strong, independent units, which will allow members to feel a sense of connection with their immediate colleagues and rely on them for support and problem solving.

(Parent and McIntosh, 2013: 235)

This study is one of the few studies of leadership and culture in the event organizing committee and is recommended to readers. This is in contrast to the plethora of studies relating to volunteer motivation.

Chapter summary and key points

This chapter has discussed the important topic of leadership, the ability to influence people in order to achieve organizational objectives. Simply put, this means getting the work done. Leadership has been discussed in the context of short-life and long-life organizations, and research on leadership and leadership models has been evaluated in terms of 'near' and 'far' leadership. There is scope for further research into leadership during the different phases of event planning and implementation, particularly since the workforce explodes in size during the operational period.

We have returned again to the topic of project management because of its similarity to event management and have stressed the importance of effective leadership in this fast paced environment, particularly where the workforce is so diverse. We have also seen that there are numerous operational variables that differentiate one event from another and research has shown that different leadership approaches such as transactional and transformational leadership are required in different event contexts.

Revision questions

1   What is leadership?
2   How does leading differ from managing?
3   How is leadership exhibited in the project management model of EMBOK?
4   List and describe a leader's sources of power?
5   Select one theory of leadership, study it in detail by reading more widely, and then evaluate the usefulness of the theory to the event team leader.

Industry voice by Kerrie Nash

I think the skill level of managers is actually a real challenge from an HR point of view because you're bringing in people who come from many different walks of life. A lot of them are operationally very sound, but not necessarily good leaders or good managers. They may have come into the role because they know how to deliver the operational aspect of the event, but they may or may not have strong people management skills. As an HR person you're called upon a lot to deal with managers who lack experience in the people management and leadership area.

You'll also find that the organizing committee will have a real mix of people with differing skills – some who are strong planners, and others who are strong operators. Most people aren't great at doing both. The ones who are, are rare gems!

You will find that in the early days planners will be fine, the operators will get very frustrated because they have been asked to do a lot of planning. Of course, once you get close to event time the operators become very comfortable and the planners can be somewhat lost and needing a lot more guidance.

Discussion question

This quote points to the importance of leaders being able to respond to situational variables in the event environment. After reviewing Chapter 8 on the topic of recruitment and the theoretical perspectives on leadership, explain your approach to selecting managers with the required leadership skills for an annual major or hallmark event.

References

Alimo-Metcalfe, B. and Alban-Metcalf, J. (2005). 'Leadership: time for a new direction', *Leadership*, 1(1), 51–71.

Avolio, B. J. and Bass, B. M. (1994). *Improving Organizational Effectiveness through Transformational Leadership*. Thousand Oaks, CA: Sage.

Blake, R. R. and Mouton, J. S. (1985). *The Managerial Grid III: A New Look at the Classic that Has Boosted Productivity and Profits for Thousands of Corporations World-wide*. Houston: Gulf Pub. Co.

Burns, J. M., Goethals, G. R. and Sorenen, G. (2004). *Encyclopedia of Leadership*. Thousand Oaks, CA: Sage.

Chin, J. L. (2010). 'Introduction to the special issue on diversity and leadership', *American Psychologist*, 65(3), 150.

Christenson, D. and Walker, D. H. (2008). 'Using vision as a critical success element in project management', *International Journal of Managing Projects in Business*, 1(4), 611–622.

Fiedler, F. E. (1967). *A Theory of Leadership Effectiveness*. New York: McGraw-Hill.

Goldblatt, J. J. (2005). *Special Events: Event Leadership for a New World*, 4th edn. Hoboken, NJ: Wiley.

Goleman, D. (1995). *Emotional Intelligence*. New York: Bantam Books.

Hanisch, B. and Wald, A. (2011). 'A project management research framework integrating multiple theoretical perspectives and influencing factors', *Project Management Journal*, 42(3), 4–22.

Hersey, P. and Blanchard, K. H. (1993). *Management of Organizational Behavior: Utilizing Human Resources*, 6th edn. Upper Saddle River, NJ: Prentice-Hall.

Locke, E. A. (2000). *The Blackwell Handbook of Principles of Organizational Behaviour*. London: Blackwell.

Maylor, H., Brady, T., Cooke-Davies, T. and Hodgson, D. (2006). 'From projectification to programmification', *International Journal of Project Management*, 24(8), 663–674.

Mintzberg, H. (1983). *Power In and Around Organizations*. Upper Saddle River, NJ: Prentice-Hall.

Müller, R. and Turner, R. (2010). 'Leadership competency profiles of successful project managers', *International Journal of Project Management*, 28(5), 437–448.

Parent, M. M. (2010). 'Decision making in major sport events over time: parameters, drivers, and strategies', *Journal of Sport Management*, 24(3), 291–318.

Parent, M. M. and MacIntosh, E. W. (2013). 'Organizational culture evolution in temporary organizations: the case of the 2010 Olympic Winter Games', *Canadian Journal of Administrative Sciences/Revue Canadienne des Sciences de l'Administration*, 30(4), 223–237.

Shone, A. and Parry, B. (2004). *Successful Event Management*, 2nd edn. Brisbane: Thomson Learning.

Silvers, J. R. (2012). *Professional Event Coordination* (Vol. 65). Hoboken, NJ: John Wiley & Sons.

Thomsett, R. (2002). *Radical Project Management*. Upper Saddle River, NJ: Prentice-Hall.

Tyssen, A. K., Wald, A. and Spieth, P. (2013). 'Leadership in temporary organizations: a review of leadership theories and a research agenda', *Project Management Journal*, 44(6), 52–67.

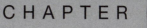
Motivation and retention

Learning objectives

After reading through this chapter you will be able to:

- Discuss the topic of workforce retention.
- Describe the differences between content and process theories of motivation.
- Use the concept of psychological contract to analyse volunteer expectations.
- Describe some approaches to reward and recognition.
- Develop strategies for workforce retention.
- Discuss issues relating to motivation of management personnel.

Introduction

When an event is staffed primarily by volunteers, motivation is a significant concern for the organizing committee who are sometimes themselves volunteers. In the business world, staff turnover is measured by the human resource department as the annual number of staff leaving as a percentage of the workforce. In the hotel industry studies have shown that the average turnover level among non-management hotel employees in the US is about 50 per cent, and about 25 per cent for management staff. Estimates of average annual employee turnover range from around 60 to 300 per cent, according to the research conducted by the American Hotel and Motel Association (Guatam, 2005). Concern for the stability of the event industry is well founded, as this is an industry that arguably offers less stability than the hotel industry.

In the event business the terms most often used are retention and attrition – attrition more commonly because many volunteers quit before they have started. For example, prior to the 2006 Commonwealth Games, there were reports that more than 1,200 Commonwealth Games volunteers had resigned their posts in the ten weeks prior to the event (Phillips, 2006).

These volunteers did not take up positions offered to them to participate in the 15,000 strong volunteer programme. The pre-event attrition issue is raised again by Nichols and Ralston (2009) who point out that for volunteers the long wait between their interview for the London Olympic Games and their role offer was de-motivating. It was also frustrating for some as it appeared that little effort was made to match their backgrounds to the roles offered.

There have been numerous studies on volunteer motivation, some of which were mentioned in Chapter 4. These studies have mostly investigated the antecedent motives for volunteering (Coyne and Coyne, 2001; Hallman and Harms, 2012; Love et al., 2011; Strigas and Newton Jackson, 2003). Essentially, the diversity of event type and scale is reflected in the diversity of motivations that volunteers put forward for volunteering. Cultural influences play an important part too, Fairley et al. (2013) finding that Korean volunteers were motivated by a sense of community. Other studies have looked at reasons why volunteers quit, Elstad (2003) finding that the top three reasons were workload, lack of appreciation and poor event organization. Cuskelly et al. (2004) did an extensive study on the behavioural dependability of volunteers, arguing that a study of behaviour is more meaningful than a study of attitudes. One of the points they make is that many event organizers deal with retention problems by overrecruiting volunteers, but are then faced with increases in the cost of selection and training, as well as the cost of uniforms, accreditation, etc. An oversupply of volunteers has the potential also to cause dissatisfaction when underutilization occurs. This is problematic as one of the highest level satisfiers is feeling skilled, useful and productive. Using the theory of planned behaviour, Cuskelly et al. (2004) found that the most consistent predictor variable was perceived behavioural control, measured as having the confidence and skills to be a volunteer.

Motivation and retention of volunteers is not however the only concern. From a risk management perspective, a much more significant concern is retention of event planning staff, those involved in the lead-up period to an event. When a key person quits at a crucial time, this can have a major effect on other members of the team, increasing their workload and impacting on goal achievement. For this reason, retention of management and other paid personnel is a significant consideration. One suggestion for retention of staff is to provide employment contracts with loyalty bonuses. Hanlon and Jago (2004) have drawn up a schema for retention of both paid and seasonal event staff working for major sporting events, which will be discussed later in the chapter.

Theories of motivation

There are two main groups of theories of motivation: content theories assume that all individuals possess the same set of needs and therefore prescribe the characteristics that ought to be present in jobs; process theories, in contrast, stress the differences in people's needs and focus on the cognitive processes that create these differences.

One example of a content theory is that of Frederick Hertzberg (1987) who proposes that job satisfaction and dissatisfaction appear to be caused by different factors (see Figure 15.1).

Hygiene factors (dissatisfiers)	Motivators (satisfiers)
Supervision	Goal achievement
Policy	Recognition
Work environment	Intrinsic nature of the work itself
Relationships with colleagues	Responsibility
Pay/reward	Advancement

FIGURE 15.1 Hertzberg's two factor theory

According to this theory, the factors listed as hygiene factors would lead to dissatisfaction if they were not up to standard. To support this concept, Elstad (2003) found that food had a significant effect on the volunteers' continuance commitment at a jazz festival. Nichols and Ojala (2009) also found that volunteers were critical of food and drink provided, as well as the lack of toilet arrangements. However, food is not a satisfier; if adequate, it is taken for granted and does not contribute to feelings of job satisfaction. The factors that do motivate are goal achievement and recognition. For management personnel, the intrinsic nature of the work itself, particularly the creative development of the event concept and plans, is also highly satisfying. To sum up and simplify, motivators provide reasons to stay, while unsatisfactory hygiene factors can provide reasons to leave.

What all process theories have in common is an emphasis on cognitive processes in determining a person's level of motivation. For example, equity theory assumes that one important cognitive process involves people looking around and observing what effort other people are putting into their work and what rewards follow. This social comparison process is driven by a concern for fairness and equity.

Expectancy theory resulted from Vroom's (1973) work into motivation. His argument is that crucial to motivation at work is the perception of a link between effort and reward. This link can be thought of as a process in which individuals calculate, first, whether there is a connection between effort and reward and, second, the probability that rewards (valences, as Vroom called them) will follow from high performance (instrumentality). The motivational force of a job can therefore be calculated if the expectancy, instrumentality and valence values are known (see Figure 15.2).

If the individual perceives that no matter how much they try they will never reach the work performance level indicated, they will not make an effort. For example, a goal may be to serve 300 banquet guests within 15 minutes. This may be regarded as unachievable due to the number of floor staff available and delays in kitchen production. However, the floor staff may also be thinking about the promise of a reward. Perhaps they were promised an early finish once and instead had to stay back to set up for breakfast the next day. The promised reward has to have a high valence, or value, and there needs to be a level of trust that rewards will be delivered.

Perception ⇨ effort ⇨ work performance ⇨ reward

FIGURE 15.2 Expectancy theory of motivation

The main contribution of process theory has been to highlight the effects of cognitive and perceptual processes on objective work conditions.

A different theory of motivation involving goal setting has been proposed by Locke and Latham (1984). This theory states that goals direct effort and provide guidelines for deciding how much effort to put into each activity when multiple goals exist, and that participation in goal setting increases the individual's sense of control.

This theory is well suited to the project management environment of event planning where goals such as audience size, throughput at turnstiles, food service during intermission, delivery times and scoring accuracy can be measured and communicated to event personnel. At a more personal level, control systems such as safety checklists, cash balancing and voucher reconciliation can provide a level of satisfaction when such goals are achieved.

Workforce expectations

Guest and Conway (2002) talk about the psychological contract in terms of perceived promises and commitments in the employment relationship, which is usually discussed in the literature in terms of employee expectations. These authors look instead at employer views on this topic. Ultimately, of course, the psychological contract works both ways, each party making promises and commitments and having certain expectations. Indeed, managing expectations is also crucial to the management of volunteers, so this concept of the psychological contract is a very useful one to use in the event context. The following quote talks about psychological contracts in the context of event volunteering:

> First, it seems that regardless of previous experience, volunteer background and reason for participating volunteers are seeking fulfillment of a psychological contract from the outset and not simply during the period of volunteer engagement during the event. As the early stages of the psychological contract are based largely on trust, then any early contact or activities are essential in validating this trust that expectations will be fulfilled. In this case, the welcome afforded to all volunteers had an impact on expectations.
>
> Second, there appears to be an ideal set of expected outcomes regarding planning, recruitment, training and communications but also a realism that expectations are not always met. Thus, there appears to be a degree of compensation afforded in circumstances where expectations are met but barely. However, it is clear that if expectations are not met with a degree of adequacy then the level of concern and in some cases withdrawal from the process can be expected. This happened for many volunteers in relation to the lack of communication between management and volunteers and in relation to transport. There is a fine line between perceptions of breach of the psychological contract and volition. Although some volunteers have more tolerance of uncertainty and unmet expectations, it would be unwise for management to become complacent. The desire to be part of a special or unique

event may attract volunteers in the first place, but it may not be strong enough to influence their attitudinal or behavioural responses to management reneging on expectations and perceived promises.

The third key issue the research raises is that such events seem to arouse optimism and positive word-of-mouth marketing not at a level expected given the perceived lack of planning. This optimism extended into expectations regarding long-term outcomes. Thus, if effectively managed, volunteers can generate a positive wave of expectation and citizenship in the period leading up to the Games. The challenge is for managers to plan these outcomes well in advance of such an event to reap the benefits of a highly charged, if temporal, volunteer workforce.

(Ralston et al., 2004: 22)

Nichols and Ojala (2009) also use the construct of psychological contract finding that for event managers volunteers bring enthusiasm, empathy with the public and of course budget savings. The expectations of volunteers were fair treatment, interesting and meaningful work, responsibility, challenge, the resources to do the job and skills development (p. 382). We will look at the psychological contract in three phases, at initial entry, in day-to-day work and in ongoing development. These three phases will be discussed here, where we look further at workforce expectations.

Initial entry-planning phase

The hype that is often a feature of the lead-up period of an event is likely to develop a strong sense of ownership on the part of employees and volunteers (Hanlon and Jago, 2004). However, as Ralston et al. (2004) point out in their study of volunteers for the 2002 Commonwealth Games, early communication with volunteers is vital. These authors also found that volunteers were motivated primarily by altruism, involvement and the uniqueness of the special event. Events of this scale have the added advantage of positive publicity contributing to building relationship between volunteer and event organization. Negative press can result in reduced enthusiasm and lower than expected numbers of volunteers committing to work from the recruitment pool. In fact, prior to the 2006 Commonwealth Games the organizers were forced to contact volunteers who had been rejected to compensate for the 1,200 who had pulled out two months before the Games.

Positive publicity is even more important for organizers who carry responsibility for the infrastructure and the programme. These external forces (often uncontrollable) have considerable impact on those in the hot seat at the time. It takes a seasoned operator to withstand this type of pressure. Thus motivation of paid staff is something that needs considerable attention. Stress and burn-out are common, some people 'falling over' just before the event and others totally exhausted before the execution phase when the highest levels of energy are needed. It is also possible that some members of the team are looking for alternative post-event employment during the final phases of planning. This, too, has implications for the organization, some of which have post-event placement programmes to assist the transition.

Retention strategies for this phase should focus on internal communication, regular and efficient meeting updates, and celebration of targets and achievements. Well-facilitated training and change management can also contribute to perceptions that the train is on track and there is light at the end of the tunnel.

Daily event operations

Motivation and retention of staff and volunteers day to day during the event operational period are essential components of the human resources plan. Such strategies can take the following forms.

Tickets

Many event volunteers expect to watch part of the performance and are provided with tickets for periods when they are not working. For many mega events this is a ticket to the rehearsal of the opening or closing ceremony. However, according to one study, volunteers' satisfaction with the opportunity to use free tickets had no impact on volunteers' continuance commitment (Elstad, 2003: 107).

Sponsor products

Quite often sponsors are prepared to provide their products as rewards for volunteers. However, good intentions can have serious repercussions if it is perceived that these rewards are distributed inequitably. As an example, Swatch provided Sydney Olympic Games volunteers with commemorative watches. However, the logistics of distribution were less than adequate and some volunteers missed out, including ceremonies volunteers who were not included in the headcount (Webb, 2001).

Loyalty schemes

Loyalty schemes have been used to assist retention of employees and volunteers. This may be a passport which is stamped for each shift and qualifies the volunteer or worker for entry in a draw for a major prize, such as a motor car. These have been used in hotels and by Games organizing committees (Byrne et al., 2002). However, the odds of winning seem slim to most and it is doubtful that the link between shift attendance and the prize is strong.

Loyalty bonuses

A loyalty bonus, as an addition to an hourly rate, may be paid on completion of all allocated shifts. This requires careful planning to ensure that work times are recorded and payroll systems modified accordingly for hourly staff.

For full-time employees on contract, a bonus on completion could make the difference between early departure and seeing it through in even the most difficult circumstances.

Celebrity meetings

Inviting high-profile people from the events committee, charity, sponsor organization or government to address the workforce can raise morale. Everyone wants to meet celebrities and this brush with fame can be accompanied by permission for large group photos with athletes and/or entertainers.

Photo boards

While many codes of conduct preclude the use of cameras at events (particularly in VIP and athlete areas), volunteers in particular love to have their photographs taken on site, and these can be displayed on notice boards (with permission, of course).

Briefings and debriefings

A pre-shift briefing is one of the most important communication strategies for the event workforce, enabling everyone to have the latest information. Likewise, debriefings allow people to contribute their concerns and suggestions. No amount of extrinsic rewards such as pins and caps can solve the frustrations of a member of a team who is bombarded with questions from the event audience and cannot answer them.

Daily newsletters

Staff newsletters, highlighting milestones and achievements, can be distributed at the start of shifts or be kept in the staff canteen area. Notice boards can be used for the same purpose. Production of the newsletter requires a budget and plan and distribution needs to cover all venues. Information of this type can also be broadcast to mobile phones.

PLATE 15.1 The workforce is formally acknowledged

Posters

Posters highlighting goal achievement, such as the size of the crowd, media stories or television coverage, all contribute to a sense of satisfaction that the event concept is being realized.

Food and beverage surprises

Support teams carrying bags of treats appear to be appreciated, particularly if they have engaging personalities and can visit staff members at remote sites. More exciting are donut days, cappuccino days and ice-cream treats. When these come as a surprise they are much appreciated. Once again a budget and planning are required.

Parade of volunteers

While some mega events have a parade of volunteers after the event, there is nothing to prevent this happening at some stage during the event so that the audience can express their appreciation.

Media support for volunteers

To obtain media support, the public relations department needs to find stories and write press releases. As with previous recognition strategies, this needs pre-planning and will be discussed in the next chapter on internal and external communications.

Games

Games are used as ice-breakers and for stress relief. The choice of games and timing are crucial. They can be simple things like competitions to guess the outcomes of matches or spectator numbers. The higher the relevance, the greater the value the game is perceived to have.

Entertainment

Entertainment in the staff area is much appreciated, although for a sporting event the link to work performance is tenuous. However, at a folk festival, volunteers would love to watch musicians rehearsing.

Concluding party for staff

Little needs to be said about the traditional post-event party. However, decisions do need to be made about when to hold the party – even pre-event is a possibility – and whether to make it a family or adult affair.

Certificates of appreciation

References and certificates of appreciation are highly valued, particularly if they are specific to the individual and to the role they played in making the event a success. A computer printout with a floral border and no individualization has little value.

Careful consideration must be given to the cost of all recognition and reward programmes. These strategies need to be planned on a day-to-day schedule for the event as it progresses with, for example, templates in readiness for staff newsletters and people allocated to writing and printing them. A budget is needed for all such activities. The budget for the Melbourne Commonwealth Games volunteer programme was A\$3 million for 5,000 volunteers. This included the cost of meals and uniforms, which are significant.

Career development expectations

At management level, the event personnel are ever mindful of their future careers. Being associated with a successful event will enhance their reputation, while an event that fails to reach expectations or is exposed to media criticism can be irredeemably harmful to

PLATE 15.2 All smiles and hugs when it is over

CASE STUDY 15.1
Volunteer contingency planning

The weather report is not good, intermittent rain is expected for the whole weekend of the food and wine festival. Many contingency plans are in place to deal with operational issues such as safety. The event workforce includes primarily:

- employees of the local authority in charge of areas such as waste management;
- police and other emergency services;
- stall holders;
- volunteers;
- the event organizing team.

Motivating the workforce in these circumstances will be a challenge, particularly as the event will run over three days.

Reflective practice 15.1

1   What can you do in preparation for the safety, comfort, motivation and recognition of the workforce?
2   What level of staff attrition will you expect?
3   Are the any contingency plans that you can put in place to co-ordinate a response to staffing shortages?

their career prospects. In traditional business environments, lack of job satisfaction is the primary antecedent to resignation. Haltom et al. (2005) show from their research that precipitating events, or shocks, are more often the immediate cause of turnover. This is a most interesting perspective and, as the authors suggest, the organization should look at strategies to manage shocks and thus improve retention. Many mega events are subjected to intense criticism in the lead-up to the event: for example, the ticketing fiasco in Sydney and the incomplete infrastructure in Athens not long before the opening ceremony. In Sochi there were major security concerns.

Tactics are needed to help staff weather such storms, which affect morale across the board. An understanding of the patterns of a mega event – the positive honeymoon period following the successful bid, then the ever-growing concern about the budget and negative reports – should be linked to the employee communications strategy. Negative press, even when 'par for the course', can be demoralizing. Some individuals don't have the stamina to deal with the lows and thus miss out on the buzz of the final, dramatic success that ensues.

TABLE 15.1 A recommended guide for retaining full-time and seasonal personnel at the Australian Open Tennis Championship and the Australian Formula One Grand Prix

Event cycle	Retention strategies for personnel categories	
	Full-time	Seasonal
Lead-up	Event's status Recognition Ownership	Event's status Recognition Ownership Timing of the event
During an event	Team debrief Team activities	Team debrief Team activities
After an event	Team debrief Thank-you function Performance appraisal Remuneration Career management programmes Updated job descriptions Re-establishing teams Positive direction from management Exit interviews Loyalty payments	Team debrief Thank-you function
During the year	Team meetings	Continuous contact (i.e. Christmas cards, birthday cards, organization's newsletter, team meetings)
	Remuneration	Career opportunities Survey needs Employed for additional events

(From Hanlon and Jago, 2004: 47. Reproduced with permission.)

To further illustrate the variables impacting on retention of staff in event management, Hanlon and Jago (2004) show from research into two major annual events that the period immediately following the event is typically flat in contrast to the adrenalin rush of the previous weeks. It is during this period that a number of retention strategies should be considered for permanent staff. Additionally, for organizations running annual events such as the Australian Open, efforts need to be made to maintain contact with seasonal workers who return annually to the event.

Table 15.1 is a guide to retaining both full-time and seasonal staff at two major annual events.

This area is undoubtedly ripe for investigation. Research into changing expectations and workforce motivation would be most valuable for human resource practitioners in this field given the rapidly changing scale of the workforce and the diversity of employment and volunteer options. No doubt as technology progresses and people working at events are able to check in and out electronically, more reliable data will be available on the level of retention of both full-time employees and volunteers.

Performance appraisal

Large event organizations that employ a permanent workforce usually have a performance appraisal programme, although for many others performance management is largely informal. A formal performance review session is an opportunity to discuss present performance and future aspirations with an employee. The elements of this programme include:

- assessing performance against goals, objectives, target and outcomes;
- providing feedback on performance, particularly positive feedback and constructive advice;
- providing an opportunity for the employee to provide feedback on their level of motivation and satisfaction;
- reaching agreement regarding action plans or learning programmes.

Ongoing performance feedback, both formal and informal, contributes significantly to clear expectations for all concerned. Long-term volunteers also require performance feedback. Performance management contributes in constructive ways to a positive organizational culture, which was discussed in Chapter 12, and in turn the event organizational culture affects volunteer retention and motivation. Some of the elements of this culture include:

- Feedback – encouragement and a sense of direction.
- Cohesion – everyone wants to feel part of a team that has a positive dynamic, as dysfunctional teams fall apart very quickly. Shared goals contribute to a sense of cohesion.
- Resources – lack of resources to do the job efficiently or correctly frustrates volunteers, while being well equipped assists productivity.
- Support – being neglected by team members or supervisors makes volunteers most unhappy, particularly those left isolated at remote spots without relief or encouragement.
- Fairness – like permanent employees, volunteers get extremely upset by inequitable treatment.
- Improvement – in the ongoing event operational environment, suggestions for improvements need to be taken seriously and acted upon.
- Information provision – to provide good service, volunteers need to be in the information loop. This also contributes to a sense of collaborative teamwork.

Performance management is a vital component of the human resource strategy. Whether the event organization is a long-life or short-life concern, everyone needs to be working at an optimal level. This involves meeting expectations, providing motivational opportunities and managing performance that is below par. For the most part, there are many intrinsic elements in the event environment that can be relied upon to maintain motivational momentum.

CASE STUDY 15.2
Staging a Shakespeare Festival

You are the organizer of a Shakespeare Festival. There will be four week-long plays performed over the summer holidays with matinee and evening performances. The event will be preceded by a main street procession. The production of the plays will be professionally managed by a theatre team using amateur performers. A number of volunteers will be assigned to minor roles in costumes, set and lighting. The administrative team will be a core of event management paid staff with support from volunteers in the ticket office, at information and on merchandising. Volunteers will also assist with ushering. You will need to suggest a naming rights sponsor and some minor sponsors. Marketing and promotions volunteers will need to be appointed early. Overall, your paid staff to volunteer ratio will be 1:4.

Reflective practice 15.2

- Identify the phases of this project, and allocate timings to the workforce appointments (paid and volunteer).
- Develop a simple organization chart for the planning of the event and another for the production period.
- Describe ideas for motivating the core team of senior staff during the pre-event phase.
- Develop strategies for motivating the workforce during the event production phase.

Chapter summary and key points

This chapter has covered some of the research pertaining to motivation, looking mainly at longer term paid staff and volunteers. Theories of motivation fit mainly into two categories: content theories prescribe a series of characteristics that should be present in jobs, while process theories stress differences in people's needs and their perceptions of the circumstances in which they find themselves. Motivation and retention strategies were considered at different points in the event cycle, from initial entry to final celebration and beyond. The concept of the psychological contract was used to analyse the relationship between the event organization and the volunteer, elaborating expectations on both sides.

Revision questions

1   What are the implications if there is poor retention of management/planning staff?
2   What are the implications of overrecruitment of volunteers?
3   Explain the idea of the psychological contract.
4   Discuss the following statement: 'to understand motivation you need to understand the planning cycle for the event'.

Industry voice by Kerrie Nash

Attrition's a funny one because at every one of the Games that I've worked on one of the first things that people ask about, and certainly that senior leadership is concerned about, is how're we going to counter attrition at Games time? My answer to that, having done lots of events now, is it's not Games-time attrition that you have to worry about because I've never experienced significant Games-time attrition at all.

The real issue is in pre-Games attrition. For example your volunteers are on standby, if you like, for so long, so if you don't continue to communicate with them and continue to inform and involve them you could lose their interest.

I think in Sydney we ended up with roughly around about 20 per cent of volunteers dropped out along the way before Games-time. That was everything from dropping out from the time they put the application in, to coming to interviews, to attending training. I've always used that 20 per cent figure as a bit of a benchmark among other Games to see how we go. Some have done slightly better, some have done slightly worse.

You will sometimes hear comment from paid people that the volunteers are all getting taken care of, so there is that little bit of jealousy. Sometimes you can kind of 'over egg' the value of the volunteers, not so much at Games time, but in the planning phases. You have to be really careful with the staff that you have a good communications and engagement programme on board. If you have that, paid staff can see that they're valued as well and that a lot of what we do is about taking care of them, not just thinking about what happens to the volunteers at Games time.

The biggest reason that I've seen for Games time attrition of volunteers anywhere is boredom. It's not doing useful, valuable work. It's one of the hardest things to get functional areas to sign up to, particularly if the leader of that functional area has not done a Games before, is to right size their team. The tendency will always be to ask for more volunteers than they need if they've not done an event before. We have to try to convince them that it is a sure fire way of getting attrition because your people will all be bored and they won't turn up for day three because on days one and two nobody wanted them and they had nothing to do.

Secondly, it's really disruptive for your operation because those volunteers are going to follow you around all day asking 'what can I do?' Instead of being able to focus on your operation you're constantly thinking 'how can I keep my volunteers engaged'? What can they do? The manager will call workforce operations saying, 'I've got ten spare volunteers can you find something for them to do?' That is how it plays out. That's a terrible thing to do; it's so disrespectful of volunteer time and commitment.

Discussion questions

1   Summarize Kerrie's experience with attrition and speculate on the reasons for high levels of motivation for events such as the Olympic Games and FIFA World Cup.
2   Many students undertaking volunteering in order to build a career profile come back feeling that their time has been wasted. Review the reasons for this and provide recommendations specifically for short-term placement of student volunteers at business events, festivals and sporting events.

References

Byrne, C., Houen, J. and Seaberg, M. (2002). 'One team', *Communication World*, 19(3), 28–32.

Coyne, B. and Coyne, E. (2001). 'Getting, keeping and caring for unpaid volunteers for professional golf tournament events', *Human Resource Development International*, 4(2), 199–216.

Cuskelly, G., Auld, C., Harrington, M. and Coleman, D. (2004). 'Predicting the behavioural dependability of sport event volunteers', *Event Management*, 9, 73–89.

Elstad, B. (2003). 'Continuance commitment and reasons to quit: a study of volunteers at a jazz festival', *Event Management*, 8, 99–108.

Fairley, S., Lee, Y., Green, B. C. and Kim, M. L. (2013). 'Considering cultural influences in volunteer satisfaction and commitment', *Event Management*, 17(4), 337–348.

Gautam, A. M. (2005). *Knowledge Flight: The Challenge of Hotel Employee Turnover*. Available at: http://www.hvs.com/article/1522/knowledge-flight-the-challenge-of-hotel-employee-turnover/; viewed 12 January 2014.

Guest, D. and Conway, N. (2002). 'Communicating the psychological contract: an employer perspective', *Human Resource Management Journal*, 12(2), 22–39.

Hallmann, K. and Harms, G. (2012). 'Determinants of volunteer motivation and their impact on future voluntary engagement: a comparison of volunteer's motivation at sport events in equestrian and handball', *International Journal of Event and Festival Management*, 3(3), 272–291.

Haltom, B., Mitchell, R., Lee, T. and Inderrieden, E. (2005). 'Shocks as causes of turnover: what are they and how organizations can manage them', *Human Resource Management*, 44(3), 337–352.

Hanlon, C. and Jago, L. (2004). 'The challenge of retaining personnel in major sport event organizations', *Event Management*, 9, 39–49.

Hertzberg, F. (1987). 'One more time: how do you motivate employees?', *Harvard Business Review*, 65, 109–120.

Locke, E. A. and Latham, G. P. (1984). *Goal Setting: A Motivational Technique That Works!* Upper Saddle River, NJ: Prentice-Hall.

Love, A., Hardin, R., Koo, G. and Morse, A. (2011). 'Effects of motives on satisfaction and behavioral intentions of volunteers at a PGA tour event', *International Journal of Sport Management*, 12(1), 86–101.

Nichols, G. and Ojala, E. (2009). 'Understanding the management of sports events volunteers through psychological contract theory', *VOLUNTAS: International Journal of Voluntary and Nonprofit Organizations*, 20(4), 369–387.

Nichols, G. and Ralston, R. (2009). 'Volunteer management at the 2012 Olympic Games, a tension between "programme" and "membership" management styles', *Problems, Possibilities, Promising Practices: Critical Dialogues on the Olympic and Paralympic Games, Eleventh International Symposium for Olympic Research.* London, Ontario, Canada: International Centre for Olympic Studies, Western University Canada, pp. 110–115. Available at: http://www.uwo.ca/olympic/files/downloads/ICOS.2012.Proceedings-TOC.pdf; viewed 3 September 2014.

Phillips, S. (2006). 'Volunteer dropouts soar', *Herald Sun*, 7 January.

Ralston, R., Downward, P. and Lumsdon, L. (2004). 'The expectations of volunteers prior to the XVII Commonwealth Games 2002', *Event Management*, 9, 13–26.

Strigas, A. and Newton Jackson, E. (2003). 'Motivation: volunteers to serve and succeed', *International Sports Journal*, 7(1), 111–123.

Vroom, V. (1973). *Work and Motivation*. Hoboken, NJ: John Wiley and Sons.

Webb, T. (2001). *The Collaborative Games: The Story Behind the Spectacle*. Sydney: Pluto Press.

CHAPTER 16

Internal communications

Learning objectives

After reading this chapter you will be able to:

- Understand the role played by internal communications.
- Understand the relationship between human resource management and internal communications.
- Discuss the importance of internal communications as a means of engagement.
- Describe the various stakeholder interests that can be supported and acknowledged in the event environment using an internal communications strategy.

Introduction

Every day, across thousands of organizations, HR and Communications teams are joining forces to develop internal communications programmes to better engage and energize their employees.

Effective internal communications can bring an organization's brand, values and objectives to life in the hearts and minds of employees. In turn, through the actions of its employees, it can ultimately shape consumer experience of the organization as well as its wider reputation.

This is certainly true in the event industry, where the majority of the workforce is customer facing – from the ticket collector to the first aid team.

Effective internal communications also plays a critical risk mitigation role, for example in the implementation of health and safety policies and procedures. An organization may have a brilliant event risk assessment and safety plan, however, unless employees know and understand the plan and are motivated to implement it, the plan has limited value.

In this chapter, we will clarify the relationship between internal communications and the HR function, as well as outline the various stages and elements which go into internal communications strategizing, planning, execution and evaluation.

Internal communications versus human resource management

Internal communications, as a field of its own, is primarily focused on the effective communication of an organization with its internal stakeholders – its employees. Internal communications draws on broader communications theory, also employed in related fields such as public relations, marketing communications and stakeholder management.

Since internal communications focuses on the employee audience, it has a natural affiliation with the HR function of an organization.

While organizations are likely to employ entirely separate teams (with communications teams focusing on a broad range of public relations, marketing, social media and stakeholder management functions, and HR teams focusing on recruitment, retention, employee leave and benefits etc.), collaboration and partnership between communications and HR teams is vital to ensure that shared objectives are achieved. Madia (2011: 20) suggests that HR should develop its recruitment strategy in conjunction with marketing and public relations resulting in 'positive publicity for a company that knows how to position itself in the online space'. However, the collaboration can be even more strategic in terms of dissemination of messages, active participation and commitment.

An example of the cross-over between communications and HR would be an organization's objective to increase employee engagement and, over time, to change employee behaviour to better reflect the organization's core values (perhaps relating to customer experience, team work, etc.). Another example could be an organization which plans to implement a new business strategy, and wants to ensure all employees understand the new strategy and are on board to help deliver it.

The event workforce itself is generally comprised of a core team, volunteers, numerous contractors and their employees as well as many other stakeholders such as government agencies and sponsors. For the purposes of this chapter, we will relate internal communications specifically to the primary event workforce, comprised by the core team, volunteers and contractors.

Employer brand and values

Internal communication plays a key role in developing and promoting an employer brand (or its benefits, offering, culture, point of difference), and ensuring its employees are aligned with the organization's core values. These values may include a commitment to social causes, sportsmanship, patriotism, environmental concerns, diversity, equality, community, individuality and many other event organization values or aspirational visions.

A key challenge for an organization is firstly to identify its core values and define what it has to offer its employees. Ideally these core values and 'internal' brand are aligned with its external brand proposition. After all, an organization that projects a very different public façade to the one it preaches internally is ultimately compromised or at best confused.

For the organization that gets it right, its internal culture will be strongly aligned to the organization's core values, its customers' experience will live up to the external brand promises, and this strong external reputation will in turn attract more likeminded potential employees.

Take the example of a music touring company specializing in world music. Its external brand might relate to 'global citizenship' (shared responsibility for global issues) and it might differentiate itself by bringing unique music from around the world to the mainstream audience. Its core values could relate to diversity, acceptance and global awareness.

In this example, it would be crucial that this organization not only hires a workforce which supports and is attracted to these values, but ongoing internal communications must work to ensure these values are well communicated, celebrated and upheld. Their communications strategy might focus on inviting regular guest speakers to discuss various global causes with staff, or perhaps a regular award for employees who embody the 'global citizenship' philosophy in their dealings with team members, musicians or festival goers.

Another event business, such as one which runs large-scale business conferences and expos, would have an entirely different external and internal brand and values. This second organization may highly value entrepreneurialism and a 'start-up' culture. In turn it could encourage its employees to come up with new marketing ideas or business opportunities and ways to encourage and support small business innovation. Ideas could be shared via a wiki page, forum and/or online voting platform.

As you can see from these two examples, employer brand and values can differ greatly from organization to organization.

The challenge for organizations is to identify their existing employer brand and internal culture and, with the help of internal communications and HR, outline the desired future values and attributes of the organization and develop the right communications strategy to achieve the desired outcome.

This can be illustrated particularly well by the effective labelling of London volunteers as 'Games Makers' in an effort to highlight the integral and valuable nature of their volunteers. The public relations impact of the volunteer programme is incalculable. The service provided by the Games Makers enhanced London's brand image, and will no doubt help to achieve the long-term aim of increasing tourism impacts of the mega-event. According to the Telegraph,

> the success of the London 2012 Games, and in particular the unfailing warmth of the volunteer Games-makers, has had such a profound effect on foreigners' perceptions that Britain has risen up an international league table of the world's most welcoming countries. As a result, Britain has leapfrogged Canada to become the fourth strongest national 'brand' in the world, according to the latest industry figures.
>
> (Rayner, 2014)

PLATE 16.1 Media stakeholders are a priority

Internal communication strategy

An internal communications strategy, like an HR strategy, is primarily informed by the organization's overarching business goals and strategy.

In this way, an internal communications strategy may help to support and communicate the organization's overarching business strategy to its employees. Alternatively, or in addition, effective internal communications may be a key deliverable of the organization's strategy, for example, where an organization's strategy includes the aim of improving employee culture and brand alignment. In a qualitative study of ten companies, Mazzei (2010: 231) suggests that the link between internal communication and human resource management systems 'contributes to organizational well-being, a collaborative environment and organizational change and in turn promotes further allegiance between the company and its employees'.

Having been informed by the organization's strategy, the internal communications strategy should focus on key, measurable deliverables and details about how this will be achieved, i.e. the tactics to be employed.

Like any communications strategy, an internal communications strategy may consider the following:

- Target audience: who are our employees, volunteers and contractors, what do we know about them, what are their needs, views and opinions about the organization, how receptive are they to organizational directives?

- Messages: what key messages, core values or attributes does the organization want to communicate, what do we want our workforce to know, think about, do?
- Channels: what formal and informal communications channels already exist, what technology platforms can we employ (e.g. intranets, social media etc.), what physical considerations need to be made (e.g. one physical head office, or remote, mobile workforce), what channels will work best and in what combination?
- Spokespeople: who is best to deliver these messages, one or more people, who will champion these messages?
- Monitoring and feedback: who is responsible for monitoring implementation and feeding back initial observations, how will that be conducted?
- Evaluation: how is success to be measured, is there scope for some form of employee research and/or are their other indicators that are tied to specific communications objectives?

CASE STUDY 16.1
Internship and volunteer programmes – communications strategy

Arts Council England provides the following guidelines for creative and cultural employers taking on interns:

- However small your business, put in place an internship and equal opportunities policy.
- Seek buy-in from all levels of the organization.
- Make sure you are adhering to employment law on work rights and pay.
- Be honest about the type of activities you are planning to ask the intern to do – changing the name of a work placement does not change someone's worker status.
- Always advertise your internships openly and transparently.
- Interns (as defined by these guidelines) should always be provided with a written contract of employment.
- Assign your interns a line manager.
- Always include a health and safety risk assessment in your preparations, and in the intern's induction.
- Make sure you have adequate insurance cover, including Employer's Liability and Public Liability insurance.

Reflective practice 16.1

This advice suggests that buy-in is necessary from all levels of the organization.

1   As the HR manager, prepare a memo to all line managers in your event organization introducing a new internship programme.
2   Ensure that guidelines relevant to their supervision of interns are explained and that the aims of the programme are highlighted.

Source: http://www.artscouncil.org.uk/publication_archive/internships-arts/. With permission from Arts Council England

Target audience

For business events the target audience is often clearly defined, particularly in the case of in-house meetings and conferences for internal employees. At the other extreme, festivals and sporting events have a significant number of external stakeholders (e.g. local authorities, emergency services), suppliers (e.g. venue management, catering), and volunteers in addition to the core team. These audiences may require different messages with different levels of engagement as clarified below.

Message development

Having outlined the overarching internal communications strategy, the next key phase is message development.

The types of messages and content will vary greatly between organizations, depending on the objectives of the strategy. Figure 16.1 illustrates an internal communications strategy for an organization's convention and in this case, objectives include inspiring, engaging, informing and educating attendees. Welch (2011: 341) differentiates between the need to emotionally engage employees (potentially volunteers in the event environment) and cognitively engage employees:

> Since engagement levels differ within workforces, the model encourages communicators to consider the communication needs of employees with varying levels of engagement. For example, a highly emotionally engaged employee may have a greater need for information to validate an ongoing sense of belonging to the organization. Likewise, employees with high cognitive engagement may value access to detailed material to facilitate their understanding of, and contributions to organizational goals. Consequently, the model encourages practitioners to evaluate employee communication needs from an engagement perspective.

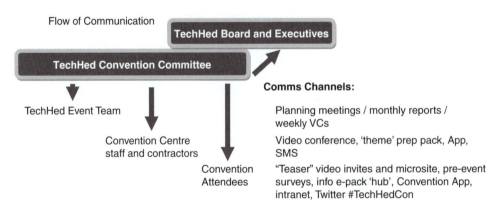

FIGURE 16.1 Communication plan and flow of communication for in-house convention

Channel development (including social media)

Communication channels typically comprise of four main categories:

- *Electronic (including social media):* Communications that are delivered electronically, either by email, intranet, video and webcasts, DVD, electronic newsletters, podcasts, blogs, wikis, SMS text messaging, screensaver or desktop messaging, and internal social media tools (e.g. internal Twitter-style sites such as Yammer).
- *Print:* Paper-printed communications. Examples include hard copy newsletters, posters, magazines, brochures, postcards and other 'desk drops' or 'toolkits'.
- *Face-to-face:* Either large/small group addresses or one-to-one meetings. Examples include 'town hall' meetings, conferences, briefings, 'paper bag' lunch meetings, team WIP meetings, whole section meetings, whole office meetings and 'focus group' style consultations.
- *Physical workspace:* The office or worksite and its surrounds. Examples can include notice boards, video screens, pictures or messages on walls near high traffic areas including kitchens, lifts, stairs other entries and exits and in some cases bathroom facilities (though many question whether this location is an appropriate venue for corporate announcements!). During an event's operation, the prime location for this channel is staff check-in, staff break area and locker room. Typically messages at these locations refer to health and safety.

Within these main categories, it is also important to consider which channels are one-way forms of communication (e.g. broadcast message from top down) and which have the ability to facilitate (or those which specifically encourage) the preferred two-way communication (a 'conversation' between the organization and its employees, a chance for feedback, response and ongoing dialogue).

When looking at these two characteristics, channels can be classified in this way:

- One-way/broadcast: video blog (no comments), newsletter, stand-alone poster, mass email, notice boards, desk drops.
- Two-way: face-to-face 'town hall' style meetings with Q&A time, blogs, wikis and podcasts with comment threads, intranets with community comment boards, electronic newsletters with feedback options and/or click throughs to online competitions, surveys or polls.

Internal communications practitioners regularly harness social media-style channels to engage with employees, and encourage peer-to-peer and 'bottom-up' communication within an organization. This is particularly the case with volunteers. Social media now influences the way many generations communicate at home and at work.

While many employees regularly use computers and mobile devices in their workplaces, it is still important to consider your organization's particular workforce and whether this is true of them. For example, volunteers on the field of play or based in remote locations are often out 'in the field' and may not be regularly connecting to the internet/intranet and email on a regular basis.

One of the key challenges is selecting the best mix of communications channels to suit the audience, availability and the objectives.

For example, when considering the audience, ask 'Who are they? What do we know about them? How do they like to access information? Where are they located? How do they go about their daily work?' It's vital to ask those questions and get a clear picture of the audience in order to assess how effective the proposed channel/s will be to engage them. Also consider many organizations may have multiple audiences, with various characteristics, preferences and requirements. In the event environment there are distinct phases, the lead up to the event and then its hectic implementation, each with different considerations for internal communications. The diverse and temporary nature of the workforce is an additional challenge.

Internal communications plan for TechHed Group convention

This internal communications plan has been designed to support the key business objectives that underpin the TechHed Group's annual global sales and entrepreneurial convention.

Objectives

To inspire, engage and re-energize our global sales team to achieve next year's sales targets.

- To inform and educate our sales team in relation to the company's strategic direction.
- To ensure a seamless experience with an 'entrepreneurial' flavour.

Key stakeholders

- Convention attendees – global sales execs
- Blue Harbour Convention Centre event staff
- Other event contractors
- TechHed Board and Executives
- TechHed Events team
- TechHed HR team.

Spokespeople

- TechHed Global CEO
- TechHed Global Director of Sales
- Global Event Manager
- Global HR Director.

Key messages

- TechHed is at the cutting edge of consumer tech innovation – we do things our way for our customers.
- At the heart of things, we're all entrepreneurs.
- We deliver new solutions to the world's businesses.
- Our TechHed people are global change makers and our best brand ambassadors.

Communications strategy

Develop Convention 'sub brand' for all communications materials.

Identify five key themes which represent categories of innovation to be presented at the conference and in line with TechHed core values. Proposed themes for work shopping include:

- Remote
- Transparent
- Connection
- Expansion
- Global.

Develop calendar of communication activities for key periods – pre-event, during-event, post-event.

No paper-based communications, rely solely on technology including a new microsite, convention App and Twitter feed as major platforms of communication for convention attendees.

Increase WebEx infiltration across the convention, to facilitate a greater 'live' event experience for sales executives unable to travel to attend the convention.

Looking further at the channel, one needs to be mindful of the context and substance of the message. For example, sensitive messages may need to be communicated face-to-face, rather than by, say, SMS text. In the event environment for example, a coded broadcast might be used on two-way radio in case of an emergency.

The next consideration is a purely practical (and budgetary) one. What channels either already exist within the organization or can easily be introduced? That's not to say that investing heavily in new platforms should be discouraged, but rather more often than not there are some pre-existing channels, platforms or capabilities that can be accessed.

Finally, timing and the flow of information must be considered. How urgent is the message? (For example, communications in times of crisis which require quick dissemination of important messages.)

Managing traffic is crucial during event implementation. For example, during the bump-in period for an event, the operations manager is dealing with a flood of incoming

TABLE 16.1 Media analysed by source, type and tone

Stage	Number of items	Source		Tone				Type		
		Melbourne	National	Melbourne		National		News/ Features	Letters	Special supplements
				Positive	Negative	Positive	Negative			
Initial euphoria	18	14	4	12	2	4	0	10	0	8
Discovering roles	11	5	6	5	0	4	2	3	0	8
Reality sets in	14	8	6	2	6	4	2	7	3	4
Immediate lead up	15	10	5	7	3	4	1	10	1	4
Post-event euphoria	7	5	2	4	1	2	0	4	1	0
Total	65									

Note: Melbourne sources included: *The Age Newspaper*, *The Herald Sun Newspaper*. National sources included: *The Australian Newspaper* (National), *The Australian Financial Review* (National), *The Advertiser* (Adelaide, South Australia), *Mercury* (Hobart, Tasmania), *The Sydney Morning Herald* (New South Wales), *The Daily Telegraph* (Sydney, New South Wales), *The Courier Mail* (Brisbane, Queensland).

calls during this pivotal time. Mobile coverage is particularly problematic at large events where the network is often overloaded. This is one reason why event managers should never be reliant on mobile phones for disseminating messages and why as much information should be provided in the lead-up to the event, rather than relying on dealing with everyone in person on the day of the event. Two-way radio can also be a far more effective method of broadcasting messages to the whole workforce as multiple users have access to the channel and control centres can override all channels during emergencies.

Managing risk

Controlling the dissemination of messages (and indeed feedback received, particularly using social media) requires consideration and ongoing attention. Employees may share too much information, expose confidential information and raise the risk of litigation. Wu (2012) provides guidance to organizations to mitigate social media security risks that may threaten the organizations and this involves enforcing social media security policies that are understandable to employees. The volunteer code of conduct for the Ottawa Folk Festival (2011) lists the following points:

- I will maintain confidentiality with respect to all Ottawa Folk Festival information and records
- I will refer questions from the media to the Ottawa Folk Festival publicist
- I will not record any folk festival performances (audio/video).

These are a few of the areas in which a member of the team might find themselves in breach of the code of conduct by spontaneous use of social media, such as posting an image or potential news story. The most important messages issued by an event organization to the news media or general public via other channels needs to be managed carefully by the communications team. In crisis situations in particular the appointment of a spokesperson is essential. This should be included in the crisis management plan (Van Der Wagen 2010). Earl et al. (2003) found that less than half of the study participants in their research into an outdoor music festival had knowledge of emergency and public health management for the festival. Furthermore, less than one quarter had knowledge of the festival's emergency management plan.

Monitoring and evaluation

When the objective of the internal communications plan is to invite participation and develop engagements then it is self-evident that management and monitoring is required. This requires collaboration between the internal communications team and human resource departments, and may involve tools such as internal engagement surveys or analysis of date including 'click through' or hit rates of online channels.

Evaluation

Bondarouk and Olivas-Luján (2013) summarize current thinking in use of social media by HR departments in their paper, 'It takes two to tango'. Finally, the internal communications strategy should be evaluated against the initial objectives.

CASE STUDY 16.2
Volunteer PR – 'good news stories'

Lockstone and Baum (2009) analyse media source, type and tone of articles relating to volunteers at the following stages of their event experience:

- the initial euphoria and volunteer recruitment;
- discovering roles and responsibilities;
- reality sets in;
- immediate lead up and the Games themselves;
- post-event euphoria.

This paper set out to investigate 'formal' press representation of volunteers and their roles during a mega sporting event as an alternative to the perspectives hitherto reported in the literature, primarily that of the volunteers themselves or event organisers. What has emerged is an image of tightly controlled and managed reporting of the volunteer cycle and the role of volunteers, dominated by effective press relations by the Games organisers except at such times when issues (generally negative) emerged. The overall positive and bland reporting may be a reflecting of media indolence, aversion or apathy when confronted by 'good news stories'; in the case of the first, effective news management and the presentation of news items about volunteers for placement are evident in that common items appeared across a number of publications in Australia simultaneously. Overall, the reporting of volunteers and the volunteering experience are consistent with the findings of other studies addressing the theme from different perspectives. However, hints at darker sides to the volunteer experience point to the need for the media to be more searching in its investigations in order to counter the impression that they are merely acting as a public relations mouthpiece for the event. There is also a case to be made that event organisers should show greater trust in the media in order to ensure credible and balanced representation of volunteering.

Source: Lockstone and Baum (2009: 52–53)

Reflective practice 16.2

1   These authors suggest that a more balanced representation of volunteering is required. Conduct your own research into reporting of event volunteering seeking to find both 'good news' and 'bad news' stories in the mainstream media and summarize your findings.
2   Now volunteers can comment on their experience through social media. Investigate comments both positive and negative and summarize your findings.
3   Write a press release for the media regarding the training provided for volunteers at an event of your choice including the potential benefits and rewards that the experience might bring. Ensure that the article is balanced by the need for realistic expectations on the part of the volunteers who often underestimate the challenges and hard work associated with the volunteering experience.

Chapter summary and key points

This chapter has highlighted the convergence of internal communications and human resource management in relation to the event industry. It is clear that there are many opportunities to better engage stakeholders, employees, volunteers and contractors. However the organization needs to have clear objectives for any internal communications strategy and an evaluation process to see whether objectives are being achieved.

Revision questions

1   Explain the convergence of the fields of human resource management and internal communications.
2   How does an internal communications campaign have the potential to influence service levels in the event environment? Give examples.
3   How can an internal communications strategy improve relationships with contractors/ suppliers? Are they an integral part of the workforce, to be included in internal communications planning (including training) or do they sit outside the remit of human resources/the event organization?
4   What are the particular communication challenges of event environments during the operational phase? Use the concepts elaborated in this chapter to support your answer.

Industry voice by Kerrie Nash

I recently worked with an event where they didn't have anyone doing internal communications and engagement early on. About twelve months out from Games they developed a communications and engagement plan. The change in the organization in three months was just unbelievable. It's all about people being informed and involved and inspired. They were the three words the internal communications team in Sydney used and I think it's such a great motto: inform, involve, inspire.

Discussion questions

- What is the difference between external and internal communications strategy?
- Why is an internal communications strategy arguably more important for an event than it is for a traditional, long-life business?

References

Bondarouk, T. and Olivas-Luján, M. (2013). 'Social media and human resource management: it takes two to tango', in T. Bondarouk and M. Olivas-Luján (eds). *Social Media in Human Resources Management (Advanced Series in Management, Volume 12)*. Bingley, UK: Emerald Group Publishing Limited, pp. xi–xv.

Earl, C., Stoneham, M. and Capra, M. (2003). 'Volunteers in emergency management at outdoor music festivals', *Australian Journal of Emergency Management*, 18(4), 18–24.

Lockstone, L. and Baum, T. (2009). 'The public face of event volunteering at the 2006 Commonwealth Games: the media perspective', *Managing Leisure*, 14(1), 38–56.

Madia, S. A. (2011). 'Best practices for using social media as a recruitment strategy', *Strategic HR Review*, 10(6), 19–24.

Mazzei, A. (2010). 'Promoting active communication behaviours through internal communication', *Corporate Communications: An International Journal*, 15(3), 221–234.

Ottawa Folk Festival (2011). *Volunteer Handbook*. Available at: http://ottawafolk.com/pdf/DRAFThandbook10may2011.pdf; viewed 3 January 2014.

Rayner, G. (2014). 'Britain sheds "stiff upper lip" image thanks to London 2012 Games-makers', *The Telegraph*, 4 January. Available at: http://www.telegraph.co.uk/earth/environment/tourism/9803790/Britain-sheds-stiff-upper-lip-image-thanks-to-London-2012-Games-makers.html; viewed 14 February 2014.

Van Der Wagen, L. (2010). *Event Management*. Sydney: Pearson Education.

Welch, M. (2011). 'The evolution of the employee engagement concept: communication implications', *Corporate Communications: An International Journal*, 16(4), 328–346.

Wu, He (2012). 'A review of social media security risks and mitigation techniques', *Journal of Systems and Information Technology*, 14(2), 171–180.

Glossary

accreditation process of granting approval for entry into a particular event area or zone, usually with badge or swipe card

action plan a plan that shows what needs to be done and when it needs to be done; projects comprise multiple action plans

activity a specific project task

audience people attending an event, also described as spectators or visitors

bidding competitive process of submitting proposals

breakdown process of dismantling event infrastructure; also called bump-out

budget estimate of revenue and expenditure

bump-in assembling event infrastructure on site, e.g. building exhibition stands or stages; also called load-in or set-up

bump-out process of dismantling event infrastructure; also called load-out or breakdown

business events meetings, incentives, conferences, exhibitions

centre business unit, department or functional area to which costs can be attributed

contingency plan alternative course of action if things don't go according to plan

contractor an organization that works independently to provide goods and services

control cost ensuring that performance meets plans by monitoring and checking

critical path timeline for project completion based on dependent tasks

crowd management techniques used to manage crowd flow through an event site

customer person who purchases goods and services; in the event environment, the audience or spectators

debrief a short meeting after a shift or an event to discuss the success or problems experienced

deliverables results required; often physical objects, but also reports, plans and written documents

duty of care legal responsibility for the safety of every person on site, including visiting workers and the general public

equal employment opportunity (EEO) providing the same opportunities for all, based on merit

event product range of goods and services captured as the purchased event product; may include performance, catering, ambience, entertainment, first aid and other services

extrinsic reward reward from external sources, e.g. praise from supervisors, certificates

functional area departments of a business that represent individual disciplines, e.g. marketing, purchasing, human resources

Gantt chart a timeline chart linking tasks with deadlines; a horizontal time scale

gap analysis an analysis of current skills against requirements; identifies skills and knowledge gaps as a result of a training needs analysis

human resource management effective use of human resources (people) to achieve organizational outcomes

human resource operational plan plan to ensure that the right people are in the right place at the right time doing the right thing

human resource strategic plan long-range plan to identify labour needs and implement workforce strategic plans and policies

induction introduction to an organization, may be formal or informal

intrinsic reward a reward that comes from an internal realization that personal goals have been achieved

job analysis systematic process of describing jobs within an organization

job description a document that describes the position and the tasks and responsibilities associated with it

job-specific training work-related training for specific job-related skills

job specification a document that describes job requirements in terms of the ideal candidate, including his/her knowledge, skill and other attributes; also called person specification

leadership directing and inspiring commitment to the organization's goals

logistics the procurement, distribution, maintenance and replacement of materials and staff

matrix organization organizational structure that uses both functional and project teams – leads to dual reporting relationships and cross-functional teams

merchandising items for retail sale consistent with the event theme

MICE meetings, incentives, conferences and exhibitions (now known as business events)

motivation an individual's interest and effort in achieving a goal

occupational health and safety (OHS) systems for worksite health and safety for all workers on site

orientation session at which the individual is introduced to the organization and its various facets (same as induction)

paid staff employees working in a paid capacity, full-time, part-time or seasonal

performance appraisal process used to give individuals performance feedback

person specification see job specification

policy intended course of action; guiding principle

precinct zone or area of an event venue, e.g. catering precinct

procedure specific series of tasks or actions for goal achievement, generally linked to policy

procurement assembling resources, mainly purchasing goods and services, needed for a project

project management planning, organizing directing and controlling a system with specific deadlines and resources

recognition acknowledging work performance in a formal way

recruitment process of attracting applicants to an organization

risk management process of identifying, evaluating and dealing with risks in relation to probability and consequence

scope of work identified parameters of a work project or action plan

selection process of selecting the best candidates for the position (with EEO in mind)

site place, usually an outdoor venue

situational management matching management style to work context variables

staffing process of recruiting, selecting, inducting and training new personnel

stakeholder organization associated with an event with significant interest in related goal achievement, e.g. police, sponsor

supplier an organization that works independently to provide goods and services

training providing the workforce with the skills and knowledge they need for successful performance

vendor an organization that works independently to provide goods and services

venue place at which an event is held, such as convention centre, athletics track

venue area part of the site which is designated for a special purpose, such as venue catering area

venue training training relating to the venue or zone, such as the chain of command and evacuation planning

venuization term used during mega events where the venue is 'taken over' by the organizing committee and the overlay for the sports, for example, is installed

volunteer unpaid worker

work breakdown structure (WBS) describes all work that needs to be done to achieve project outcomes; used as the basis for costing, scheduling, organizational design and work allocation

workforce everyone working, including paid staff, contractors and volunteers

zone specific area of an event venue or site

Appendix: assessment project

You are required to develop the human resources strategy for a multi-venue, multi-session event. This can be for any one of the following: international conference, exhibition, music festival, sporting event, street festival, awards ceremony, community celebration or an event of your own conception.

For this project you need to be mindful of the scope that this event provides for human resource planning so at least some of the following challenges need to be addressed:

- scope of the event – a multi-venue event provides logistics challenges;
- size of the event – the total workforce should number at least 200;
- unique nature of the event – if the concept is untried the challenges will be greater;
- volunteer management – consider the use of volunteers if you choose a community or non-commercial event;
- themed event – service, ambience and congruence with the theme will influence planning;
- stakeholder involvement – a range of contractors, government agencies and emergency services may be part of the planning;
- outdoor or unique venue – infrastructure has to be built from the ground up;
- risk – the level of risk associated with staffing, such as involvement of high-profile VIPs, celebrities or royalty.

Clearly, not all of the above would be part of the concept; however, if the event is too simple, it will not allow you to adequately demonstrate your planning skills.

Your Human Resources Plan should include the following headings and sections:

1   executive summary;
2   event overview (with an emphasis on the concept and the staffing considerations presented by the concept);
3   human resources strategic plan (including a labour force analysis; a rationale for the workforce composition; a human resources risk prevention and contingency plan);
4   human resources operational timelines (including tasks and timelines for significant elements such as recruitment, selection and training);

5   compliance review (a review of HR legal obligations and insurances);
6   job analysis (rationale, organization chart and sample job descriptions/job specifications for key positions as appendices);
7   recruitment and selection plan (identify source of labour, tasks and timelines);
8   training plan (include orientation, venue and job-specific training);
9   policies and procedures (identify which policies and procedures are necessary);
10 organizational culture and communication (review communication plans);
11 leadership, motivation and retention (provide strategies for human resource management);
12 human resources evaluation plan (outline ways in which the quality of service and management of personnel can be evaluated during and post event);
13 references;
14 appendices.

When presenting this report you may wish to include some components as appendices at the end of the report, for example, a copy of a policy and procedures for accreditation or a training guide. In each case you need to refer to the appendix in your main document.

Index